P9-CKH-308

About Island Press

Island Press is the only nonprofit organization in the United States whose principal purpose is the publication of books on environmental issues and natural resource management. We provide solutions-oriented information to professionals, public officials, business and community leaders, and concerned citizens who are shaping responses to environmental problems.

In 2002, Island Press celebrates its eighteenth anniversary as the leading provider of timely and practical books that take a multidisciplinary approach to critical environmental concerns. Our growing list of titles reflects our commitment to bringing the best of an expanding body of literature to the environmental community throughout North America and the world.

Support for Island Press is provided by The Bullitt Foundation, The Mary Flagler Cary Charitable Trust, The Nathan Cummings Foundation, Geraldine R. Dodge Foundation, Doris Duke Charitable Foundation, The Charles Engelhard Foundation, The Ford Foundation, The George Gund Foundation, The Vira I. Heinz Endowment, The William and Flora Hewlett Foundation, W. Alton Jones Foundation, The John D. and Catherine T. MacArthur Foundation, The Andrew W. Mellon Foundation, The Charles Stewart Mott Foundation, The Curtis and Edith Munson Foundation, National Fish and Wildlife Foundation, The New-Land Foundation, Oak Foundation, The Overbrook Foundation, The David and Lucile Packard Foundation, The Pew Charitable Trusts, Rockefeller Brothers Fund, The Winslow Foundation, and other generous donors.

The Good in
Nature and Humanity

The Good in

Nature and Humanity

Connecting Science, Religion,
and Spirituality with the Natural World

EDITED BY
Stephen R. Kellert
and Timothy J. Farnham

ISLAND PRESS
Washington ◆ Covelo ◆ London

Copyright © 2002 Island Press

All rights reserved under International and Pan-American Copyright Conventions. No part of this book may be reproduced in any form or by any means without permission in writing from the publisher: Island Press, 1718 Connecticut Avenue, N.W., Suite 300, Washington, DC 20009.

ISLAND PRESS is a trademark of The Center for Resource Economics.

We express grateful acknowledgment for permission to reprint previously published material: "The Mappist" from *Light Action in the Caribbean*, by Barry Lopez, published by Alfred A. Knopf, Inc. Reprinted by permission of Sterling Lord Literistic, Inc., and the author. Copyright © 2000 by Barry Lopez. A selection from *LEAP*, by Terry Tempest Williams, published by Pantheon. Reprinted by permission of Brandt & Hochman Literary Agents, Inc., and the author. Copyright © 2000 by Terry Tempest Williams. A selection from *Heartsblood*, by David Petersen, published by Island Press. Reprinted by permission of the author. Copyright © 2000 by David Petersen.

Library of Congress Cataloging-in-Publication Data
The good in nature and humanity : connecting science, religion, and spirituality with the natural world / Stephen R. Kellert and Timothy J. Farnham, editors.
　　p.　　cm.
Includes bibliographical references and index.
　　ISBN 1-55963-838-9 (alk. paper)
1. Religion and science. 2. Nature—Religious aspects. 3. Human ecology—Religious aspects. I. Kellert, Stephen R. II. Farnham, Timothy J.
　　BL241.G66　2002
　　261.5'5—dc21　　　　　　　　　　　　　　　　　　　　　　　2001008404

British Cataloguing-in-Publication Data available.

Printed on recycled, acid-free paper

Manufactured in the United States of America
09 08 07 06 05 04 03 02　　8 7 6 5 4 3 2 1

Dedicated to the memory of H. Boone Porter, who did
so much to reveal the good and the God in nature and humanity

Contents

Preface

This book, and the conference that inspired it—"The Good in Nature and Humanity," held at Yale University in May 2000—originated in the conviction that the root causes of modern society's environmental and spiritual crises cannot be understood nor effectively resolved until the split between religion and science, or, more generally, between faith and reason, has been effectively reconciled. By comprehending and strengthening the bonds between spirituality, science, and nature, we may come closer to achieving an environmental ethic that better equips us to confront two of the most imperiling crises of our time—global environmental destruction and an impoverished spirituality. By bridging the gap between rationality and religion through the concern of each for understanding the human relation to creation, we may better pursue the quest for a more secure and meaningful world.

Scientists traditionally examine the natural environment in seeking knowledge that enhances our physical and mental security. The religious or spiritual practitioner analogously pursues an understanding of creation that points the way toward meaning and salvation. For both scientists and the spiritually and religiously inclined, the recognition grows that in our abuse of the earth we diminish our moral as well as our material condition. This mutual realization forges an understanding of the link between an environmentally degraded planet and a spiritually depauperate humanity. Conservationists, ever more cognizant of this connection, have increasingly acknowledged that both scientific and spiritual understandings are necessary in achieving an ethical sensibility capable of confronting the global crisis of pervasive environmental pollution, resource depletion, atmospheric degradation, and enormous biodiversity loss.

This book is based in the premise that neither science nor religion by itself can resolve the prevailing malaise of environmental and moral decline. The contributors to this volume pursue an ethic of right relation between nature and humanity that balances theory with practice and relates each to the enormous challenge of generating a practical ethic for managing the natural environment. Scientists, theologians, spiritual leaders, and writers, working with foresters, farmers, fishers, wildlife managers, and land developers, embrace an environmental perspective that links utilization of nature with the preservation of its beauty, health, and integrity. A basic objective is to advance human wisdom in order to avert environmental catastrophe but, more affirmatively, to achieve a more harmonious human relationship with the natural world that moves us toward a measure of goodness and grace. The phrase *the good in nature and humanity* reflects the realization that in pursuing a more nurturing relationship with the natural world, we see our own salvation in the preservation of the health, integrity, and beauty of creation.

The book originated, as noted, in a conference, organized by the Yale School of Forestry and Environmental Studies, the Yale University Divinity School, The Wilderness Society, and the National Religious Partnership for the Environment. Over a period of four days, some seven hundred participants confronted issues of science, religion, spirituality, and the natural world and the related challenge of ethical environmental and resource management. Most of the conference speakers contributed to this volume. Some not represented in the book include Sylvia Earle, Paul Gorman, Gary Nabhan, and Seyyed Hossein Nasr, occasionally cited in the chapters that follow.

The volume is organized in three parts. Corresponding chapters are introduced in greater detail at the beginning of each part; what follows is a brief overview. Part I, "Scientific and Spiritual Perspectives on Nature and Humanity," explores how science, spirit, and religion can guide our experience and understanding of the good in nature and its relevance to our ongoing relationship with the natural world. Richard J. Wood, former dean of the Yale University Divinity School, introduces this part with a thoughtful reflection on the relevance of traditional philosophical approaches to ethics in the generation of an environmental ethic grounded in both scientific and religious understandings of creation. Part II, "Linking Spiritual and Scientific Perspectives with an Environmental Ethic," written largely by resource managers and users, focuses on how the integration of science and spirituality can equip us to make wiser choices as procurers and consumers of resources obtained from the natural world. William H. Meadows, president of The Wilderness Society, introduces this part by calling for a land ethic wherein advocacy based in moral passion leads us to land and resource use that honors the sacredness of the earth. Finally, part III, "From the Perspective of the Storyteller," embraces a more narrative understanding of the relation between science, spirit, and nature.

Stephen R. Kellert and Timothy J. Farnham

Acknowledgments

This book, and the conference that preceded it, came into being as a result of the considerable assistance and inspirational guidance of others. We owe particular thanks to Robert Perschel of The Wilderness Society, Paul Gorman of the National Religious Partnership for the Environment, and Dr. Richard J. Wood, dean emeritus of the Yale University Divinity School, all of whom were instrumental in the organization and realization of the conference. The original concept and implementation of the meeting benefited greatly from the creativity, commitment, and hard work of Greg Hitzhusen, a joint degree student at the Yale School of Forestry and Environmental Studies and the Yale University Divinity School. Richard Fern, a professor at the Yale University Divinity School at the time, was an important intellectual force in the conference's development. We owe special thanks to Nature Johnston, a student at the Yale University Divinity School, for her remarkable energy and competence in helping to organize the conference, as well as the invaluable assistance of many other students at the Yale School of Forestry and Environmental Studies. We also received material and moral support from Professor Mary Evelyn Tucker of Harvard University's Forum on Religion and Ecology and Gus Speth, dean of the Yale School of Forestry and Environmental Studies. Additionally, we thank Nathan Garland for his superb design of the conference program and poster. Finally, we very much appreciate Barbara Dean's invaluable editorial suggestions and advice in the development of this book.

Implementation of the conference and publication of the book would not have been possible without the generous financial support of many institutions and individuals. We especially thank The Nathan Cummings Foundation, the Heinz Family Philanthropies, the Oliver S. and Jennie R. Donaldson Charitable Trust, the Edward J. and Dorothy Clarke Kempf Fund at Yale University, the Center for Resource Economics, the H. Boone Porter and Violet M. Porter Charitable Foundation and the family of H. Boone Porter, Reverend Albert Neilsen, The Wilderness Society, the Yale School of Forestry and Environmental Studies, the Yale University Divinity School, the Forum on Religion and Ecology at Harvard University, Ms. Josephine Merck, Ms. Jeanie Graustein, and Mr. Strachan Donnelley.

We also want to thank Cilla, Ellen, and Anabelle for their considerable patience and support.

Chapter 1

Building the Bridge: Connecting Science, Religion, and Spirituality with the Natural World

TIMOTHY J. FARNHAM AND STEPHEN R. KELLERT

There is a perception in modern society, as reflected in many of the chapters that follow, that a significant divide exists between science and religion. These two modes of inquiry—the empirical and the faith-based—represent ways we search for answers to questions both practical and timeless. Yet in Western culture the two are often envisioned as occupying different realms of thinking and practice. The goal of this collection is to find connections, through humanity's relation to the natural world, that help bridge the chasm separating the scientific from the spiritual and religious.

But as often occurs when two entities have grown apart, there exist fundamental language and communication problems that obstruct a possible reconciliation. The words themselves impede what could be fruitful exchanges between science and religion concerning the human ethical relationship with nature and creation. As William H. Meadows comments in his introduction to part II of this book, "we are still in search of the right language, the comfortable language." George W. Fisher similarly declares in chapter 8 that a significant language problem exists when we converse outside the familiar confines of a faith or a discipline. David Petersen, in his essay on hunting and spirituality (chapter 13), further notes the need for a "lexicon" that allows discussions of spirituality and nature to move freely between secular and religious worldviews. In short, we need a common vocabulary, a language that allows thoughtful people to cross over safely and share ideas about science, religion, spirituality, and the natural world.

1

Definitions, of course, are the basis of any language, especially one seeking to bring together separated constituents. While the words *science* and *religion* obviously have complex, multilayered meanings, we can propose relatively simple characterizations that partially reveal how contemporary culture often understands each term. For example, the *Oxford English Dictionary* observes that the modern notion of science has become "restricted to those branches of study that relate to the phenomena of the material universe and their laws," whereas in past centuries the term *science* often enjoyed a broader usage indicative of the search for knowledge in a wide variety of fields.[1] In contemporary times, the practice of science typically involves specialized instruments that measure quantities and qualities in the context of experiments or carefully controlled studies specifically designed to test hypotheses. This activity derives from and results in theories that seek to explain the workings of the natural world through physical causation alone. Investigators who use the scientific method generally ask questions that can be answered only by experimental or controlled testing procedures, and the answers must meet certain levels or standards of proof. Science implies the use of reason and the pursuit of empirical "facts" to increase our understanding of how the universe functions.

By contrast, again quoting the *Oxford English Dictionary,* religion represents the "recognition on the part of man of some higher unseen power" and the beliefs, traditions, and ceremonies that formally represent this understanding and recognition.[2] Often, this "unseen power" is considered responsible for the origin of life and may even be regarded as continuing to exercise a measure of control over present and future human activities and other aspects of creation. Whatever the specific details, religion and spirituality require some degree of belief in, reverence for, and worship of a higher power. Moreover, because this power typically is believed to possess qualities existing beyond the known material world (hence the term *metaphysical*), religious and spiritual thought incorporates a significant element of mystery and questions whose answers cannot be demonstrated or proven by scientific and empirical examination alone. In apparent opposition to science and reason, spirituality and religion depend on faith, the human recognition of and deference to the unknowable, and the related realization that answers to some of life's most profound questions can exist beyond complete human understanding.

Using these broad definitions as a foundation, we recognize that the pursuits of both science and religion can have their extremes, and perhaps here is where the divide between the two becomes most evident. For example, as Ursula Goodenough notes in chapter 2, something exists deep within humans that resists scientific explanation because of "a fear of reductionism." This fear involves the view that science entails an impulse toward continuous analysis, a dissection (and, by implication, destruction) of the whole in search of the mechanism. Science is seen as neglecting the larger emergent and holistic qualities of nature that humans intuitively experience without the aid of a microscope. These reductive practices represent what biologist Edward O. Wilson calls "scientism" or "science run rampant."[3] In an effort to describe the fear that science often elicits, Wilson quotes scientist and social critic C. P. Snow, who expresses well the frequent protest of science's analytic ways:

> Science reduces and oversimplifies
> Condenses and abstracts, drives toward generality
> Presumes to break the insoluble
> Forgets the spirit
> Imprisons the spark of artistic genius[4]

In addition to having concerns about reductionism, many people regard science's close connection with modern technology as representing a dangerous liaison. As Jeremy Benstein notes in chapter 9, this relationship frequently implicates science in an increasing mechanization and dehumanization of society, resulting in a weakening of the physical, cultural, and spiritual ties between people and the natural world. Some further believe our technological prowess encourages an exaggerated obsession with and focus on the material and physical. As Goodenough observes, many fear that science and its offspring technology directly conflict with religious and spiritual values, forcing us to "encounter our context in [only] material form." Moreover, Goodenough continues, "to lose our spirituality, we fear, is to lose our humanness, our soulfulness, our capacity for transcendent experience. We fear we will become automatons." Such an end would seem to befit a society excessively focused on the mechanical and physical properties of the world.

Religion and spirituality can easily be perceived as the victims of this struggle with modernity and a hegemonic scientific perspective of creation. The importance of faith may seem diminished by a constant onslaught of scientific discoveries purporting to reveal and enable us to "know" the inner workings of the universe. But religion and spirituality cannot be so readily cast as innocents, given that they are often complicit in helping build the divide with science. Critics of religion, for example, note its seeming inflexibility and doctrinaire qualities, and many observe that spiritual thought has often lost its relevance for many, if not most, citizens in modern society. Moreover, faith is frequently depicted as a crutch; reliance on it is seen as a surrender to ignorance that is crippling precisely because faith requires no physical proof nor can ever be proven wrong. A familiar example of religious immobility in the Christian tradition is literal adherence to the story of creation. As Margaret A. Farley notes in chapter 7, even though the facts of this story are "contradicted by the findings of modern science," some believers refuse to accept or even consider the theory of evolution. The battle between evolutionists and creationists is well documented, and some scientists evoke images of fundamentalists who insist the earth was created in six days to illustrate how traditional religious thought contradicts accepted science. Certainly, many believe a doctrine of creation is not incompatible with an evolutionary perspective, but those who choose to interpret religious texts most literally often find their beliefs in conflict with science and modernity.

Thus, one of the strongest critiques of religion and spirituality is that of "blind faith." While many fear the scientific tendency toward overanalysis, the corresponding fear of religion involves a lack of analysis. In a society in which individuality, inquiry, and independence are prized, traditions demanding submissiveness and the suppression of doubt tend to be rigorously criticized. Religion in the extreme often seems to leave little room for discovery and innovation. In many ways, Goodenough's description of people's worry of becoming automatons under the domination of science can also be applied to religion. The fear of spiritual and religious zealotry is based in part on a perception that it causes adherents to lose their desire and ability to explore and discover.

These are unpleasant characterizations, and they should not be exaggerated. But it is important to recognize that both science and religion have aspects that people fear and resist. Both possess the potential to deny or suppress essential facets of our humanity and our relation to nature and creation. For this reason, we must look for ways in which science and religion can prevent such extremes from dominating, as well as ways they can share common goals and language that offer guidance, particularly regarding our effects on the natural world. As Calvin B. DeWitt suggests in chapter 3, science and religion can and should be necessary complements in our modern worldview. Both seek understanding of, and answers to questions about, the world that humans experience. Both pursue the "truth," and this pursuit lies at the crux of the connection between science, religion, spirituality, and nature. Both share, in this search for truth and knowledge, the same ultimate objective of revealing the underlying causes in the patterns of the universe and determining our place in these patterns.

René Dubos, in his book *The GodWithin*, offered eloquent words to express these potential connections between religion and science:

> Religion and science . . . constitute deep-rooted and ancient
> efforts to find richer experience and deeper meaning than are
> found in the ordinary biological and social satisfactions. . . . Both
> the myths of religion and the laws of science . . . are not so much
> descriptions of facts as symbolic expressions of cosmic truths.
> These truths may always remain beyond human understanding, but
> at every stage of human development glimpses of them have
> enriched man in experience and comprehension.[5]

Scientists may take exception to the notion of their discoveries being "symbolic expressions" analogous to the "myths of religion." But Dubos, a molecular biologist, two-time Nobel laureate, and seminal environmental thinker and conservationist, offered a perspective that elevates science above the limited role of providing only facts while reminding us that religious and spiritual myths can contain as much truth as can accepted scientific discoveries. To Dubos, facts as mere "descriptions" are marginally important, but as "symbolic expressions of cosmic truths" they retain the magic that scientists experience when they seek to decipher the mysteries of the natural world. Facts as the gateway to more profound revelations can be an accurate description of the motivation of many scientists. Similarly, myths as symbolic expressions allow us "glimpses" of truths, enriching our understanding of the world beyond everyday experience. Science and religion can thus become unified through their ultimate goal.

Yet finding a common language and engendering trust between science and religion, especially regarding matters of the human relationship with the natural world, have proven difficult. Many scientists and conservationists avoid discussing their interests and endeavors in religious or spiritual terms. For example, David Takacs, in his book *The Idea of Biodiversity,* asked various conservation biologists a wide range of questions, including whether or not they found spiritual or religious value in their work and their efforts to preserve biodiversity. Most of the biologists expressed difficulty with the word *religious,* and some flatly declared their distaste for the ritualistic and restrictive beliefs they associated with an organized faith. The term *spiritual* elicited a wider range of responses, although many of the scientists seemed stymied by the word, claiming that the lack of a clear definition for such a "fuzzy" adjective, as one called it, made it difficult to express useful observations about the spiritual value in their work. Some further relied on scientific terms to explain spiritual feelings as biological or psychological adaptations humans acquired during our evolutionary development. Others, faced with questions they regarded as falling outside their professional training, simply declined to consider possibilities beyond the scientific frame of reference.[6]

One scientist remarked when asked whether he found religious or spiritual value in his work:

> Not at all, no. Zero. I'm just a traveler in time, that's it. . . . As a scientist, you can't be an atheist and you can't be a believer because you can't test the hypothesis. So your only recourse is to be an agnostic. There is no other possibility if you're a real scientist.[7]

But interestingly, when asked what had motivated him to become an entomologist, this scientist related having experienced the following feelings when observing the beetles he studied:

> You see it and it's just, God, it's just beautiful, absolutely beautiful. How did it come about? The process behind it must be even more beautiful, more intricate, more complex, more sophisticated, whatever. And it's a challenge to the human mind to figure that out.[8]

Aside from the irony of invoking God to express what he saw when looking at a tiny life-form, this scientist unknowingly described the shared goal of science and religion as Dubos had earlier identified: Both of them search for origins; both seek an understanding of the mysterious processes through which life develops.

Science and religion can each reveal the curiosity, humility, and reverence humans experience when confronting expressions of creation far more complex than any single entity or being. Perhaps, as the entomologist asserted, no apparent way exists to test for God or some fundamental force in the universe, but it seems that the "process" of creation he described inspires an awe similar to the religious emotion felt by those worshiping in ways other than by studying insects. This shared sense of wonder emphasizes the similarities in science and religion rather than the differences between them.

The celebration of creation is perhaps the strongest link between the scientific and religious worldviews. The study of the earth and the complex relationships that link life together offers a common ground for both scientific and spiritual revelation. Dubos, again, provided wise words on the subject, suggesting that the broad field of ecology offers the prospect of a future relationship between science and religion:

We may . . . be moving to a higher level of religion. Science is at present evolving from the description of concrete objects and events to the study of relationships as observed in complex systems. We may be about to recapture an experience of harmony, an intimation of the divine, from our scientific knowledge of the processes through which the earth became prepared for human life, and of the mechanisms through which man relates to the universe as a whole. A truly ecological view of the world has religious overtones.[9]

Ecology holds the promise of revealing the connections between living things and their environment. Rather than abandoning the effort to learn about the mechanics of the world, ecology emphasizes how these mechanisms serve to link humans and other life-forms to the surrounding world. This perspective can lead to an "experience of harmony" or, more strongly, "an intimation of the divine," which Dubos saw as a pathway to a "higher level of religion."

The ecology Dubos envisioned is not simply an effort to understand how nature works, a search for mere descriptions. A truly ecological view perceives complex systems of intertwining relationships that allow us to hear what Dubos termed "religious overtones." These overtones serve as a clarion call for humans to discover how to act in relation to the natural world. Ecological interdependence implies a moral obligation to consider how our activities affect the earth. Here we discern the potential convergence of scientific, religious, and spiritual thought, a means for considering ethical duties to nature that invoke the perspectives of both science and religion. Decisions about our role in conserving other living beings in an interdependent ecological system require us to combine scientific knowledge with our sacred beliefs. Science can lead to an understanding of our influence on other life and on the natural environment, but in becoming cognizant of this knowledge, we face choices that have spiritual consequences.

The successful completion of a bridge between science and religion will depend on the respect and reverence for the natural world cultivated on both sides of the spiritual and scientific divide. Ethics serves as the keystone, and if the bridge is carefully built, we can anticipate a free and fruitful flow in the exchange of scientific and spiritual views. This collection of essays will, it is hoped, offer a strong base from which to start constructing this enduring edifice.

Part I

Scientific and Spiritual Perspectives of Nature and Humanity

Part I explores the connections between science, spirit, and religion and how these may facilitate the human experience and understanding of the "good" in nature. Richard J. Wood, dean emeritus of the Yale University Divinity School, introduces this part with a thoughtful reflection on the relevance of traditional ethical approaches in conceiving an environmental ethic inspired by religious, spiritual, and scientific understandings of nature.

In chapter 2, Ursula Goodenough, professor of biology at Washington University, provides an insightful perspective on the spiritual dimensions of science. She notes how many contemporary religious thinkers are disturbed by society's diminished faith and a corresponding reliance on scientific views and interpretations of the world. Goodenough offers a different perspective, one that allays these fears and suspicions of the scientific method and the explanations it provokes. She asserts that the scientific desire to comprehend the "astonishing materiality" of the universe does not lessen the value of more subjective ways of knowing and experiencing creation. On the contrary, she declares, if we ignore the material workings of nature, we neglect elements crucial in our understanding of our place in the universe. She offers a framework that helps us see how scientific understandings of nature can contribute to moral, spiritual, and religious wholeness and well-being. Drawing on the work of Thomas Berry, she describes how we can reconcile scientific understandings and the religious impulse by employing three principles reflected in the terms *differentiation, subjectivity,* and *communion.* Goodenough reveals how, with development of a common language for both science and spirituality, these two realms of understanding can converge, and how each, in the context of the other, can gain meaning through the pursuit of "questions of Ultimacy" that drive their respective searches.

In chapter 3, Calvin B. DeWitt, director of the Au Sable Institute of Environmental Studies and professor of religion at the University of Wisconsin–Madison, continues the theme of the potential complementarity of science, spirituality, and nature. DeWitt notes that religion, especially the Judeo-Christian tradition, has been depicted as a major contributor to the modern environmental crisis. He notes that several prominent scientists and conservationists have recently voiced a contrary viewpoint of religion potentially offering an integrative forum through which ethics and spirituality can help science to conserve nature. DeWitt addresses these links between science and religion through examination of definitions and etymologies and a close ecological reading of scriptural teachings. He notes four ecological ethics found in the Bible and encourages us to identify how each of these perspectives can support a scientific knowledge of the natural world. Finally, DeWitt emphasizes that a scientific and religiously derived ethic must be connected to everyday life (what he calls *praxis*) and calls for a thoughtful and constructive activism informed by both spiritual and secular knowledge.

Stephen R. Kellert, in chapter 4, begins by noting a fundamental divide that has historically separated science and spirituality, centering on questions of the origin and evolution of life. He suggests the possibility of a "middle ground" that connects human evolution, spirituality, emotion, aesthetics, and ethical relation to nature. He proposes that an environmental ethic can emerge from a perspective of science and spirituality rooted in the hereditary needs and traits of our species. To make this case, he invokes the concept of biophilia and nine related values of nature to explain how humans biologically depend on the richness of their experience of nature to achieve physical, emotional, intellectual, and spiritual well-being. He begins his description of these values with a personal anecdote of warblers during their spring migration near his home. In this anecdote and the subsequent delineation of the nine values, Kellert argues that a broad anthropocentric ethic can be tied to the human experience of the natural world and its enormous diversity. But, he argues, these values of biophilia, while biologically based, rely on adequate learning and social support to become fully and functionally manifest. He suggests that when humans degrade nature, particularly their ongoing experience of it, they not only compromise their material well-being but also give rise to a profound and alienating loss of psychological and moral bearings. Kellert concludes that an ethic of care and responsibility for the natural world can emerge from the adaptive expression of all nine values of biophilia, not just the more obvious utilitarian and moral perspectives. He suggests that even our fears of and aversions to nature can be a necessary basis for recognizing the awesome power, splendor, and magnificence of creation.

In chapter 5, Mary Evelyn Tucker, professor of religion at Bucknell University, offers a multiple-faith perspective at the intersection of what she calls the compatible "cosmologies" of science and religion. Tucker believes that those who search for ethical guidance can learn much from the various religious worldviews of diverse cultural traditions. She identifies compatible perspectives among religious cosmologies of the human relationship with the "good" and the natural world as well as connections between the spiritual articulations of these various traditions and our modern, scientific sensibilities. Tucker argues that religion in Western society has often been considered an inadequate intellectual means for achieving a modern scientific understanding, with the religious perspective frequently omitted from discussions of humanity's place in the natural world. By contrast, her analysis of the scriptures of three religious traditions—the Psalms (Israel), the Vedas (India), and the Book of Changes (China)—identifies various ways in which the wisdom of these ancient faith traditions can inform our evolutionary understandings of and ethical inclinations toward nature. Tucker concludes that the search for moral and environmental guidance requires both scientific and religious understandings of the patterns of the cosmos that help us harmonize our inner selves with "the deep cosmological rhythms in nature." She asserts that the universal pursuit of harmony constitutes a significant source of mutual quest and inspiration for both religion and science. She concludes that we need both religion and science to cultivate a cosmology true to what we know as well as what we feel.

No collection would be complete without a provocative dissent. In chapter 6, Dorion Sagan and Lynn Margulis assert that nature is "intrinsically neither good nor evil" and declare ethics an entirely human construct, one with identifiable evolutionary roots. The authors offer several provocative examples of activities in the natural world that humans find ethically abhorrent—murder, cannibalism, incest—and assert that we cannot judge nature by a human-based morality, for nature is amoral. Thus, they conclude, it is fruitless to search for a concept of "good" beyond that defined by human subjectivity. They advocate instead a view of life in its entirety—the theory of Gaia, a perspective of the earth as constituting "intertwined ecosystems with a global physiology" and a biota that collectively regulates planetary environmental conditions instrumental to maintaining life itself. This cooperation, they suggest, is not the consequence of some mystical or moral inclination or consciousness but rather is an evolutionary response to changing environmental conditions and gradients. From such a planetary vantage point, concepts of good, evil, and spirituality are merely peculiar to a "minute component" of the global whole—that is, humans—that "late Holocene upright ape whose destiny is incessant chatter and the physiological need for reassurance and community, a basic prerequisite to production of healthy offspring." The "good" from this perspective exists only in the human mind, playing a very small role in the larger scheme of the universe. Still, one is left to wonder whether notions of Gaia and biotic cooperation might not imbue in humanity the intuitive recognition of a "goodness" inherent in preserving that living mantle which is both instrumental and genetically related to one's ultimate survival.

A very different outlook prevails in chapter 7. Margaret A. Farley of the Yale University Divinity School, eloquently responding to the ways in which religious and spiritual identity can contribute to an understanding of nature and humanity, offers a religious framework to help "protect, not destroy, the earth and all that dwells therein." Farley proposes three tasks—critique, retrieval, and reconstruction—central to understanding the relevance of certain ideas and stories among various religious traditions, particularly Christianity, to the modern challenge of fostering ethically responsible treatment and stewardship of nature. In the idea of critique, Farley examines how we can look at our historical beliefs about God, creation, and the human condition with a special awareness of how these perspectives bear on contemporary thinking. Through retrieval, Farley suggests, theological "articulations" in Christian thought can resonate with understandings of modern life and the natural world. Finally, through the act of reconstruction, we may take what we have learned through critique and retrieval and build a new understanding of nature and creation, one that will serve as the basis for a kind of spiritual conversion. All these tasks can occur within any religious tradition and are essential to religion's continued vitality and relevance in addressing the contemporary environmental crisis.

In chapter 8, George W. Fisher of the Department of Earth and Planetary Sciences at Johns Hopkins University offers insight regarding the links between geology and theology. He believes these links are necessary to our achieving a "livable future," one that not only sustains us physically but also "gives life meaning beyond mere existence." Fisher initially considers the geologic history of the earth, particularly how the planetary system makes life possible through a unique and perhaps unlikely combination of events. He believes that this understanding underscores humanity's complete dependence upon maintaining a particular range of environmental conditions on earth. Yet an exploding human population and the current scale of consumption and resource exploitation bring humanity ever closer to the absolute limits of what the global ecosystem can provide. As we approach these limits, questions of "livability" arise, questions of not only geologic but also moral sustainability. Fisher turns here to theology, noting several significant messages all people should hear no matter what their faith. He particularly emphasizes humility, stewardship, and "ultimate concern," arguing that religion and spirituality remain essential components of any sustainable vision of the future. He suggests that the confluence of geology and theology can provide us with a clearer perspective of the "beauty, intricacy, and . . . exuberance of life," forcing us "to stand in awe at the sheer privilege of being here."

Finally, in chapter 9, Jeremy Benstein concludes part I with a critical examination of the effects of technology and related ideas of power and progress. Benstein does not argue with the numerous benefits derived from our growing ability to manipulate the material world, but he notes, "For all that has been gained, much has been lost, and growing piles of debris line the pathways of the technological motorcade." Not the least of these problems are the effects of our technological and scientific prowess on the natural environment, as well as on the ability of individuals and societies to choose their own destinies. Technology frees us from many arduous tasks, but, Benstein argues, accompanying this "progress" is often a "disempowerment" resulting from increasing globalization and corporate control of economics and policy-making institutions. He suggests, "Ordinary people are losing their ability to democratically shape their societies and ensure the well-being of their environments." He also suggests that a particularly problematic price is paid in the spiritual realm, in which a sense of purpose becomes obscured by an obsession with controlling and exploiting the physical world. Benstein believes we must shift away from a preoccupation with material and physical comfort, become more aware of our future adverse environmental influence, and look to "the world that is coming" (the *alma de'atei*) with self-restraint for the sake of preserving the creation for future generations. Benstein supports his position by reinterpreting several biblical passages within a framework of both physical and spiritual sustainability. Finally, he argues, we have both too much and too little power, and this should cause us to pause and consider our essential requirements in a world where materialism has become rampant and "progress" deserves closer examination.

Introduction to Part I

Ethics and the Good in Nature and Humanity

RICHARD J. WOOD

In reexamining the relationships among science, religion, and the natural world, this book gives a great deal of attention to ethics. It is clear that thinking seriously about the environment raises deep questions about the basis of moral judgment and action, and about the meaning of human existence. From my perspective as dean emeritus of the Yale University Divinity School, I would like to suggest briefly a framework that might be helpful in engaging the chapters that follow.

For many years, much of philosophical ethics—and not a little of religious ethics—has been an attempt to figure out the extent to which *results* determine obligations. Various forms of utilitarianism try to make results central to defining our obligations. After all, ethics is a matter of doing good, which has to involve the results of our actions. The generic problem with utilitarianism, a problem that is intensified greatly when we consider the environment, is giving an adequate account of the good. In the context of this volume, it simply will not do to suggest that *good* is defined by human preferences. Environmental ethics points us beyond the human to a wider order, and beyond the needs or preferences of a given generation of humans to issues of intergenerational justice. Rule utilitarians often invoke a postulate such as "One ought to act following rules that will bring about the greatest good to the greatest number of people in the long run." But when we consider the environment and the place of humans in it, both *of people* and *in the long run* become problematic. If, as modern astrophysics suggests, our solar system has a life expectancy of 5 billion to 8 billion years, the long run is long indeed, and it is hard to imagine deriving useful rules of conduct from it beyond the imperative (which I believe very important) to pay serious attention to sustainability—that is, to inter-generational justice.

Other influential ethical views, often called "deontological," ground obligation in our rationality or our capacity to be self-legislators. Immanuel Kant urged us to think of ourselves as legislating, in our actions, for an ideal society of rational beings. The generic difficulty here is that such approaches need some kind of accounting of results. This has led to attempts by leading American moral philosophers, from William Frankena to John Rawls, to mix utilitarian and deontological theories, for they do seem to require each other, if one pushes the issues far enough. Clearly, good results have something to do with right action, but experience shows that the meaning of *good* in regard to nature is problematic and the term cannot be defined in purely anthropocentric terms, such as what is good for humanity or what brings pleasure to humanity. Finally, I hold that the "good" cannot be defined at all but is the basic ethical concept in terms of which everything else is defined—a position that goes back to Plato and has recently been defended by English philosopher and novelist Iris Murdoch.

All these humanistic ethics run into difficulty when we consider fundamental issues in the environment such as the preservation of biodiversity—the avoidance of species destruction. Why should biodiversity be an ethical issue? There is, of course, a purely instrumental humanistic argument for species preservation, one that should not be ignored. That argument, in a sentence, is a counsel of caution: Maximize biodiversity to protect options to preserve the human species.

The deeper issue this observation raises can be put this way: There seems to be in the universe, and in the very notion of creativity, a drive from the simpler to the more complex (including, at some levels of complexity, deliberate resimplification, as in abstract art). Whether or not one considers this driving force "divine," it is difficult to find a basis for values if it is purely mechanical. And somehow it lies at the very core of the question of value—of the Good in nature and humanity.

Somehow, reducing the value of preservation of other species to human self-preservation seems to be inadequate and to do injustice to our intuitive sense of the beauty and goodness of diversity. On the other hand, we should not beg the question by assuming that diversity as such is good. Many of its forms are quite destructive. So we need a broader perspective within which this kind of question can be meaningfully pursued. Some will find that in religion. If my Yale colleague Robert Adams and I are right in seeing the Good as God (a position to which Iris Murdoch comes very close), then Professor

Adams is also right in suggesting, "The perspective of omniscience must be less bound to the human than ours, and the creator of a universe of which humanity occupies so small a part may be presumed interested in other things in it besides us."[1]

As demonstrated in detail in this book, when we think about environmental ethics, these issues take interesting forms. To what extent can an environmental ethic be derived from nature or the sciences of nature? Or might both "nature" as a concept and the conceptual frameworks of the sciences of nature be shaped by visions of the Good, or God? In his book *Finite and Infinite Goods,* Adams observes: "A conception of the good as transcending the human has a distinct advantage over purely humanistic conceptions that insist on tracing all value to human preferences and the goods of human life. The latter sort of view is hard-pressed to account for the values of nature and the kind of respect many of us intuitively think we owe them." I follow Professor Adams in his suggestion that follows closely on this quotation: "The question of the intrinsic value of natural objects and natural kinds is at any rate a broadly religious question."[2]

How we are to understand the complexity of this universe we occupy is more problematic than it might first seem to be. Many environmentalists in North America seem to identify "nature" with wilderness, that is, nature without human influence. This view, in a way, is as one-sided as are anthropocentric views of nature, since instead of putting the human species at the center, it excludes humanity altogether. As a specialist in Japanese thought, I have long been struck by the difference between the widespread identification of nature with wilderness in parts of Western culture and the widespread Japanese view that nature is something with which humans can cooperate, that it is in some sense a work in progress. Aristotle made an analogous comment when he commented at the beginning of his *Politics* that the civil state is the most natural of human organizations, and we are to be grateful to the person who invented it. Is it so with the good of nature?

How shall we think about the good in nature and humanity? In her slim but important book *The Sovereignty of Good,* Iris Murdoch argues that the Good has authority precisely because it requires a kind of realism—a kind of intellectual ability to perceive what is true—and therefore it requires a suppression of self: "The necessity of the good is then an aspect of the kind of necessity involved in any technique for exhibiting fact."[3] In this sense, the sciences of nature are central contributors to our understanding of the good in nature and humanity. They require a sharpening of our ability to perceive what is true, and to that end they also require a suppression of self. Contrary to some early modern positions on scientific inquiry, these features do not require that scientific inquiry be value-free. What is important is that the values governing scientific inquiry (or, for that matter, theological inquiry) support the search for truth— for example, rigorous logic, respect for data. Modern philosophy has quite decisively demolished the myth of value-free inquiry, for values are fundamental to the most basic of scientific decisions: deciding what is *worth* studying. Yet the relation of careful observation, rich description, and the values that govern where we look is very complex. Maybe this is why there is truth in the cliché that both God and the Devil are in the details.

Chapter 2

The Contribution of Scientific Understandings of Nature to Moral, Spiritual, and Religious Wholeness and Well-Being

Ursula Goodenough

Aldo Leopold wrote a passage, in *A Sand County Almanac,* that takes us right to the heart of the matter:

> No important change in ethics was ever accomplished without an internal change in our intellectual emphasis, loyalties, affections, and convictions. The proof that conservation has not yet touched these foundations of conduct lies in the fact that philosophy and religion have not yet heard of it. In our attempt to make conservation easy, we have made it trivial. . . . We can be ethical only in relation to something we can see, feel, understand, love, or otherwise have faith in.[1]

Leopold wrote this passage in 1949, and it can certainly be said that religion and philosophy have since come to hear about conservation, in good part because of the environmental movement Leopold so helped to catalyze. But I hear him saying something more. I hear him saying that it is not enough to *appreciate* Nature. It is also crucial that we *understand* it, deep in our bones.

Several years ago, I attended a workshop at which the participants described various ways in which environmental topics had been effectively woven into college curricula. Many interesting programs were outlined by faculty and administrators. In not one presentation, however, was there any mention of science courses. Indeed, the *S*-word was never used in the entire two

19

hours of discussion. *Sustainability,* yes, and *stewardship* and *subsidies* and *self-restraint.* But not *science.*

To illustrate why I am troubled by this omission, let me take a short detour. Environmentalism has, since the middle of the twentieth century, shared the stage with a key social movement that we can loosely call cultural sensibility. We have come to realize that in order to have an appreciation of a culture other than one's own, it is essential to leave one's own culture-laden perspectives behind. To take in another culture requires a deep understanding of its language, its history, its dynamics, and its story from the perspective of those who inhabit that culture, from those who indwell. We insist on hearing their voices.

In the same way, I would argue, to understand a tree is not just to think of it as beautiful, or as a habitat for birds, or as a provisioner of shade for ferns or loam for the forest floor. A tree is all these things, to be sure. But it also carries out photosynthetic electron transport and cyclic and noncyclic phosphorylation and nicotinamide adenine dinucleotide phosphate (NADP) reduction and deoxyribonucleic acid (DNA) replication and lignin biosynthesis. To say that these vital activities of the tree are not very interesting or are too difficult to understand seems dismissive to me, or even arrogant, like someone saying he wants to observe an Oceanic culture through his own lenses, on his own terms, wants to pull up in a cruise ship and buy a few postcards and leave. To my mind, it is our *obligation* to understand how genes work and evolution happens and galaxies collide and water freezes and brains think and stars burn. This is the language and the history of our entire context. Trees speak in electrons and carbon and chemical bonds and DNA. How could a curriculum on environmentalism leave these things out?

In response, we might begin with the perception that "these things" are not very interesting or are too difficult to understand. To be sure, our schools in the main do a terrible job of making science interesting and an excellent job of making it incomprehensible. And to be sure, the perceived linkage between scientific understanding and the technological use of scientific understanding fuels an anti-science bias in persons who are alarmed by the technological juggernaut, although to my mind this bias stems from a misunderstanding of how the science–technology linkage works.[2]

But I pick up on something more here, something deeper: I encounter a *resistance* to scientific explanation. Resistances don't usually come from cognitive sources. They come from the gut. Therefore, I suggest that much of the resistance to scientific explanation comes from what can be called a fear of reductionism. We fear, however inchoately, that to view the sun in terms of its language of thermonuclear reactions and gravitational pressures will destroy our experience of the sun's majesty and its sunset beauty. We fear that to view life as the product of genes interacting with environment is to destroy the meaning of both life and environment. We encounter, that is, the ominous specter of "scientific materialism," which sounds for all the world like "dialectical materialism" or perhaps even "diabolical materialism." We shudder, a long existential shudder, and then we scurry back to thinking about Nature on our own aesthetic and political terms.

In fact, I would argue, to experience the sun is *also*—not just, but also—to take in its astonishing materiality: its fissions and fusions, its unimaginable heat and density, its finitude. To understand the sun is to take in its language, its history, its dynamics, its story. In the same way, to take in life is to understand how it works, all the way down, and to understand how it evolves, all the way down. Our scientific understanding of Nature tells us, more than any other voice, what Nature is, how Nature works, how Nature came to be and evolves over time.

So the real resistance, I submit, is embedded in our fear that we will somehow lose what we call our spirituality by encountering our context in material form. And to lose our spirituality, we fear, is to lose our humanness, our soulfulness, our capacity for transcendent experience. We fear we will become automatons.

Here is what I say to my undergraduate students when we arrive at this potentially gloomy juncture: "Okay, suppose a good-looking guy walks by and I feel my pulse quicken and my face flush. Do I say to myself, 'Aha—norepinephrine released from my sympathetic neurons has stimulated my sinoatrial node to generate increased cardiac output?' Of course not. I say to myself, 'Wow, that's a really good-looking guy!'" It's not as if I can't go there. I can certainly reflect on how interesting it is that the experience I just had was mediated by action potentials and calcium influx. But, I assure them, this doesn't wreck the experience. It's just a second way to think about it. The immediate experience, the subjective experience, is uncompromised. Subjectivity, in the end, is immune to anything but its own inherent experiential manifestations.[3]

◆ ◆ ◆

So now let's turn all this on its head. Let's say I've convinced you that to take in and absorb our scientific understanding of Nature is to acknowledge Nature's nature, to accord Nature her due respect. But is it indeed the case, as many suppose, that these understandings are nothing more than dry-as-dust facts that we must dutifully ingest? What if they in fact have spiritual potential?

Religious potential? Moral potential? That is, to paraphrase the title of this chapter (a title suggested by Stephen R. Kellert), how can scientific understandings of Nature contribute to spiritual and religious and moral wholeness and well-being?

In the remainder of this chapter, I will offer some of my own responses to this question, the goal being to encourage subjective responses in my readers. My responses will be organized along the lines articulated by Father Thomas Berry. Berry suggests, in his seminal collection of essays *The Dream of the Earth,* that the universe functions on three principles: differentiation, subjectivity, and communion.[4] For me, this typology works well to describe the three components of a religious orientation, and indeed, since Berry is seeking to articulate a religious orientation in the universe, the convergence is probably not fortuitous.

Berry uses the word *differentiation* to connote the fact that the universe is not some "homogeneous smudge or jellylike substance" but rather is made up of radiation and particles manifesting "an amazing variety of qualities." In religious terms, I would suggest that the apprehension of differentiation is closely linked with our search for Origins, for a Creator of the myriad differentiations. For a theistic person, differentiation can connote the experience of Otherness with respect to God, the unmoved mover. It is a statement about Ultimacy.

One of my favorite Thomas Berry quotes, offered in conversation, is this comment: "Come on. Nobody is ever going to know *anything* about God." If we take this statement as the core understanding of the Abrahamic traditions, as I do, and combine it with the equally powerful sense of Ultimate Mystery that pervades the Eastern and indigenous traditions, then we arrive—all of us, theists and nontheists alike—at the same place. We recognize, with profound humility, that there are questions of Ultimacy that we cannot answer, most of which can be summarized by the question, Why is there anything at all, rather than nothing?

Science has no answer to this question and, indeed, does not ask it. But what science does bring to us is a dazzling, detailed, and extraordinary account of what Is: galaxies, quarks, proteins, ecosystems, the whole shebang. As we seek ways to orient ourselves in the universe, these Is-es present themselves as vibrant substrates for our quest. The important thing, to my mind, is the quest. To take the universe on—to ask, Why are things as they are?—is to generate the foundation for everything else. For some, this foundation comes to take the form of a system of theistic belief—God as Mind, or God as Process, or God as Source—while for others it takes the form of a deep, wondrous agnosticism. Our theological diversity is a testimony to the diversity of the human spirit, and attempts to impose theological homogenization are both futile and tragic.

We can next consider the second component in Berry's trilogy: subjectivity. I will work with this concept in religious terms as the analogue to what is usually called spirituality, although I prefer the term *interiority* to describe this dimension of our religious lives. Our interior selves struggle with a different set of religious questions from those that beset our search for Ultimacy: Who am I? What is my value? How do I transcend the mundane? And the big one, How do I reconcile myself with my materiality and its core manifestation, my mortality? Our religious and artistic traditions offer us many ways to approach these questions, but so do our scientific understandings.

Offered here are two short passages from my book *The Sacred Depths of Nature* to suggest how this can work. The first has to do with our quest for self-value. Prior to this passage, I have been explaining molecular biology to my reader in the context of the concept of emergence, which can be summarized as the "something-more-from-nothing-but" that occurs when novel combinations of proteins give rise to new adaptive traits. Emergence pervades all of evolutionary history—indeed, it can be said to define evolutionary history—and it is manifested with particular elegance during the unfolding of the genetically scripted developmental programs that give rise to multicellular organisms from fertilized eggs. I conclude the discussion as follows:

> At the baptismal ceremony at my church, the parents hand the shining baby over to the minister. He looks down lovingly, dips his hand in the water, touches the luminous little head three times, and says "I baptize you in the name of the Father, and the Son, and the Holy Spirit. You are a child of the Covenant, called by name, cherished, known, blessed by the grace of God."
>
> Called by name. This brand new creature, called by name. I gasp every time I hear the words. The self, the soul: Created, Known, Immortalized, Saved. I was taught to sing "Jesus loves *me* this I know," and to "pray the Lord *my* soul to take." What do I do with my yearning to be special in some ultimate sense?
>
> I have come to understand that the self, my self, is inherently sacred. By virtue of its own improbability, its own miracle, its own emergence.
>
> I start with my egg cell, one of 400,000 in my mother's ovaries. It meets with one of the hundreds of millions of sperm cells produced each day by my father. Astonishing that I happen at all, truly

astonishing. And then I cleave, I gastrulate, I implant, I grow tiny fetal kidneys and a tiny heart. The genes of my father and the genes of my mother switch on and off and on again in all sorts of combinations, all sorts of chords and tempos, to create something both eminently human and eminently new. Once I am born, my unfinished brain slowly completes its maturation in the context of my unfolding experience, and during my quest to understand what it is to be a person, I come to understand that there can be but one me.

And so I lift up my head, and I bear my own witness, with affection and tenderness and respect. And in so doing, I sanctify myself with my own grace. To the extent that I know myself, I am known. My yearning to be capital-K Known is relegated to the corridors of arrogance, and I sing my own song, with outrageous gratitude for my existence.

With this comes the understanding that I am in charge of my own emergence. It is not something that I must wait for, but something to seek, something to participate in achieving, something to delight in achieving.[5]

The second passage relates to our interior struggle to find any kind of meaning in death. From my perspective, an evolutionary understanding of multicellularity has given us much to work with here. Multicellular organisms partition the job of being alive between two kinds of cells: the sexual germ-line cells, which are responsible for transmitting genetic instructions to the next generation, and the somatic cells, which are responsible for seeing that sexual transmission occurs—they negotiate the environment, provide nurture to immature offspring, and so on. Fecund as this arrangement has been for the radiation of the multicellular creatures that we know and love, including ourselves, it carries with it the built-in fact that the soma is biologically dispensable once the germ line has been transmitted. And so it dies. My reflection includes the following:

One of the somatic parts of my body is my brain, the locus of my self-awareness, my interiority. My brain developed with nary a backward look at gene transmission or immortality. The whole point was to make synapses, strengthen them, modulate them, reconfigure them, with countless neurons dying in the process and countless more dying during my lifetime. It is because these cells were not committed to the future that they could specialize and cooperate in the construction of this most extraordinary, and most here-and-now, center of my perception and feelings.

So our brains, and hence our minds, are destined to die with the rest of the soma. And it is here that we arrive at one of the central ironies of human existence. Which is that our sentient brains are uniquely capable of experiencing deep regret and sorrow and fear at the prospect of our own death, yet it was the invention of death, the invention of the germ/soma dichotomy, that made possible the existence of our brains.[6]

And further on:

When I wonder what it will feel like to be dead, I tell myself that it will be like before I was born, an understanding that has helped me to cope with my fear of *being* dead. But what about the fact that I will die? Does death have any meaning?

Well, yes, it does. Sex without death gets you single-celled algae and fungi; sex with a mortal soma gets you the rest of the eukaryotic creatures. Death is the price paid to have trees and clams and birds and grasshoppers, and death is the price paid to have human consciousness, to be aware of all that shimmering awareness and all that love.

My somatic life is the wondrous gift wrought by my forthcoming death.[7]

Finally, we come to communion, the foundation for any ethic. Communion draws us out of our private interiority, compelling as it is, and reminds us of our context and our obligations to that context. And certainly our scientific understandings offer rich resources here. During the course of biological evolution as we now understand it, a common unicellular ancestor served as the founder for the three great radiations of life—the bacteria, the archaea, and the eukaryotes. During the post-Cambrian radiation of the eukaryotes, there occurred countless kinds of unicellular and multicellular incarnations. The current tally indicates that we humans share 47 percent of our genes with yeast and 74 percent of our genes with the worm *Caenorhabditis elegans*. These data, these numbers, insist that we encounter our deep interrelatedness, our deep genetic homology, and hence our vibrant fellowship, with the rest of the living world.

I will end with a reflection on this theme from *The Sacred Depths of Nature:*

Fellowship and community are central to the religious impulse. Children of Israel. United in Christ. Umma in Islam. A friend who was raised Roman Catholic and who travels frequently to foreign cities tells me that she often seeks out the local church when she arrives, finding there the shared ritual, the known liturgy and prayers, the haven. Those of us who find a religious home feel deep affinity with those who have moved through with us and before us, congregating, including, supporting. We offer and receive sympathy and affection. The musicians sing their hushed responses or chant their solemn rhythms and we breathe together, sense our connectedness, heal.

Religion. From the Latin *religio,* to bind together again. The same linguistic root as ligament. We have throughout the ages sought connection with higher powers in the sky or beneath the earth, or with ancestors living in some other realm. We have also sought, and found, religious fellowship with one another. And now we realize that we are connected to all creatures. Not just in food chains or ecological equilibria. We share a common ancestor. We share genes for receptors and cell cycles and signal transduction cascades. We share evolutionary constraints and possibilities. We are connected all the way down.

I walk through the Missouri woods and the organisms are everywhere, seen and unseen, flying about or pushing through the soil or rummaging under the pine needles, adapting and reproducing. I open my senses to them and we connect. I no longer need to anthropomorphize them, to value them because they are beautiful or amusing or important for my survival. I see them as they are; I understand how they work. I think about their genes switching on and off, their cells dividing and differentiating in pace with my own, homologous to my own. I take in the sycamore by the river and I think about its story, the ancient algae and mosses and ferns that came before, the tiny first progenitor that gave rise to it and to me. I try to guess why it looks the way it does—why the leaves are so serrated and the bark so white—and imagine all sorts of answers, all manner of selections and unintended consequences that have yielded this tree to existence and hence to my experience.[8]

And then a poem by Mary Oliver:

> You do not have to be good.
> You do not have to walk on your knees
> for a hundred miles through the desert, repenting.
> You only have to let the soft animal of your body
> love what it loves.
> Tell me about despair, yours, and I will tell you mine.
> Meanwhile the world goes on.
> Meanwhile the sun and the clear pebbles of the rain
> are moving across the landscapes,
> over the prairies and the deep trees,
> the mountains and the rivers.
> Meanwhile the wild geese, high in the clean blue air,
> are heading home again.
> Whoever you are, no matter how lonely,
> the world offers itself to your imagination,
> calls to you like the wild geese, harsh and exciting—
> over and over announcing your place
> in the family of things.[9]

> Blessed be the tie that binds. It anchors us. We are embedded in the great evolutionary story of planet Earth, the spare, elegant process of mutation and natural selection. And this means that we are anything but alone.[10]

The land ethic that flows forth from these understandings, canonized in the writings of Aldo Leopold, was given pithy summary by Oren Lyons, Faithkeeper of the Onondaga Nation, in an address to delegates of the United Nations:

> I do not see a delegation for the four-footed. I see no seat for the eagles. We forget and we consider ourselves superior, but we are after all a mere part of the Creation. And we must continue to understand where we are. And we stand between the mountain and the ant, somewhere and there only, as part and parcel of the Creation. It is our responsibility, since we have been given the minds to take care of these things.[11]

My father, Erwin Goodenough, was a professor of the history of religion at Yale University for many decades, and he therefore gets the last word. "Life is a coral reef," he would say to us children. "We each leave behind the best, the strongest deposit we can so that the reef can grow. But what's important is the reef."

Chapter 3

Spiritual and Religious Perspectives of Creation and Scientific Understanding of Nature

Calvin B. DeWitt

We have come to recognize that human society is on a path that degrades and threatens the integrity of the biosphere. Scientific understanding of nature and nature's degradation have not been sufficient to correct our course; neither has the ethical and moral compass of religion. Consequently, many scientific and religious leaders have advocated that science and religion work together in complementary fashion to address our environmental situation. This raises two basic questions. First, Do spiritual and religious perspectives of creation complement scientific understanding of nature? And second, assuming a positive answer to the first question, Does a partnership of religion and science hold promise for the integrity of the biosphere?

In seeking answers, we can reasonably invoke Aldo Leopold, the scientist who extended ethics to embrace the environment in his essay "The Land Ethic." Moreover, since he also had good knowledge of the Bible, his thought is a particularly appropriate place to begin. In this well-known essay, Leopold states, "An ethic, ecologically, is a limitation on freedom of action in the struggle for existence."[1] Killing of whoever gets in the way of human ambition is constrained by convention or commandments such as "Thou shalt not kill." Noting that the biblical Ten Commandments applied to the personal and individual level, Leopold sought an ethic that extended to land and its biotic communities. Knowing that land was incorporated in the ethics of the biblical prophets Ezekiel and Isaiah, and informed by his Bible study as a student at Yale University and afterward, he could write, "Individual thinkers since the days of

Ezekiel and Isaiah have asserted that the despoliation of land is not only inexpedient but wrong."[2]

Leopold declared the biblical prophet Ezekiel "a woodsman and an artist," Isaiah "the Roosevelt of the Holy Land," and Joel "the preacher of conservation of watersheds." Job he labeled "the John Muir of Judah." Each had vital ecological understanding coupled with an ethical commitment to the rightness of preserving creation. Their ecological understanding and ethical understanding were complementary, one mutually fulfilling and completing the other.[3]

Complement means "to make whole, to fulfill, to complete." A complement is "something which, when added, completes or makes up a whole—each of two parts which mutually complete each other or supply each other's deficiencies." As a verb, *complement* means "to make complete or perfect, to supply what is wanting."[4] From the perspective of Leopold, Roosevelt, Muir, and the biblical prophets, ecological knowledge (science) is incomplete unless joined with knowledge of what ought to be. Mirroring the land–ethics connection of the prophets, Leopold reconnected what had been joined before—science and ethics.

Prophets, then and now, expose and describe environmental degradation and call upon its perpetrators to mend their ways. Today, most prophets are scientists, who "more than any other single segment of [the] general public . . . more, even than most mainline preachers," are telling us that "our world is in critical shape and . . . the human element is chiefly to blame for it."[5] Exposing and describing the way things are, challenged by a cross fire of intentional confusion and misinformation, these scientists are looking for ethical partners. And recently, they have joined key religious leaders to make their appeal.

The "Joint Appeal by Religion and Science for the Environment"

In their "Joint Appeal by Religion and Science for the Environment," made in Washington, D.C., on May 12, 1992, scientists and religious leaders announced:

> We are people of faith and of science who, for centuries, often have traveled different roads. In a time of environmental crisis, we find these roads converging. As this meeting symbolizes, our two ancient, sometimes antagonistic, traditions now reach out to one another in a common endeavor to preserve the home we share. . . .

We humans are endowed with self-awareness, intelligence and compassion. At our best, we cherish and seek to protect all life and the treasures of the natural world. But we are now tampering with the climate. We are thinning the ozone layer and creating holes in it. We are poisoning the air, the land and the water. We are destroying the forests, grasslands and other ecosystems. We are causing the extinction of species at a pace not seen since the end of the age of the dinosaurs. . . .

We believe that science and religion, working together, have an essential contribution to make toward any significant mitigation and resolution of the world environmental crisis. What good are the most fervent moral imperatives if we do not understand the dangers and how to avoid them? What good is all the data in the world without a steadfast moral compass? . . .

Insofar as our peril arises from a neglect of moral values, human pride, arrogance, inattention, greed, improvidence and a penchant for the short-term over the long, religion has an essential role to play. Insofar as our peril arises from our ignorance of the intricate interconnectedness of nature, science has an essential role to play. . . .

We believe that the dimensions of this crisis are still not sufficiently taken to heart by our leaders, institutions and industries. We accept our responsibility to help make known to the millions we serve and teach the nature and consequences of the environmental crisis, and what is required to overcome it.[6]

The "Joint Appeal" urges reconnection of the break between scientific knowledge and the "moral compass" of religion, advocates preservation of our biospheric home, finds it necessary for people of science and religion jointly to address the environmental crisis, and appeals to people to live rightly and responsibly, to cherish and protect all life and natural treasures, and to spread the word.

The Importance of Religion

The "Joint Appeal" sees religion, lately perceived as the cause of the environmental crisis,[7] as necessary for its solution. "For most of my adult life I believed, as many environmentalists do, that religion was the primary cause of ecological crisis," wrote environmental philosopher Max Oelschlaeger. But, he continued, "I lost that faith by bits and pieces. . . . My conjecture is this: There are no solutions for the systemic causes of ecocrisis, at least in democratic societies, apart from religious narrative."[8] A similar strain was echoed by Sierra Club director Carl Pope: "Many of us have inherited and uncritically accepted the 19th century idea that religion could be discarded because it had been superceded by science. We failed to realize—as some eminent scientists now tell us—that science and religion offer two distinct approaches to knowledge, and that neither has a monopoly on the truth." Pope stated pungently, "We acted as if we could save life on Earth without the same institutions through which we save ourselves . . . it is time to recognize our allies in the faith community." Recognizing integration of the ethical, spiritual, and scientific in the Sierra Club's creator, he commended his readers to the "frankly spiritual writing of our founder John Muir."[9] Earlier, physicist and Nobel laureate Max Planck wrote, "Human beings need science in order to know; religion in order to act," and "Beliefs about the universe can as little take the place of knowledge and skills as the solution of ethical problems can be achieved through pure intellectual knowledge."[10] Religious ethics and science are reciprocally fulfilling; one does not substitute for the other.

Religion and Religation

Wayne C. Booth, distinguished professor emeritus of English at the University of Chicago, defines religion as follows:

> Religion is the passion, or the desire, both to live right—not just to live but to live *right*—and to *spread* right living, both desires *conceived as responses* to some sort of cosmic demand—that is, to a demand made to us by the *way things are,* by the way the world is, by the nature of Nature (as some would say) or by God himself (as explicitly religious people put it).[11]

Within this definition of religion is complementarity of the kind we are evaluating here. The desire to live right and spread right living requires an understanding of what ought to be (ethics), whereas to know the way things are requires knowledge (science). *Within* religion, therefore, we have the necessity for both science *and* ethics, one completing the other to enable right action in the world (praxis).

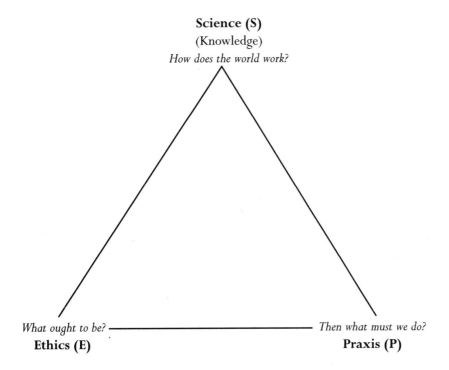

Science, broadly defined to include all knowledge, linked with ethics and praxis, can be related in a "science-ethics-praxis triad." This triad, and the principal question each of its corners addresses, is illustrated in the figure.

Science, ethics, and praxis are connected here with three ligaments. When any ligament is degraded or torn, one or all corners are freed from the constraints and contributions of the others, with consequent problems: Science without ethics may produce praxis that results in degraded human–environment relations, weapons of destruction, and impoverished genetic diversity. Ethics disconnected from science may bring removal of dead wood and other signs of death from forests at the expense of soil building, or unwise use of pesticides to erase evidence of "The Fall." Praxis separated from science and ethics (just "doing something") may result in cities built on floodplains or houses built on geologic fault lines. All three elements of the triad need to be connected; ideally, each should be complementary to the others. And this brings us to our question.

Do Spiritual and Religious Perspectives of Creation Complement Scientific Understanding of Nature?

Recalling our definition of *complement,* we ask, Does scientific understanding of nature complement ethical imperatives derived from spiritual and religious perspectives of creation? There are at least four routes for evaluating such complementarity: (1) individual scientists who adhere to a religious perspective; (2) definitions of religion; (3) etymology of the word *religion;* and (4) scriptural teachings within the Judeo-Christian-Islamic tradition.

1. Complementarity in Individual Scientists

A potent source for answering our question is the scientists who profess a particular religious belief. Their scientific and religious confessions can be found in various books, such as *Ecology and Religion: Scientists Speak; Professors Who Believe;* and *Real Science, Real Faith.*[12] Here are examples of scientific and religious perspectives joining together within individual people. Complementarity can and does exist for science and religion at the level of individuals.

2. Complementarity within Definitions of Religion

In seeking complementarity, we also can look at definitions of religion, such as this restatement of Wayne C. Booth's definition:

> Religion is the passion or desire both to live *right* and to *spread* right living as desires *conceived as responses* to some sort of cosmic demand made to us by the *way things are,* by the nature of nature, or by God, who orders creation and holds all things together with integrity.

Either this or Booth's original has complementarity built into it. Living rightly according to the way things are—in response to the nature of nature—requires complementarity. If religion is the passion to live rightly with respect to nature, or with respect to God, who orders creation, then it must complement a scientific understanding of nature.[13]

3. Complementarity in the Etymology of Religion

Although Cicero connected the word *religion* with *religĕre,* "to read over," later authors connected it with *religāre,* "to bind" or "to religate." The latter etymology was chosen by subsequent writers. Closely related words are *ligate,* "to tie with a ligature," and *ligature,* "something used to bind" or "the action of binding or tying." Also related are *religate,* "to bind up or back," and *religation,* "the action of tying up."[14] This means that whenever religion, science, and ethics are ligated and religated, they must of necessity be complementary.

4. Complementarity in Religions and Religious Texts

In taking this fourth route, we need first to recognize the wide array of religions and to respect the differences among them that are vital to their individual worth and worthship. Yet all share in the human habitation of the biosphere, in environmental use and degradation, and in concern about environmental degradation and caring for creation. Their shared commitment is indicated in *The Assisi Declarations,* an interfaith statement that tells us the following:

- "Destruction of the environment and the life depending upon it is a result of ignorance, greed and disregard for the richness of all living things" (Buddhist).
- We should "declare our determination to halt the present slide towards destruction, to rediscover the ancient tradition of reverence for all life" (Hindu).
- "Now, when the whole world is in peril, when the environment is in danger of being poisoned and various species, both plant and animal, are becoming extinct, it is our . . . responsibility to put the defense of nature at the very center of our concern" (Jewish).
- We "repudiate all ill-considered exploitation of nature which threatens to destroy it" (Christian).
- People as God's trustees "are responsible for maintaining the unity of His creation, the integrity of the Earth, its flora and fauna, its wildlife and natural environment" (Muslim).[15]

This shared commitment among religions is also seen in statements of the Alliance of Religions and Conservation:

- "The grandeur and diversity of the natural world are purposeful reflections of the majesty and bounty of God" (Baha'i).
- "All life is inter-related," and believers "are called to show compassion to every living thing" (Buddhist).
- "Conserve ecology or perish" is the Bhagavad Gita's injunction (Hindu).
- Avoiding "violence towards all of nature" is a fundamental doctrine resulting in "reverence for all life in all forms" and leading to "compassion for all living beings" (Jain).
- "The purpose of humanity is to serve the world and to protect all of creation" (Sikh).
- "Humanity follows the Earth, the Earth follows Heaven, Heaven follows the Tao, and the Tao follows what is natural" (Taoist).

- "The world belongs to God and humanity has a place as leader and custodian of the natural world, responsible to God" (Jewish).
- God's creation and sustenance of the earth motivates people "to properly care for the land" (Christian).
- Humanity's role is "Trustee of God, on earth"—people "are entrusted by God with its safekeeping" (Muslim).[16]

Each of these religions shows complementarity with science in the sense that it recognizes creation's order and integrity; is committed to addressing human arrogance, ignorance, and greed; and is dedicated to protecting and caring for creation. Seyyed Hossain Nasr, professor of Islamic studies at George Washington University, expressed it well:

> The person who speaks for the life of the Spirit today cannot remain indifferent to the destruction of that primordial cathedral which is virgin in nature, nor maintain silence concerning the harm human beings do to themselves as immortal beings by absolutizing the "kingdom of man" and as a consequence brutalizing and destroying everything else in nature in the name of the earthly welfare of members of that kingdom.[17]

The complementarity of these and other religions can perhaps be summed up in the belief that people should "walk in beauty," as the Navajo put it.[18] However, as these basic statements indicate, we may not create the fiction that all these religions are one without doing them a disservice; and it would not be practical to cover each of them individually here.

Some religions encourage or require withdrawal from wider human society so that adherents might live a simpler or even monastic life that is less manipulative of the environment, thereby achieving a kind of benign harmony in creation. Others engage with the goings-on of the wider world and society, requiring more manipulation of the environment, and therefore find it necessary to constrain behavior that otherwise might be destructive. The religions of Judaism, Christianity, and Islam are generally of the latter type. Understandably, they also have strong connections with the origins and history of science and technology. All three are Abrahamic monotheistic religions and hold the Bible in high regard among their textual material. Their adherents—the "People of the Book"—share the Judeo-Christian-Islamic tradition.[19] For the remainder of this chapter, the scope of the discussion will be limited to the People of the Book and, more specifically, the Bible.

Complementarity of Persistent Qualities

Taking the Bible first with a rather grand sweep, historian of science Colin Russell, in his book *The Earth, Humanity, and God,* concludes that its persistent qualities are in concord with current science: It perceives the earth and the heavens as unified within the same universe under their creator; it affirms consistent and lawful operation of the earth and the universe; and it puts the earth in its place within the universe (e.g., as God's footstool).[20]

Eight Biblical Ethics

At a more specific level, there is a need to examine particular teachings, and it is appropriate again to have Aldo Leopold open the Book for us.[21] In his essay "The Forestry of the Prophets," he cites Ezekiel 34:18, in which the prophet asks: "Is it not enough for you to feed on the green pastures? Must you also trample them with your feet? Is it not enough for you to drink the pure water? Must you also muddy it with your feet?" And also Isaiah, who prophesies: "Woe to them that join house to house, and add field to field, that they may take away something of their neighbour's."[22]

Leopold's opening is an invitation to numerous biblical ethical teachings on human dealings with creatures and creation. Among these are eight basic ethics: four on the economy of the biosphere[23] and four on the economy of human behavior:

A. Economy of the Biosphere: Four Basic Ecological Ethics

1. Earthkeeping Ethic: As the creator keeps and sustains us, so must we keep and sustain the creator's creation.
2. Fruitfulness Ethic: We must ensure flourishing of the biosphere.
3. Sabbath Ethic: We must not relentlessly press creatures and ecosystems.
4. Fulfillment and Limits Ethic: We must provide for the earth's fulfillment in biodiversity and abundant life, within the earth's finite limits.

B. Economy of Human Behavior: Four Basic Human Behavioral Ethics

5. Sabbath Buffer Ethic: We must not press the biosphere's absolute limits.
6. Contentment Ethic: We must seek contentment, not material accumulation.
7. Priority Ethic: We must seek first biospheric integrity rather than self-interest.
8. Praxis Ethic: We must not fail to act on what we know is right.[24]

These appear to be complementary to corresponding scientific knowledge.[25] I have selected three of these ethics, Earthkeeping, Fruitfulness, and Sabbath, for elaboration here and have added a fourth, Con-service. Each is presented .with references to specific books of the Bible (Genesis, Exodus, Leviticus, Numbers, Deuteronomy, Psalms, Isaiah, Ezekiel, John, Colossians, etc.), in which chapter and verse are separated by a colon.

Earthkeeping Ethic

The Earthkeeping Ethic is derived from Genesis 2:15, in which God expects Adam to *keep* the garden. The Hebrew word translated as *keep* is *shamar,* and it merits careful attention. It also appears in the blessing of Aaron (Numbers 6:24): "The Lord bless you and *keep* you" (emphasis added). This does not look for a preservationist keeping, as would *natsar,* but a full dynamic keeping. Both *natsar* and *shamar* are applied to keeping the Law, which must be both preserved and kept. And given the availability of both words, it is significant that *shamar* is used for keeping people and keeping the garden. For people, it is expected that God's keeping will nurture human life-sustaining and life-fulfilling relationships with vibrant wholeness and dynamic integrity—social relationships with parents, mates, children, siblings, and neighbors. For the garden, it is expected that human keeping of the garden will respect and nurture life-sustaining and life-fulfilling ecological relationships with and among land, air, water, and other creatures, imaging God's love for the world.

As in "people keeping," so in "earthkeeping." Earthkeeping maintains and ensures the dynamic vitality, energy, and beauty of the garden and its creatures. Informed by science, we know that such keeping involves a fine balancing of constructive and destructive processes. In people and other vertebrates, it includes the dynamic re-formation of the skeletal system of dynamic creatures in a dynamic world. Osteoblasts build up bone where needed even as osteoclasts tear it down where superfluous, in a controlled and finely tuned process that maintains a strong skeletal system responsive to the needs of a changing body under changing stresses. Elsewhere in nature, this dynamic re-formation includes the formation of living systems from previously living systems in a dynamic biosphere. Photosynthesis builds up material and energetic resources energized by the sun while respiration and decomposition break down dead materials to energize and perpetuate species and ecosystems. All this is controlled by constraints of material and energy budgets that sustain life as a flowing stream of biotic intricacy, complexity, and diversity.

When people *keep* the garden and creation, they do so in this deep, full, and dynamic sense. Reflecting God's keeping of them, they profess and confess in deeds and actions that creatures under their care must be kept with dynamic integrity. They must be preserved, maintained, and enabled to maintain proper connections with members of their own kind and with many other creatures with whom they interact—and with the soil, air, and water upon which they depend for life and fruitfulness. They must be maintained, in ways complementary to our scientific understanding of the world, within the trophic cycles of life and death—within the trophic energy and material transfers upon which the life of the biosphere depends.

We must keep and sustain God's creation as God keeps and sustains us.

Fruitfulness Ethic

The fish of the sea are accorded God's blessing of fruitfulness. So are the birds and other living creatures: "Let the water teem with living creatures, and let birds fly above the earth across the expanse of the sky" (Genesis 1:20), and "Be fruitful and increase in number and fill the water in the seas, and let the birds increase on the earth" (Genesis 1:22). This blessing is also given to creation's caregivers, as next we read in Genesis 1:28.

God's creation reflects God's fruitful work of giving to land and life what satisfies, as Psalm 104:10–13 proclaims:

He makes springs pour water into the ravines;

it flows between the mountains.

They give water to all the beasts of the field;

the wild donkeys quench their thirst.

The birds of the air nest by the waters;

they sing among its branches.

He waters the mountains from his upper chambers;

the earth is satisfied by the fruit of his work.

Just as God's fruitful work brings fruit to creation, so should people's work. Imaging God, people should also provide for the creatures. And just as Noah spared no time, expense, or reputation when God's creatures were threatened with extinction (Genesis 6–9), neither should we. Countering "development" at the expense of other creatures, our knowledge of human behavior and population provides a base for the proclamation of the prophet

Isaiah: "Woe to you who add house to house and join field to field till no space is left and you live alone in the land" (Isaiah 5:8).

The Jewish teaching of *bal taschit*—Hebrew words that mean "Do not destroy!"—is an expression of the Fruitfulness Ethic: "When you lay siege to a city, you must not destroy the fruit trees" (Deuteronomy 19:19–20). We may take of the fruit of creation, but using our knowledge of requirements for maintaining the lineages of species, we must not destroy creation's fruitfulness. And "When you come across a mother bird on its nest with young, you may take the young but not the mother" (Deuteronomy 22:6–7). Thus, even though we might never take birds, if we do so, we must not destroy the ability of the bird to produce more offspring; we must preserve its fruitfulness.[26]

Speaking strongly to the Fruitfulness Ethic are parallel passages in the Psalms and Ezekiel. In Psalm 23:2:

> He maketh me to lie down in green pastures;
>
> He leadeth me beside the still waters;
>
> He restoreth my soul.

This divine provision for contented living and peaceful fulfillment is paralleled by the passage from Ezekiel quoted by Leopold (Ezekiel 34:18):

> Is it not enough for you to feed on the green pastures?
>
> Must you also trample them with your feet?
>
> Is it not enough for you to drink the pure water?
>
> Must you also muddy it with your feet?

In using the gifts of creation, human beings are restored and satisfied. But we are admonished not to make a mess of these gifts—we are not to go beyond grateful and reasonable use of them. And, after the example of Noah, we must *keep* creation's biodiversity and the biosphere, with all their dynamic integrity.

We should enjoy, but must not destroy, creation's fruitfulness.

Sabbath Ethic

Exodus 20 and Deuteronomy 5 require that one day in seven be reserved for rest by people and animals. The biblical reason is that God also rested after making the heavens and the earth. Just as human beings and animals are to be given their times of Sabbath rest, so is the land. Exodus 23 commands, "For six years you shall sow your land and gather in its yield; but the seventh year you shall let it rest and lie fallow." In Leviticus 25:20, a question arises: "You may ask, 'What will we eat in the seventh year if we do not plant or harvest our crops?'" God answers in Leviticus 25:26: "I will send you such a blessing in the sixth year that the land will yield enough for three years." God is saying, in essence, Do not worry, but practice this law so that your land will be *fruitful:* "If you follow my decrees and are careful to obey my commands, I will send you rain in its season, and the ground will yield its crops and the trees of the field their fruit."

More than a legal requirement, the Sabbath Ethic is a principial one. In Mark 2:27, Jesus describes the meaning of the Sabbath in terms of its benefi-ciaries; the Sabbath is for the ones served by it. Thus, observance of the Sab-bath year protects land from relentless use. By resting, the land rejuvenates itself and gets things together again. The Sabbath Ethic for land prevents all creatures and the biosphere from being relentlessly pressed. Failure to observe this divine command results in depopulation of degraded land, and, no longer inhabited by people, "the land will rest and enjoy its sabbaths. All the time that it lies desolate, the land will have the rest it did not have during the sabbaths you lived in it."

We must provide for creation's Sabbath rests.

Con-service Ethic

Beyond recognizing the full meaning of *shamar* in Genesis 2:15, it is helpful for us to attend to the word *'abad,* which precedes it. In *Young's Literal Translation of the Holy Bible,*[27] it is rendered as follows: "And Jehovah God taketh the man and causeth him to rest in the garden of Eden, to *serve* it, and to *keep* it." The term is also used in the book of Joshua: "Choose for yourselves this day whom you will *serve.* . . . But as for me and my household, we will *serve* the Lord."[28] Although the concept of serving the garden or creation might have a peculiar ring to it, we should consider its meaning for Eden, a garden planted by God,[29] where hoe, shovel, and plow might have simply been out of place. Eden could be more like gardens of some tropical peoples where interplanting and high diversity are the rule. It might best be viewed as not amenable to turning of the ground but still open to service.

In Christian teaching, the human role as servant is widely taught; even Jesus is described as someone who took the form of a servant. The biblical expecta-tion is that human work in the garden is an act of service. Clearly, not only do we serve the garden; the garden also serves us and other creatures. Creation's service is returned with our service to creation. One reciprocally serves the other. When supplied with the prefix *con,* the word *service* becomes *con-service.* People are expected ethically to be about the business of con-servancy. While the reciprocal relation between people and the garden can be service, it also can take the form of human abuse and creation's retribution. Intended and unintended abuse of creation can have severe consequences. When people fail to serve, and instead abuse, creation, they have reason to expect a reciprocal in-kind payment.

When dominion is seen as license to serve one's self-interest, it is a misappropriation of the image of God, and in Christianity it is a failure to follow the example of Jesus. The key to proper service always is to consider one's service as Christ's service. One's service should reflect God's love for the world.[30] Responsible reflection of God's love seeks not itself but the Kingdom of God. Responsible imaging of God's love and law reflects God's goodness, righteousness, and holiness. It employs intellectual powers, natural affections, and moral freedom to reflect the wisdom, love, and justice of God. It expresses the depths of one's soul in responsible praxis.

We must con-serve creation.

Ethics–Science Complementarity

These four biblical ethics can be examined for complementarity:

	ETHIC	SCIENCE
Earthkeeping	We must keep the earth and the biosphere with their dynamic integrity.	The integrity of the earth and the biosphere can be and is degraded by human action.
Fruitfulness	We must behave in ways that ensure continued fruitfulness and biodiversity.	Biodiversity and the flourishing of life can be diminished and degraded by human action.
Sabbath	We must provide creatures and creation with times for restoration and regeneration.	Relentless exploitation of the earth and the biosphere can work against their sustainability.
Con-service	We must return the service we derive from the earth and its creatures with our own.	Continuous taking from the earth and the biosphere degrades and tends to deplete it.

These four ethics complement our scientific understanding of the natural world, with science describing the world and the consequences of human action in it and biblical ethics describing what human beings ought to be doing in the world. However, complementarity has little significance if the ligaments are broken. And broken ligaments pose problems.

Linkage of the kind advocated by the "Joint Appeal by Religion and Science for the Environment" is necessary for achieving complementary contributions of ethics and science. Such linkage does not equate science and ethics; rather, it recognizes the distinct contribution of each. The religation respects the language and role of each and in partnership provides a basis for acting upon what we know and believe. But how are we to religate both of these with praxis? That is the problem we ultimately must squarely face.

Complementary Praxis

I began by noting that scientific knowledge of the nature and causes of environmental degradation does not necessarily bring corrective action; nor do ethical imperatives of religion. Thus, in the context of the desire expressed in the "Joint Appeal" to work together for the environment, we have looked for complementarity between religion and science. In seeking ethical teachings from religion and scientific understandings that complete each other—that supply each other's deficiencies—we have positive findings. We now need to ask whether science and religion, working together in complementary fashion, can bring corrective action to our environmental situation and, more specifically, whether our praxis complements our scientific and ethical understanding of nature and creation. Since religion and science have been operating with long-standing complementarity (without much cooperation), we can ask whether there is clear evidence that our science and ethics are working for the good of nature and creation. Unfortunately, the answer is not an unequivocal yes.

Here is what we can see through the eyes of two twentieth-century witnesses, Aldo Leopold for the first half of the century and Tony Ends, director of the Michael Fields Agricultural Institute, for the second. Leopold, in his unpublished 1947 foreword to *Great Possessions,* a manuscript precursor to *A Sand County Almanac,* observed:

> During my lifetime, more land has been destroyed or damaged than ever before in recorded history. . . . Concurrent growth in knowledge of land, good intentions toward land, and abuse of land presents a paradox that baffles me, as it does many another thinking citizen. Science ought to work the other way, but it doesn't. Why?[31]

Tony Ends continues in the same theme:

> I ask you to reflect with me about what I have witnessed in my lifetime. . . . There were 89,000 more farmers on the land in Illinois

when I was 4 years old. There were trees and flowering shrubs along many of the roadsides. There were small orchards, berry patches and vegetable gardens in the farmyards. There was livestock visible in the pastures. . . . Almost every vestige of that world has been swept away with those 89,000 farms and with them a rich culture, healthy communities and vibrant rural economies. Most of the barnyards that remain are silent, empty islands in oceans of bare ground, crop residue or stubble, which lap up against the very sides of dilapidated buildings. How can we live our faith in such a setting, knowing what our created world and its nurturing, spiritual qualities looked like such a short time ago?[32]

We human beings know much about what environmental integrity means, and we believe it ought to be maintained; yet we degrade the earth. The biblical description of this problem is, "what I do is not the good I want to do; no, the evil I do not want to do—this I keep on doing" (Romans 7:19). "I discover this principle then: that when I want to do right, only wrong is within my reach. In my inmost self I delight in the law of God, but I perceive in my outward actions a different law, fighting against the law that my mind approves."[33] This problem can be identified as "the human predicament."[34]

"Science ought to work the other way, but it doesn't. Why?" asked Leopold. He answered this in part with his essay "The Land Ethic." We respect, appreciate, and honor his work. "The Land Ethic" is a wonderful contribution, and it has had some wonderful effects, but, by and large, the degradation described by Aldo Leopold and Tony Ends has continued. Now, more than fifty years later, we ask a question parallel with Leopold's: "Ethics should work the other way, but it doesn't. Why?" Its connections with science and practice are broken. When the praxis connections—the ligaments connecting praxis to science and ethics—are degraded or torn, praxis is freed from the constraints and benefits of science and ethics. But praxis needs to be connected with science and ethics in complementary fashion. Praxis needs to be informed, shaped, and constrained by science and ethics.

Arrogance, Ignorance, and Greed

In search of the causes of this disconnect, each semester I ask my forty-two students in environmental science at the University of Wisconsin to identify the most serious environmental problems. Next, they work in groups to discover the underlying causes of all these problems. Over the years, the most frequently identified causes have been human arrogance, ignorance, and greed.[35] Environmental crises are accompanied often by an arrogance that elevates our immediate exploitative capabilities while neglecting and obscuring the long-standing natural processes that have brought us present benefits: We are quick to say that we know and then to act upon our knowledge as if the world might have a life not much longer than our own. Our ecological crises often are accompanied by ignorance—an ignorance that eschews understanding of both the short-term and long-term effects of our actions. We prefer, it seems, to act before we understand the consequences of our actions; we might even work to preserve ignorance of the earth's sustaining ecosystems and of the effects of human actions on the earth's integrity. And our greed brings our society to convert long-standing components of the biosphere into short-term personal or corporate gain even when superseding the long-term interests of a sustainable biosphere and continued integrity of the earth. Unchecked by scientific knowledge of nature and ethical understanding, we might hunt whales to total annihilation, destroying entire species as well as prospects for whaling in the future.

Greed is the term we apply to (1) seeking first our own gain, (2) adapting our belief systems to self-interest, and (3) cultivating a mind-set that emphasizes winning over participating. My students' findings are informed by a statement of Lynton K. Caldwell: "The environmental crisis is an outward manifestation of a crisis of mind and spirit. There could be no greater misconception of its meaning than to believe it to be concerned only with endangered wildlife, human-made ugliness, and pollution. These are part of it, but more importantly, the crisis is concerned with the kind of creatures we are and what we must become in order to survive."[36]

"The kind of creatures we are" is a principal focus of religion. "If we consider human behavior to be the product of evolution and that our actions are influenced by genes and are at least in part 'hardwired,' doesn't this suggest that unpleasant aspects of human behavior such as aggression and violence cannot easily be modified?"[37] "Seek first yourself—preserve and transmit your own genes" would seem to be our evolutionary heritage. But religion counters this selfishness, as Mahatma Gandhi reminded us in his talk to the Economic Society at Allahabad University, India, in 1916. He told his audience he had read the most basic book on economics. Identifying this book as the New Testament, Gandhi paraphrased Matthew 6:33: "Let us seek first the Kingdom of God and His righteousness and the irrevocable promise is that everything will be added to us." Countering an economics that places self-interest as a principal presupposition, he concluded: "These are real economics. May you and I treasure them and enforce them in our daily lives."[38]

The context of this "biospheric" (or "ecumenical") economics is the Sermon on the Mount (Matthew 5–7), in which "one is free to leave one's best interest in God's hands and to respond to others out of love rather than self-interest."[39] Seeking the Kingdom of God is first:

> After this manner therefore pray ye: Our Father which art in heaven, Hallowed be thy name. Thy kingdom come. Thy will be done on earth. . . . Lay not up for yourselves treasures upon earth. . . . For where your treasure is, there will your heart be also. . . . Ye cannot serve God and mammon. . . . Consider the lilies of the field, how they grow; they toil not, neither do they spin: and yet I say unto you, that even Solomon in all his glory was not arrayed like one of these. . . . But seek ye first the kingdom of God, and his righteousness; and all these things shall be added unto you.[40]

Addressing the Human Predicament

How do we who participate in creation's degradation come to grips with the human predicament? Economist John Maynard Keynes proposed in his *Essays in Persuasion* in 1930 that we address it by harnessing greed to achieve the good:

> I see us free, therefore, to return to some of the most sure and certain principles of religion and traditional virtue—that avarice is a vice, that the extraction of usury is a misdemeanor, and the love of money is detestable, that those who walk most truly in the paths of virtue and sane wisdom [are those] who take least thought for the morrow. We shall once more value ends above means and prefer the good to the useful. We shall honour those who can teach us how to pluck the hour and the day virtuously and well, the delightful people who are capable of taking direct enjoyment in things, the lilies of the field who toil not, neither do they spin.[41]

"But beware!" he warned. "The time for all this is not yet. For at least another hundred years we must pretend to ourselves and every one that fair is foul and foul is fair; for foul itself is useful and fair is not. Avarice and usury and precaution must be our gods for a little longer still. For only they can lead us out of the tunnel of economic necessity into daylight."[42] And perhaps never:

"Market arrangements not only minimize the need for coercion as a means of social organization, they also reduce the need for compassion, patriotism, brotherly love, and cultural solidarity as motivating forces behind social improvement."[43]

Keynes wrote that someday we shall honor "the delightful people who are capable of taking direct enjoyment in things, the lilies of the field who toil not, neither do they spin." But, as pointed out by theologian Joseph Sittler in his "Ecological Commitment as Theological Responsibility," examination of this text shows that this is not the focus of the religious invitation:

> When the New Testament . . . reports Jesus as saying, "Behold the lilies of the field" (Matt. 6:28), one is precisely *not* saying, "Look at those lilies!" The word "behold" lies upon that which is beheld in a kind of tenderness which suggests that things in themselves have their own wondrous authenticity and integrity. . . . To behold means to stand among things with a kind of reverence for life which does not walk through the world of the nonself with one's arrogant hat on . . . it is . . . a rhetorical acknowledgement of a fundamental ecological understanding of man whose father is God but whose sibling is the whole Creation. . . . We must somehow bring under question the notion that man . . . is so set apart from the rest of God's Creation that he can deal with it with Olympian arrogance as if it had no selfhood of its own by virtue of the Creation.[44]

The arrogation of the biospheric economy by a monetary economy with self-interest as its principal presupposition is the latest manifestation of the human predicament. Religions address self-interested arrogation by instilling reverence for life in its wondrous authenticity and integrity. More than this, religions have the capacity to address the human predicament. Religious responses to the problem of society's walking a path we do not wish to take—toward degradation of creation and the biosphere—are available to us. These responses can repair the broken connections among science, ethics, and praxis. Beyond this, they also can set the path of human society toward personal and biospheric integrity. Assisting in this are scientists bold enough to describe the way things are; journalists, writers, editors, and publishers daring enough to describe the human predicament as revealed in the present; ethicists forthright enough to engage in pursuit of what ought to be; builders, engineers, economists, designers, planners, and managers disciplined enough to confine their work within the bounds of what ought to be in nature and creation; and religious leaders committed enough to practice what they preach. Religion in all its fulness, as the the binding together of science, ethics, and praxis,[45] can thus nurture the passion both to live *right* and to *spread* right living in response to the cosmic demand made to us by the *way things are,*[46] by the nature of nature, and by God, who orders creation and holds all things together with integrity.[47]

Chapter 4

Values, Ethics, and Spiritual and Scientific Relations to Nature

STEPHEN R. KELLERT

A fundamental divide historically separating scientific from spiritual and religious perspectives of nature and humanity has centered on questions of the origin and evolution of life, most particularly human life.[1] Modern biology, particularly Darwinian perspectives, asserts that species evolved in selective response to contextual environmental pressures and survival requirements, with particular biological traits genetically favored that conferred adaptive capacity and reproductive advantage. To the evolutionary biologist, issues of human morality, ethics, spirituality, and religion are relevant insofar as these inclinations and behaviors enhance an organism's survival and fitness over time.

This perspective strikes many who are religiously and spiritually motivated as excessively materialistic and deterministic, removing and denigrating the human will and related capacity to choose to seek a state of goodness, grace, and ultimate meaning. The religiously and spiritually oriented often emphasize the human ability to achieve a condition of harmony and fulfillment that transcends the merely physical and biological. Moreover, attaining this level of revelation and salvation typically requires a reverence and faith that extend beyond the merely empirically and objectively observed and scientifically determined.

Our challenge is to determine whether a middle ground is possible in which scientific and spiritual outlooks of nature and humanity can be reconciled, one that helps elucidate our ethical responsibilities to the natural world. This chapter offers a rough articulation of how this might be so. It suggests that an ethical regard for nature can be found at the intersection of an empirically based science and a deeply held spiritual faith in the value of creation. It suggests that an environmental ethic can be identified based on an expanded understanding of human evolutionary self-interest that connects human spirituality and morality with physical and material well-being, each indicative of the human dependence on the health, beauty, and integrity of the natural world. It conversely suggests that when our relational ties with nature are impoverished and degraded, we inevitably diminish the likelihood of achieving the spiritual as well as material sustenance and well-being necessary for evolutionary fitness and, ultimately, survival. In effect, this chapter argues that we may achieve our most fulfilling and enriching humanity—a state of both moral grace and physical security—by celebrating our secular as well as spiritual bonds with other life and creation.

This reconciliation of scientific, spiritual, and religious views of the natural world is reflected in the views of two pioneering ecologists, Aldo Leopold and Edward O. Wilson. Each intimates, in the quotes that follow, how an understanding of evolution can be connected with human spiritual and ethical responsibilities for the natural world. Leopold suggested, for example, that

> *ethics . . . is actually a process in ecological evolution. . . .* An ethic may be regarded as a mode of guidance for meeting ecological situations so new or intricate, or involving such deferred reactions, that the path of social expediency is not discernible to the average individual. . . . *Ethics are possibly a kind of community instinct in the making. . . .* All ethics so far evolved rest upon a single premise: that the individual is a member of a community of interdependent parts. . . . The [environmental] ethic simply enlarges the boundaries of community to include soils, waters, plants, and animals, or collectively: the land. . . . An [environmental] ethic . . . presupposes the existence of some mental image of the land as a biotic enterprise. We can be ethical only in relation to something we can see, feel, understand, love, or otherwise have faith in. [Emphasis added.][2]

Wilson, like Leopold, ties human evolutionary fitness to our ethical and spiritual relation to nature in his defense of biological diversity:

> What humanity is now doing [by the current scale of species extinction] will impoverish our descendants for all time to come. Yet critics often respond "so what"? The most frequent argument is one of material wealth at risk. This argument is demonstrably true but contains a dangerous flaw—if judged by potential value,

species can be priced, traded off against other sources of wealth, and when the price is right, discarded. . . . The species-right argument . . . , like the materialist argument alone, is a dangerous play of cards. . . . The independent-rights argument, for all its directness and power, remains intuitive, aprioristic, and lacking in objective evidence. . . . A simplistic adjuration for the right of a species to live can be answered by a simplistic call for the right of people to live. . . . In the end, decisions concerning preservation and use of biodiversity will turn on our values and ways of moral reasoning. A sound ethic . . . will obviously take into account the immediate practical uses of species, but it must reach further and incorporate the very meaning of human existence. . . . *A robust, richly textured, anthropocentric ethic can instead be made based on the hereditary needs of our species, for the diversity of life based on aesthetic, emotional, and spiritual grounds.* [Emphasis added.][3]

Both Leopold and Wilson provide an inspirational articulation of the connection between human evolution, spirituality, emotion, aesthetics, and ethical relations to nature. In this chapter, I will try to elaborate on these critical and seminal insights by exploring how an environmental ethic can be derived from a perspective of science and spirituality rooted in the hereditary needs of our species. I will suggest that people possess an inherent inclination to affiliate with the natural world that encompasses the quest for empirical understanding as well as the search for spiritual meaning and transcendence, each and more instrumental in the human striving for physical security and moral fulfillment. I will present the idea of biophilia and a related description of nine basic values of nature to help elucidate the many ways we humans depend on the richness of our experience of nature for physical, emotional, intellectual, and spiritual sustenance and security.[4] These values reveal collectively how a broad anthropocentric ethic of nature can foster a sense of beauty, meaning, purpose, and grace.

First, a personal anecdote is offered. Like other similar stories, it may seem at first idiosyncratic and tangential, but I hope it will render more vivid the many ways our values of nature can enhance human material and moral capacity. The story recounts a brief moment, like many such epiphanies, when the invisible processes of creation become fleetingly revealed in a passing moment of brilliance and exuberance. It was a time of year when my mind turned to small birds called warblers who migrate northward; a time when I bore witness to tiny spirits racing toward ancient breeding grounds; a time

when I wondered, angels being both beautiful and mighty, gentle and powerful, whether warblers could be considered angelic. I wrote at the time:

> A flicker of movement catches the corner of my eye as I tap elec-
> tronic letters on the computer screen. I sit before the desk, facing
> the large window looking east, on the third floor of the tall house.
> It always feels a little like being in a tree house, perched high
> among the tall oaks marching from the neighbor's house through
> mine on to the next. The first tree lords over the others—four
> hundred years old, twenty feet around, branches resembling entire
> trees. The pistils hang like tassels in the brisk morning air, leaves
> barely emergent, and I can still see between the tangles of branches
> out onto the horizon. In the distance looms the large vertical trap
> rock. Along its base a meandering river winds a path to the nearby
> ocean.
>
> I struggle to keep my mind on the shimmering light of the mon-
> itor's glow. Deadlines and commitments draw me back into the
> screen's reality. But, a second flicker passes among the branches,
> distracting me again. Glints of animation on the move, dancing
> within and between the flowering tassels. I cannot resist the temp-
> tation to look, and rushing for my binoculars, I remember the time
> of year. Warblers on the move. Reproductive fever urging tiny
> birds northwards in great waves, irresistibly seeking their ancestral
> breeding grounds. Returning to the desk, I scan the canopy, frus-
> trated now by the absence of movement. Then, remembering their
> diminutive size, far smaller than the symbol of spring they occupy
> in my mind's eye, I slow down.
>
> Again I catch the flicker of movement. Skipping along new
> leaves and branches among treetops. Closing in, I find and then
> capture my visual prey. A chestnut-sided warbler! Then another. A
> third. A magnolia and a blackburnian! Restless spirits of arresting
> color and exuberant life ceaselessly on the move. Absent yesterday,
> they take possession of the trees today as if the forest can hardly
> exist without them.
>
> I stare at the colors and glorious patterns. A motif of rich sienna
> arches along the white body of the chestnut-sided, a brilliant yel-
> low capping its head. The blackburnian blazes in brilliant orange,
> edged by an emphasizing black; the magnolia in bright yellow and
> black striping, calling for attention.
>
> But these warblers signal much more than beauty to me. The

motion, the eruption of energy, the ghostly specter—all suggest the restless and expansive character of Spring, a time of fresh creation. I welcome, too, their practical role in the cycling of nutrients, their complicated contribution to the continuity of associated plants, their place in a stream of ecological functions and processes on which all life, even my own, ultimately depends. From a more immediate perspective, I am reassured by their contribution to protecting trees of the northern forest, sources of timber and paper, from insect damage and disease.

These migrating wonders also rekindle an elusive youth. Seeking them indulges my passion for discovery, excites my curiosity, feeds my desire for adventure. Today I pursue the feathered storm from the window, but tomorrow I will be in the forest and along the river. There might even be, as there has been, risk and danger in probing where I should not, and sometimes entering the dark forests will call forth a foreboding I never can entirely mute. Their quick beauty represents a fundamental element of their appeal, but they also engender an inquisitive impulse, a competitive urge to find, locate, and identify, a willingness to confront the uncertain and the unknown.

I thrill at their reappearance, but an underlying lament lingers about a future lacking this spirited reminder of the glory and wonder of the returning Spring. Great gaps of cleared and converted forest already fragment vast swaths of wintering, migratory, and nesting grounds. Annual counts suggest population declines of various species. Ecological adages from the past echo inside my head: Rachel Carson[5] and the specter of a "silent spring," Aldo Leopold[6] and the reminder to "think like a mountain." A world without warblers would be mute and barren, lacking the richness of sound, color, the promise of hope, rebirth, and transcendence. Their exuberant passage reaffirms connections with the miracle of tenuous life. Their diminution contracts our tiny world of organized and purposeful matter and spirit; without them, the edge of a more universal deadness and dissolution advances.

The red cliff, the winding river, the spreading floodplain, lacking the wonder of life the warblers signify, offers but a stony silence. The warblers transform this deadness of rock, soil, and water into a fountain of energy and animation. Through them I discern a living essence in the forest and the mountain and the river.

Through them I recognize a vibrant core that converts this heap of inanimate matter into an ecological super-organism, not exactly alive, but organized and, most of all, giving rise to life.

The warblers represent one tiny thread among the many countless cords of relationship that bind the human experience to the great tapestry of life amidst and joining non-life. Standing at the pinnacle of creation, we recognize the apex is only as strong as its base. A modern ecological insight mingles with the wisdom of an ancient nursery rhyme:

Surely, wisdom is given
To all living things,
And the tiniest of creatures
Are the teachers of kings.[7]

As I shut down the computer, my eye catches another flicker of movement. A black and white warbler, less obviously colorful than the others, but striking contrasts nonetheless seductive. I am drawn in. Along with the bird my eye skips from tassel to branch to flower. Among the branches, I am carried by the wind, my self taking wing. My backyard becomes a place of enchantment. My bounded universe becomes an entire world. Along with the warbler, my mind and spirit soar among the treetops. Like the warbler I bathe in the warmth of the early spring. Blazing a trail to the north woods, dissipating remnants from the winter's weariness, re-igniting hope for another year, the warblers lift and inspirit me.[8]

Embedded within this anecdote, and countless other narratives like it, is the idea that human physical and mental well-being is nurtured and enhanced by the quality of our experience of the natural world. These stories intimate an environmental ethic derived from an aesthetic appreciation, spiritual reverence, emotional connection, sense of intellectual challenge, and more regarding nature, each relationship to the natural world related to our evolutionary fitness. The idea that people possess a genetic inclination to attach physical, emotional, intellectual, and moral meaning to nature is called "biophilia," a human biological affinity for life and lifelike processes reflected in nine basic values of the natural world.[9] Each of these values is connected to the anecdote of the warblers, each forming a basis for an instrumental ethic of care and responsibility for nature.

Much of the remainder of this chapter describes these values and connects each to an environmental ethic contingent on human physical, emotional, intellectual, and moral self-interest. Moreover, this environmental ethic embraces both scientific and spiritual perspectives of the natural world. Limited space necessitates only a brief description of each value, its instrumental significance, and its relation to the story of the warblers. To facilitate this discussion, abbreviated definitions of the nine values are noted, in alphabetical order, in the box.

An *aesthetic* value underscores the physical attractiveness and beauty of nature. This perspective has been instrumental in developing the human capacities for recognizing and promoting order and organization; developing ideas of harmony, balance, symmetry, and grace; and evoking and stimulating curiosity and imagination.[10] Few experiences in human life exert as consistent and powerful an influence as that of the beauty and physical attraction of nature. Even the most hardened criminal, when suddenly exposed to a beautiful sunset or even a Blackburnian warbler, would very likely be unable to resist some degree of aesthetic appreciation. This largely involuntary response has developed and persisted because, like all human biological tendencies, it fosters a range of adaptive benefits linked to its consistency and intensity. Beauty in nature inspires and instructs, providing a prototype and a template for

AESTHETIC:	physical attraction and appeal of nature
DOMINIONISTIC:	mastery and control of nature
HUMANISTIC:	emotional bonding with nature
NATURALISTIC:	exploration and discovery of nature
MORALISTIC:	moral and spiritual relation to nature
NEGATIVISTIC:	fear and aversion of nature
SCIENTIFIC:	knowledge and understanding of nature
SYMBOLIC:	nature as a source of communication and imagination
UTILITARIAN:	nature as a source of material and physical reward

action. Through mimicry and ingenuity, people capture analogous expressions of excellence and refinement in their lives. The spring warbler provides a glimpse of perfection in a world where chaos, frailty, shortcoming, and death are far more pervasive and normative. People also favor landscapes that enhance safety, sustenance, and security—for example, ones with water, that foster sight and mobility, and that have bright flowering colors and other features that, over evolutionary time, have proven instrumental in human survival.[11] The human aesthetic for nature is fundamentally an act of attraction, of being drawn to the most "information-rich" environment we will ever encounter. In being so attracted, we nurture our tendencies for wonder and curiosity, which lead to exploration, imagination, creativity, and discovery. And in recognizing this beauty, we become ethically inclined to defend and protect this source of wonder and inspiration.

A *dominionistic* value reflects the inclination to master and control the natural world. Adaptive benefits include an enhanced sense of independence and autonomy, greater safety and security, and a willingness to take risks, show resourcefulness, and cope with adversity. People hone their physical and mental fitness through subduing and mastering nature. We no longer rely on besting prey or eluding menacing predators or surviving in the wild, but the strength and prowess we derive from physical and mental competence in confronting nature remains instrumental in our physical and mental well-being. By demonstrating the capacity to function under difficult and challenging circumstances, we emerge surer and more confident of ourselves. Spotting and observing warblers hardly constitutes a test of survival, but by finding, locating, and "capturing" this visual prey under somewhat novel and demanding circumstances, we affirm the ability to persevere, succeed, and master challenges and the unknown. We develop self-confidence and self-esteem by demonstrating the ability to succeed in the face of adversity. And the catalyst for this enhanced well-being can become the recipient of our greater appreciation, admiration, and ethical regard.

A *humanistic* value reflects strong affection for and emotional attachment to the natural world. The development of such feelings enhances human capacities for intimacy, companionship, trust, relationship, and the giving and receiving of affection. The natural world has always been a focus of human affection, especially in bonding, affiliation, and companionship with other creatures, but also in occasional identification with certain plants and landscapes.[12] These subjects of pronounced affection provide the chance for closeness, connection, and the expression of feelings that suggest at times even a sense of love and kinship. Isolation and aloneness constitute heavy burdens for a highly social species such as our own. People typically crave companionship and affiliation, and emotionally identifying with elements of nature can be a valued means for establishing strong relationships and expressing and receiving affection. We covet responsibility for others and, in turn, gratefully welcome their seeming devotion and allegiance. This feeling of connection is powerfully evident in our ties not only to domesticated animals but also to charismatic wild species such as elephants and bears—and sometimes, with familiarity and cultivation, even warblers. We cherish and protect these objects of affection and attachment, extending to them ethical standing and a willingness to defend their interests and well-being.

A *moralistic* value reflects a spiritual and moral affinity for the natural world. Benefits associated with this perspective include a sense of order, meaning, and purpose; a feeling of shared moral conviction; and an enhanced inclination to treat nature with kindness and respect. Nature is a source of deep and persistent spirituality and religious inspiration, in part because of a sense of underlying and fundamental connection of nature with humanity. Despite incredible variability in the natural world—for example, 1.7 million classified species among an estimated 10–100 million extant species and the disappearance of nearly all species that ever existed—most people are astonished by the fundamental commonality uniting most of life as we know it. The great majority of creatures share common molecular and genetic features, analogous circulatory and reproductive structures, and parallel body parts. This and more, much of it intuitively grasped, suggests a remarkable web of relationship connecting a fish in the sea, a warbler in the treetops, and a human in a modern metropolis. This unity and relation provides a sense of meaning and order and a cornerstone of spiritual and religious belief in a world where disorder and disconnection are far more common. When we discern universal patterns in creation, we give shape to our existence. Through shared moral conviction in an underlying harmony and purpose in life, we acquire strength, a sense of cohesion, and feelings of mutual commitment. These spiritual and moral sentiments prompt the view that at the core of our existence lies a fundamental logic, worth, and even goodness. Faith and confidence emerge through the recognition of a unity transcending one's individuality, separateness, and aloneness. This sense of unity was poignantly expressed by John Steinbeck:

> It seems apparent that species are only commas in a sentence, that each species is at once the point and the base of a pyramid, that all life is related. . . . And then not only the meaning but the feeling about species grows misty. One merges into another, groups melt into ecological groups until the time when what we know as life

meets and enters what we know of as non-life: barnacle and rock, and earth, earth and tree, and rain and air. And the units nestle into the whole and are inseparable from it. . . . And it is a strange thing that most of the feeling we call religious, most of the mystical outcrying which is one of the most prized and used and desired reactions of our species, is really the understanding and the attempt to say that man is related to the whole thing, related inextricably to all reality, known and unknowable. This is a simple thing to say, but a profound feeling of it made a Jesus, a St. Augustine, a Roger Bacon, a Charles Darwin, an Einstein. Each of them in his own tempo and with his own voice discovered and reaffirmed with astonishment the knowledge that all things are one thing and that one thing is all things—a plankton, a shimmering phosphorescence on the sea and the spinning planets and an expanding universe, all bound together by the elastic string of time.[13]

This perspective fosters an inclination to protect and preserve the natural world. We conserve nature as much because of moral and ethical belief as because of any calculated materialism or regulatory fiat. When people discern a fundamental relation between themselves and creation, they inevitably temper their tendencies to harm and destroy its constituent parts. Even a tiny warbler can become the means for discerning the splendid and sublime, a pathway for divining harmony, meaning, and grace.

A *naturalistic* value emphasizes an interest in close and direct contact with the natural world. Adaptive benefits include enhanced tendencies for exploration, discovery, and imagination; increased self-confidence through demonstration of skill and competence; and greater calm and peace of mind through heightened awareness and spatial and temporal immersion in nature. Intimate relation with the many rhythms and details of the natural world engenders curiosity, imagination, and an interest in exploration and discovery. Every creature is like a "magic well"; the more one explores and draws from it, the more is revealed in an endless flow of wonder and curiosity.[14] People mine physical, emotional, and intellectual ore from deep and detailed immersion in nature's rich tapestry of shapes and forms. In the process, they achieve physical fitness and mental acuity, an expanded inclination for adventure, and an enhanced capacity for reacting quickly, resolving new and challenging situations, and exploiting and consuming with efficiency. This intimacy with nature can generate a clearer sense of priorities, greater strength and resolve, and improved feelings of self-confidence and self-worth. Pursuing warblers offers a chance for deep and timeless involvement, a respite from the modern temper, which all too often is marred by transience, tenuous relations, and conflicted identity. One feels, as a consequence, gratitude, appreciation, and an ethical inclination to defend and protect this source of physical and mental security.

A *negativistic* value reflects the tendency to fear, avoid, and sometimes disdain aspects of nature. Adaptive benefits include avoidance of harm and injury, minimization of risk and uncertainty, and, more positively, nurturance of a sense of awe and respect for nature's power. The natural world has always been a source of some of our deepest fears and anxieties.[15] Sharks, snakes, swamps, fierce storms, large predators, and more often elicit much anxiety and fright. Avoidance and fear of nature can provoke irrational and highly destructive acts, although more typically these inclinations are moderately and rationally expressed. Avoiding certain creatures and environmental circumstances can prevent harm, injury, and even death. When reasonably manifest, advantages accrue in isolating and on occasion eliminating threatening aspects of the natural world. Human well-being has always depended on skills and emotions acquired through a healthy distancing from potentially injurious elements in nature. Lacking this awareness, people often behave naively, building structures where they do not belong or ignoring their inevitable vulnerability before uncertain and powerful forces. Moreover, we should not presume that our fears of and aversions to elements of nature always provoke contemptuous or destructive tendencies. Deference to and respect for nature can arise as much from appreciation and recognition of its capacity to defeat and destroy us as from feelings of affection and allegiance. Awe combines reverence and wonder with fear, a knowing recognition of what the anthropologist Richard Nelson called the "luminescence of power."[16] Elements of the natural world stripped of their strength and prowess—a caged lion or a shark swimming inside a tank—often become objects of mere entertainment and condescension. Species and habitats utterly subdued provoke little admiration, humility, or respect. Warblers in an aviary rarely evoke the same meaning and ethical regard as those spied, perhaps at some personal risk, in a treetop or a steep ravine.

A *scientific* value of nature underscores the knowledge and understanding people derive from the empirical study of nature. Functional advantages include increased intellectual and cognitive capacity, enhanced critical thinking and problem-solving abilities, and greater appreciation and respect for maintenance of natural processes and diversity. People possess a universal need to know and understand their world with authority, a tendency independent of culture and history in which intellectual prowess is facilitated through study and observation of nature.[17] This perspective exists among all cultures, even so-called primitive peoples such as the Foré of New Guinea, who possess 110 names for the 120 scientifically classified bird species in their forest home, most of which lack obvious material or commodity value.[18] What the natural world offers all humanity, "primitive" and "modern" alike, is a varied and always stimulating context for developing critical thinking skills, problem-solving abilities, and analytic capacities. Observing and comprehending natural diversity provides countless opportunities for acquiring knowledge, developing understanding, and honing evaluative aptitudes. These cognitive capacities develop in other learning contexts, particularly in a modern world of advanced electronics and communications. But the natural world offers an especially accessible and engaging context for pursuing intellectual competence, especially for the young and inquiring mind. Moreover, over time and simply by chance, the knowledge and understanding obtained from study and observation of nature yields practical and tangible gains. Examining any portion of the natural world expands our realization of how much we can learn from even obscure organisms and natural processes. The more we know and understand these creatures and environments, the more astonished we are by the extraordinary ingenuity of the biophysical enterprise. Knowing warblers well not only increases our knowledge but also elevates our ethical regard for them and ourselves.

A *symbolic* value reflects nature's role in shaping and facilitating human communication and thought. Adaptive benefits include enhanced capacities for language acquisition and taxonomy, psychosocial development, and the ability to communicate through image and symbol. People employ nature as raw material for expediting the exchange of information and understanding. We accomplish this through metaphor, analogy, and abstraction and by employing language, story, myth, fantasy, and dream.[19] Nature as symbol is especially instrumental in language acquisition. Learning of language depends on the developing capacity to render ever more refined distinctions, categories, and taxonomies. The young encounter in nature numerous, readily available, emotionally salient, and especially distinguishable objects to differentiate and classify. When we examine young children's reading materials, we encounter a world replete with animal characters and images of nature.

Symbolizing and fantasizing nature further assists children in confronting difficult maturational dilemmas of identity and selfhood, authority and independence, order and chaos, good and evil, love and sexuality, in a disguised yet tolerable and often instructive manner. Children's stories and fairy tales, legends and myths, totems and taboos, and fantasies and dreams use metaphor and narrative to confront and address enigmatic, complicated, and often painful issues of conflict, need, desire, meaning, and purpose.

People also employ natural imagery in the language of the street, in the metaphor of the marketplace, and sometimes in great oratory and debate. Moral discourse exploits the imagery of nature for powerful and evocative communication. The Bible speaks of "laying waste the mountains and hills, and drying up all the herbage . . . [,] turning the rivers into islands, and drying up the pools."[20] We argue abstractly but often depend on natural images and symbols to advance forcefully our ethical and moral discourse. Nature provides a substrate for symbolic creation analogous to the way genetic variability offers a biochemical template for laboratory discovery. Each uses nature's clay to mold and fabricate solutions to life. Warblers may be mere birds, a speck of animate matter here today and gone tomorrow. But at a much deeper level, they are the coda for capturing ineffable moments of unity and connection with the rest of creation.

Finally, a *utilitarian* value underscores the material and commodity benefits derived from nature, including enhanced physical security associated with agricultural, medical, and industrial productivity; various ecosystem services, such as pollination and decomposition; and the self-confidence and self-esteem we obtain by demonstrating craft and skill in exploiting the land and its resources. Despite this utilitarian significance, modern society often prides itself on having achieved material independence from the natural world by domesticating the wild, eliminating natural competitors, and converting untamed land into cultivated and artificial landscapes.[21] This belief is an illusion, however; even today, people rely on natural processes and diversity as an indispensable source of basic food stocks, medicines, building and decorative supplies, and other commodities. Moreover, healthy ecosystem functioning sustains all life, including our own, through basic life support functions such as oxygen and water production, nutrient cycling, seed dispersal, and more. This utilitarian dependence on nature most likely will greatly expand in the future as a result of rapid developments in molecular biology, genetic prospecting, and bioengineering, which will allow people to exploit countless genetic solutions for survival fashioned over millions of years of evolutionary trial and error.

Even in the absence of necessity, we continue to exercise our utilitarian dependence on nature as a wellspring of physical, mental, and spiritual well-being. We reap practical benefits from these activities, but just as important, we nourish our passion for skillfully extracting a portion of our sustenance from the land. Beyond the obvious practical gains, we harvest physical and mental fitness and affirm our connection with ancient cycles of energy, matter, and spirit. Warblers help us to see how soil, stone, water, air, and matter are a "superorganism" of flowing and related nutrients, including ourselves.

Conclusion

The nine values of biophilia—the biological inclination to affiliate with nature—reflect the richness of the human reliance on nature for physical, emotional, intellectual, and spiritual sustenance and security. They intimate how in degrading the natural world we diminish our capacity for experiencing beauty, meaning, and significance in our lives. Ethical respect, moral regard, and spiritual reverence for nature thus depend less on compassion and pity for the weak and downtrodden than on a profound realization of self-interest that recognizes how the natural world shapes our bodies, minds, and souls. The writer Henry Beston suggested:

> Nature is a part of our humanity, and without some awareness and experience of that divine mystery man ceases to be man. When the Pleiades and the wind in the grass are no longer a part of the human spirit, a part of very flesh and bone, man becomes, as it were, a kind of cosmic outlaw, having neither the completeness and integrity of the animal nor the birthright of a true humanity.[22]

But biophilia, while rooted in biology, relies—like so much of what it means to be human—on experience, learning, and social support for its functional expression. Wide variations exist in the content and intensity of our basic values of nature as a result of socialization, choice, and free will, but these cultural constructs are bounded by biology. If our biophilic values of nature are insufficiently or inordinately developed, they become dysfunctional and self-defeating. Modern society has chosen in so many ways to compromise and degrade the health and integrity of the natural world. Widely evident symptoms include extensive chemical contamination and pollution, atmospheric perturbation and disruption, resource depletion and exhaustion, loss of biological diversity, and a hemorrhaging of life on earth. A less obvious but serious consequence of this environmental degradation is the slow and insidious decline in our experience of and relationship with the natural world. Degrading nature does more than material harm. It fosters as well a profound and alienating loss of psychological and moral bearings and the debasement of the human spirit.

An ethic of care for the natural world and responsibility for sustaining its beauty, health, and integrity necessitates the functional and adaptive expression of all values of biophilia. An environmental ethic can and should be advanced based on defending human material interests. This utilitarian ethic encourages us to protect and sustain elements of nature that contribute to human material and economic welfare. An environmental ethic based on this value perspective alone, however, would be insufficient and possibly self-defeating. Most creatures and habitats never yield tangible advantage to people and society, and one can question whether the seeds of destruction are sown in an ethic that extends moral consideration to a fraction of the natural world, intimating the expendability of those parts with little or no market value.

A moralistic value constitutes another powerful basis for an environmental ethic. People justifiably extend kindness, compassion, and concern to creatures that experience pain or suffering or to particular plants and landscapes spiritually cherished in collective myth and memory. The efficacy of this environmental ethic has been noted by students of religion, who observe, "No corps of secular [environmental] police however dedicated can receive the respect and obedience due to the Maker."[23] People act with prudence and restraint when motivated by spiritual and religious belief, their commitment to protect nature stemming as much from moral and ethical principles as from any cost–benefit calculation or legal mandate.

But even a moralistic and spiritual perspective of nature provides only a partial basis for an effective environmental ethic. If all creatures are accorded equivalent moral value, for example, what do we do when confronted with difficult moral choices between competing "goods," such as eliminating creatures to save human lives, destroying natural habitats to house and feed the hungry and impoverished, or draining wetlands to build factories that provide jobs for the poor and destitute? An environmental ethic that awards all nature equivalent value, or that implies the rejection of human in favor of nonhuman interests, convinces few and provides little practical guidance in those ethical situations in which we need it the most.

An environmental ethic advanced on utilitarian and moralistic grounds alone is, thus, necessary but not sufficient. Advocated here instead is an environmental ethic extending beyond these two values to embrace all values of biophilia and their related capacity to confer physical, emotional, intellectual, and spiritual rewards. All these values contribute ethical threads that collectively stitch a moral garment strongly binding the human condition to the beauty, health, and integrity of the natural world. Even our aversions and fears of nature can be a portal for recognizing the awesome power, majesty, and magnificence of nature. As with reverence for God, we see in creation both forces of love, kindness, and compassion and an authority and strength far greater than our own and humbling to us.

Aldo Leopold suggested that the idea of ecology was among the most important discoveries of the twentieth century.[24] He implied that individuals, communities, societies, and species are all products of their relational dependencies upon one another and the natural world. The notion of a single, unitary being, independent and autonomous, is a delusion. In the deepest sense, we are all the consequence of our ecological connections, related by bands of energy, matter, and spirit to that incredible fabric we call nature. A broad anthropocentric ethic of duty and responsibility for the natural world reaffirms our complicated and unyielding ties with creation. We draw ethical nourishment and moral guidance from recognizing and celebrating this commonality. Conversely, degrading our relation with nature engenders more than material harm. It leads, far more profoundly, to a loss of identity, meaning, and purpose. Again, the wisdom of Henry Beston:

> What has come over our age is an alienation from Nature unexampled in human history. It has cost us our sense of reality and all but cost us our humanity. . . . True humanity is no inherent and abstract right but an achievement, and only through the fullness of human experience may we be as one with all who have been and all who are yet to be, sharers and brethren and partakers of the mystery of living, reaching to the full of human peace and the full of human joy.[25]

Chapter 5

Religion and Ecology: The Interaction of Cosmology and Cultivation

Mary Evelyn Tucker

The environmental crisis presents distinctive challenges to both religion and science as we seek paths toward a sustainable future. While science and technology are indispensable to this task, religions are also necessary, though not sufficient, partners in this quest. Although we recognize that religions have their dark side in institutional rigidities and certain constraints on thinking, they have also functioned throughout human history as grounding and guiding forces in human life. The potential for religion to be ecologically aware and ethically efficacious is enormous. On the basis of this recognition, Harvard University's "Religions of the World and Ecology" conference series and the ongoing Forum on Religion and Ecology arose out of a concern for the growing environmental crisis and the seemingly muted response of the world's religions. It is becoming clear that the moral force of religion may be instrumental in alerting people to the ethical implications of what we are doing to the planet by unbridled industrialization, wanton use of resources, and spreading pollution of air, water, and soil.

There are many hopeful signs that change is occurring as we begin to learn that progress needs to be redefined, that growth for the sake of growth is not necessarily desirable, that ecological economics is a growing field, that green businesses are emerging, that alternative energies are feasible, that organic agriculture is gaining ground, that ecological design is essential, and that many people care deeply about preservation of the environment. Indeed, we find in this time of overload with bad news that there are many insightful and even heroic voices calling for change. One of the foremost of these has been the cultural historian Thomas Berry, whose book *The Great Work* evokes a vision of mutually enhancing human–earth relations within the context of the unfolding process of our evolving universe.[1] In *The Dream of the Earth,* Berry sees this broadened context of the universe story, with its rich cosmological dimensions, as a primary means of reorienting humans to living in a universe of meaning and mystery. Our response, he suggests, should be one of reciprocity, reverence, and care for the earth and for future generations. This vision, which brings together the scientific story of evolution with the mystique of religious sensibility, is an example of the deep integration of science and religion now possible in our times. The growing dialogue between science and religion may be fostered by the intersection between the cosmology of science and the cosmologies of various religious worldviews.

In discussing the cosmological dimension of religions, I wish to avoid the dualistic approach of those who claim "truth" lies on the side of rationalistic science while dismissing religion as mythical, magical, or superstitious. Rather, it is more helpful to see science and religion (like mathematics and literature) as different but complementary ways of knowing in the human community. While we understand the cosmology of science to operate with distinctive premises and methods drawn from scientific research, at the same time we observe that the religious traditions of the world are repositories of cosmological worldviews reflecting particular views of nature. Investigating these cosmologies is a critical task because they point toward ways in which different cultures have seen their embeddedness in and responsibility toward nature. Although derived from prescientific worldviews, these cosmologies may nonetheless be significant in the formulation of ethical attitudes of respect toward nature.

What I am suggesting is that the interconnection of cosmology and ethics (or self-cultivation) may be a fruitful perspective for understanding the role of the world's religions in fostering more sustaining relations with nature. Part of the contemporary destruction of the environment has arisen because we have regarded nature as something to be used for our own immediate needs rather than respected and valued in itself and for the support of future generations. In other words, the question is whether nature is to be perceived as a utilitarian object solely or whether it is to be seen as the matrix out of which all life has emerged. The attitudes of religions toward nature are relevant here, and their cosmological perspectives in particular are instructive in this regard.

If we put this in more personal terms, what I am asking is for us to consider how we reflect on certain questions in our own lives: Where do we come from? Why are we here? Where are we going? Scientific and religious cosmologies inform our answers to these questions. Our emerging knowledge of the vast, unfolding universe in which we live is complemented by a sense of awe that this knowledge evokes. At the same time, we need to think not just of these large cosmological questions but also of how we respond to moments in nature that move us—whether we are affected by the changing of the seasons, how a beautiful sunset touches us, why we seek places of rest in nature such as mountains or oceans, what it is we experience when we see a line of geese flying overhead or a great blue heron landing on a pond. Why are children so fascinated with nature, and how do we lose that fascination?

In other words, we are constantly interacting with our environment and drawing on its power and inspiration, both in its macrophase of evolutionary magnificence and in its microphase of bioregional beauty. It is here in the midst of the relational field of the natural and human worlds that a larger, numinous reality is experienced and named in the world's religions.[2] All religions have developed rich and distinctive expressions for describing the matrix of relationships we see in the natural world. Indeed, many of the most powerful symbols and rituals of our religious traditions are dependent on our primal encounter with nature, especially in its seasonal cycles. This is true in the Christian understanding of the birth of Christ coordinated with the winter solstice and the return of the light, as well as with Easter linked with the vernal equinox and rebirth of life. We can multiply these kinds of examples in other religions as well.

While there are strong tendencies in many religions toward transcendence beyond this world, there are also strong cosmological orientations that ground human–earth relations. The cosmological approaches of various religions toward nature are quite different, yet they converge in four areas:

1. Seeing nature as metaphor—a stepping-stone to the divine
2. Seeing nature as mirror—a reflection of the divine
3. Seeing nature as matrix—a meeting place for the divine
4. Seeing nature as maternal—a nurturing presence for the divine

The first and second perspectives more generally describe the Western religions and the South Asian traditions; the third and fourth generally describe the East Asian and indigenous traditions. These frameworks are meant to be suggestive, not exhaustive, in discussing the world's religions. In each of these perspectives, nature is valued and cherished, but a different set of environmental ethics emerges from these distinctive cosmological frameworks. What we will explore here with particular examples is the varied nature of religion as containing cosmological symbols, myths, and rituals that orient humans to a natural world of meaning and mystery, pointing even beyond itself. This is what we would call the numinous experience of nature, as seen through the cosmological frameworks of metaphor, mirror, matrix, and maternal images.

The End of Nature and Human Autism

My thesis is that in the contemporary world, we have manipulated our environment so extensively that it is difficult for us to experience this numinous character of the natural world. Bill McKibben wrote of the "end of nature" because of our extensive tampering with it.[3] Indeed, Thomas Berry said we have become "autistic" in encountering the natural world and thus have become caught in a technological trance.[4] Our fascination with technology is evidenced by our preoccupation with television, movies, video games, the Internet, and virtual reality. Somehow we have shifted the focus of our imaginative creativity from the encounter with nature and other humans to an insatiable obsession with technology as a new kind of magical realm continually feeding the senses.

How, then, to reexperience in fresh ways the numinous dimensions of nature is a primary challenge for each of us as individuals and for our educational and religious institutions as well. Without this, the destruction of the environment will no doubt continue unabated. With it, we may reclaim the voices of religions in understanding the sacred dimensions of nature, appreciating the rich creativity of nature's cosmological processes, and identifying our special role in fostering this continuing creativity for a sustainable future. Thus, through a fuller exploration of the cosmology of the world's religions, we may reinvigorate our understanding of how natural processes and religious symbol systems are deeply and subtly intertwined. In pursuit of this goal, I hope to suggest a context for rethinking human–earth relations in a more comprehensive manner, with implications for both social and environmental ethics. First, however, it may be important to explore the nature of religion itself so that we can recognize its remarkable potential for cosmological orientation and ethical grounding.

The Nature of Religion: Origin and Impulse

In exploring the nature of religion, we might consult various scholars who have elaborated particular theories on the origin and impulse of religions, especially in the late nineteenth century and early twentieth century. These include Lucien Lévy-Bruhl (1857–1939), who wrote *How Natives Think* (1910) and *Primitive Mentality* (1922). His conclusion was that early peoples were mystical and prelogical. Moreover, he believed, they had a sense of "feeling participation" with the natural and the human worlds. Max Müller (1823–1900), who edited the *Sacred Books of the East,* held that the earliest understanding of the divine was in personifications of natural phenomena as seen in the Hindu scriptures called the Vedas. James Frazer (1854–1941), who published twelve volumes of *The Golden Bough* between 1907 and 1915, suggested that religion arose in sympathetic magic and progressed eventually to science. For E. B. Tylor (1832–1917), there was also a developmental context, from the animist consciousness he described in *Primitive Culture* (1871) to so-called higher civilizations. For him, the generative source of religion lay in the idea of animism—the concept that the universe is alive with spiritual beings. These are only some examples of the various themes of the origins and impulse of religion. Most of these fed into the later-twentieth-century Western Enlightenment version of the progress of civilizations from religion toward science.

This developmental reading of history in the West began with Marquis de Condorcet (1743–1794), who believed humans would progress from "superstition and barbarism to an age of reason and enlightenment."[5] It included Comte de Saint-Simon's (1760–1825) view of religion as moving through stages of polytheism, monotheism, and metaphysics toward positivistic science. This was further elaborated by Auguste Comte (1798–1857), who believed that human consciousness progressed through three stages, namely, theology, metaphysics, and science. In this theory, theology is a necessary first step but will inevitably be surpassed by science.

Even in the twentieth century, many contemporary sociologists of religion predicted that with advances in science and technology, religion would become less necessary. In other words, they thought modernity would usurp religion. This has proven to be a drastically inaccurate prediction. We see this in the resurgence of traditional religions in Russia and China, in the rise of fundamentalisms around the world, and in the remarkable interdisciplinary dialogue between religion and science that began in the last few decades of the twentieth century.[6]

Nonetheless, a significant sector of the modern West has inherited and further developed Enlightenment attitudes that privilege rational thought and undervalue religious experience and that, in certain circles, foresee religion as eventually being superseded by science. A post-Enlightenment version of religion values individualism and personal salvation and sees God as similar to a clockmaker and removed from creation. In this scenario, religion in the West has become the province of the individual and of a creator God, while science has moved into the arena of the relationship with nature. Western religions have become concerned with matters of conscience in the human order and matters of salvation in the afterlife. They have largely retreated from the natural world and become locked into traditional concerns with redemption rather than creation. Except for the process theologians, they have, until recently, ignored or rejected real engagement with scientific cosmologies. The Yale University conference "The Good in Nature and Humanity" represented an important effort to overcome this split. So does the research of countless historians and anthropologists of religion who in the twentieth century helped us to understand other religious worldviews beyond those of the West. I would like to underscore here the importance of seeing religion in its multicultural forms, not just its Western modes, so that the dialogue of science and religion is more than an interaction between science and the biblical traditions.

To return, then, to the search for the origins of religion, it is not like discovering in this century, because of certain empirical evidence, that Fred Hoyle's steady state theory of the universe is seen as less credible than the big bang theory. Affirmation of the big bang theory occurred first in the theories of Edwin Hubble and other scientists and then in the background radiation heard by Robert Wilson at the Bell Telephone Laboratories in New Jersey, and it was finally mapped out in exquisite patterns by the Cosmic Background Explorer satellite in 1989 under the supervision of scientists from the Lawrence Berkeley National Laboratory. Evidence for the "big bang" also remains in the fossil records of the first three minutes after the explosion, namely in hydrogen, helium, and lithium.

In seeking the origins of religion, we will never be assured of such extraordinary discoveries as science gave us in the twentieth century. And yet, is this not somehow consoling? Yes, we can certainly outline patterns of religion, from personal religious experience to its communal institutionalization. This was one contribution of the distinguished historian of religion Mircea Eliade of the University of Chicago.[7] But ultimately, this great mystery of religion and religious experience lies beyond the vision of even our most powerful microscopes and telescopes—like dark matter, it eludes detection. It is as elusive as the human heart, as stunning as the discovery of relativity, as unique as a fleeting snowflake, as alluring as a loon's call, as beautiful as clouds at sunset, and as haunting as a forest at night. It is important to note once again that religions also have their distortions in rigid orthodoxies, perverse practices, and intolerant messianic campaigns, such as the Crusades or the Inquisition.

Awe and Assent: Key Religious Sensibilities

What is this thing called religion, and from whence does it arise? I should say, again, no one knows definitively, although many have surmised. But perhaps I can begin with two stories from Loren Eiseley. One relates an experience of his, described in his book *The Immense Journey,*[8] of floating on his back in the Platte River on a spectacular sunny summer afternoon. Suddenly, he was transported *into* the river and all its connecting tributaries—melting, moving, gliding down the Missouri River into the great Mississippi and into the vast currents of ocean beyond. He moved from a particular place and moment on the high plains to a sense of the whole and holy other; he was transported from the skin of his body to skinless identity with the earth's body. For Eiseley, this was an experience involving both the power of water and the flow of evolution:

> Once in a lifetime, perhaps, one escapes the actual confines of the flesh. Once in a lifetime, if one is lucky, one so merges with sunlight and air and running water that whole eons, the eons that mountains and deserts know, might pass in a single afternoon without discomfort. The mind has sunk away into its beginnings among old roots and the obscure tricklings and movings that stir inanimate objects. . . . One can never quite define this secret; but it has something to do, I am sure, with common water. Its substance reaches everywhere; it touches the past and prepares the future; it moves under the poles and wanders thickly in the heights of air. It can assume forms of exquisite perfection in a snowflake, or strip the living to a single shining bone cast up by the sea. . . .
>
> I, too, was a microcosm of pouring rivulets and floating driftwood gnawed by the mysterious animalcules of my own creation. I was three fourths water, rising and subsiding according to the hollow knocking in my veins: a minute pulse like the eternal pulse that lifts Himalayas and which, in the following systole, will carry them away.[9]

This flowing of the self toward the world, this feeling of the individual person (microcosm) for the macrocosm of the universe, this relation of the part to the whole, is one of the most fundamental movements of the human that we may call religious. It rests especially on a feeling of awe and wonder. Indeed, this urge to be identified with something larger than oneself—the lure of the universe itself and what is beyond—is, in some profound sense, religious.

A second story of Loren Eiseley, also in his book *The Immense Journey,* comes to mind. This one is called "The Judgment of the Birds." Eiseley has fallen asleep by a stump on the edge of a glade. Suddenly he is awakened by the cries of two birds, parents to a captured nestling. A huge black raven is devouring the small red nestling. The other birds, not daring to attack the raven, nonetheless join in the anguished chorus of the parents. Then, after the loss is over, the birds quiet down. And suddenly, one by one in the silence of the woods, the birds begin to sing. Eiseley describes it this way:

> The sighing died. It was then I saw the judgment. It was the judgment of life against death. I will never see it again so forcefully presented. I will never hear it again in notes so tragically prolonged. For in the midst of protest, they forgot the violence. There, in that clearing, the crystal note of a song sparrow lifted hesitantly in the hush. And finally, after painful fluttering, another took the song, and then another, the song passing from one bird to another, doubtfully at first, as though some evil thing were being slowly forgotten. Till suddenly they took heart and sang from many throats joyously together as birds are known to sing. They sang because life is sweet and sunlight beautiful. They sang under the brooding shadow of the raven. In simple truth they had forgotten the raven, for they were the singers of life, and not of death.[10]

As Eiseley suggests, there is affirmation and continuity in the face of death and struggle, even in the animal kingdom. Life itself is utterly precious, inexplicably valuable, and worthy of survival. And here is our second experience of the religious—affirmation in spite of all. Affirmation in the face of apparent meaninglessness, continuity in the midst of death, joy juxtaposed with sorrow. It is here that the great movements of human aspiration and struggle occur, and it is here that the religious impulse is forged.

For if the first story illustrates the human desire to move outward and to identify with all that is awesome and more mysterious, the second story calls us to move inward and to affirm life in its vulnerable manifestations.

To identify with the all and to affirm in spite of all—these are two key impulses that we may describe, in some sense, as religious or spiritual. I speak here of the experience not of the institutions that bind that experience into rigid stories, scriptures, or codes but of the powerful, ever-renewing sense of awe and assent. The pull outward and the call inward—these are mechanisms for situating ourselves in a universe of vast beauty, awesome mystery, and inexplicable suffering. What draws these two instincts together is patterning and organization. The inward pull and outward identification are linked by patterns that connect. As Eiseley describes it:

> Men talk much of matter and energy, of the struggle for existence that molds the shape of life. These things exist, it is true; but more delicate, elusive, quicker than the fins in water, is that mysterious principle known as "organization," which leaves all other mysteries concerned with life stale and insignificant by comparison. For that without organization life does not persist is obvious. Yet this organization itself is not strictly the product of life, nor of selection. Like some dark and passing shadow within matter, it cups out the eyes' small windows or spaces the notes of a meadow lark's song in the interior of a mottled egg. That principle—I am beginning to suspect—was there before the living in the deeps of water.[11]

He continues to reflect on the meaning of his experience in the Platte River, to which he has returned in the winter. It is snowing:

> The temperature has risen. The little stinging needles have given way to huge flakes floating in like white leaves blown from some great tree in open space. In the car, switching on the lights, I examine one intricate crystal on my sleeve before it melts. No utilitarian philosophy explains a snow crystal, no doctrine of use or disuse. Water has merely leapt out of vapor and thin nothingness in the night sky to array itself in form. There is no logical reason for the existence of a snowflake any more than there is for evolution. It is an apparition from that mysterious shadow world beyond nature, that final world which contains—if anything contains—the explanation of men and catfish and green leaves.[12]

We may speak, then, of religion as a means of cosmological orientation in the midst of the powers of the universe and a means of ethical relationship in the midst of human affairs. Yet religious experience is always contained in the mystery of the patterning of life itself—that patterning is embedded in both order and chaos, as we know now from chaos theory.

Patterning and Ordering

We seek to connect to the deep inner patterning of things—in nature and in human life. This drive to see and understand pattern, coherence, and chaos in the universe is in part what motivates many scientists. It moves the astronomers and the microbiologists to seek the mysteries of matter in its far reaches and in its inner depths. Religions promise something of that connecting link through myths and symbols, rituals and prayers. They seek to weave a web (as would a spider) from our inner structures to those complex structures that hold life together. The complementarity of science and religion can be seen in this search for patterns in the natural world reflected by patterns established in the human world. Scientists seek to probe these structures of reality while religionists seek to align human rituals and ethics with the deep order of creation. Thus, science, through its probing of pattern, can provide a perspective that aids religion in understanding the human link to creation and the natural world. And religions, through cultivation, may guide us through the intricate and complex world revealed by science. Together, they offer a cosmology that reveals our place in the evolutionary process.[13]

This patterning is called by many names in various religions. In Hinduism and Buddhism, it is *Dharma,* or law; in Confucianism, it is *Li,* or principle; in Taoism, it is the *Tao,* or the Way; in Judaism, it is *Seder bereishit,* or order of creation; in Christianity, it is *Logos,* or word; in Islam, it is *Shariah,* or law. For Native American Algonquians, it is *Manitou,* or spirit presence. Among the Walpiri people of Australia, it is *Tjukurpa,* which is sometimes translated as "Dreamtime" but refers to law or pattern in the landscape.

To apprehend and support this patterning, we balance ourselves between the outward pull of cosmological processes and the inward pull of the wellsprings of personal authenticity and collective communion. Many religious traditions organize themselves around the patterns their practitioners perceive in nature. For example, indigenous peoples seek to embody the cosmos in their own persons as well as in the actions they undertake and the structures they create in bioregions, such as subsistence activities and organization of habitat.[14] Hindu society has organized itself into sacrificial ritual patterns analogous to the great sacrifice at the origin of the world, and Chinese religious thought has developed complex rules of correspondences based on how individuals are to live in relation to the patterns of nature. This includes geomancy (*feng shui*) and meditative exercises such as *t'ai chi ch'uan* and *ch'i gong.* Religions thus mediate between the patterns of nature and those of the individual by creating stories of our origins, rituals to ensure continuity through the various stages of life from birth to death, and codes of behavior that aim to maximize harmonious relations and thus survival itself. In its simplest form, then, religion consists of a worldview embracing cosmology and cultivation. These are linked by patterns (or rituals) connecting self, society, nature, and the larger field of being in which they exist.

Defining Cosmology

In further defining terms, it may be helpful to distinguish between *worldview* (weltanschauung) and *cosmology*. Although these are sometimes used interchangeably, we take *worldview* to be a more general and less precisely defined perspective, whereas *cosmology* reflects a more specific, focused description of reality often associated with story or narrative. Thus, *worldview* refers to a broad set of ideas and values that helps in the formulation of basic perspectives of societies and individuals.[15] *Cosmology* is more specifically linked to an explanation of the universe (mythical or scientific) and the role of humans in it. A cosmology may or may not include a cosmogony (a story of origins). Cosmologies of particular world religions, however, usually include explanations for the way things are in the universe or the way things ought to be. Science includes the former but not the latter.

Cosmologies of world religions, however, imply a metaphysics, an ethic, or both to give orientation and meaning to human life. In this sense, cosmologies of religions contain "principles of order that support integrated forms of being"[16] and thus give moral direction to a person's life.[17] This is true because of both the orientation and openness religious cosmologies provide for self-cultivation. *Self-cultivation* is a term used in Chinese religions to refer to specific means of personal development (such as meditation or moral education) that unify a person's inner and outer life. In the classical Confucian tradition, this involves the cultivation of virtue to enable the individual to contribute to the social and political order. In the neo-Confucian tradition, this involves abiding in reverence and investigating things. In many religious traditions, this dialectic between inner and outer life is maintained in a delicate balance.

In attempting to formulate the theoretical grounds for describing cosmology and its functions, Gregory Schrempp wrote:

> What do we mean by "cosmology"? In part we seem to point toward formulations that involve a quest for *ultimate* principles and/or grounds of the phenomenal world and the human place in it. But cosmology often—and this aspect stems perhaps from the Greek notion of kosmos—seems to carry for us a concern with wholeness and integratedness, as if cosmological principles are not only ultimate principles, but also principles of *order* in the broadest sense, that is, principles engendering and supporting a way of being that is cognitively and emotionally integrated and whole. In these two kinds of concerns—the impetus to seek the "ground" of the present order, and the impetus toward integratedness and wholeness—there is already a potential tension, since the quest for

a ground is implicitly a resting of one thing on another, and thus involves a regression from any given state, whereas the impetus toward wholeness may engender the task of finding closure, as a condition for wholeness.[18]

Something of this tension between "grounding" and "growing" is what interests me in proposing a dialectic of cosmology and cultivation. If *cosmology* in Schrempp's sense has within it an "is/ought" tension, then *cultivation* is the work toward resolving that tension or living that tension through an ongoing deepening and broadening of one's personhood and ethical life. The deepening is the inner grounding, whereas the broadening is the growing outward.

Cosmology and Patterning

More than ever before, our challenge today is to reorient ourselves to the universe—to know its vastness and its limits and to attune our rich inner space to the rhythms of this universe—which is, in essence, a religious act of boldness, of imagination, and of courage in the midst of staggering odds and enormous obstacles. This is the challenge of the evolution of religion to respond to the complex story of the universe.

In short, we are seeking to reattune our cultural coding and religious symbol systems to be in touch with the genetic coding and natural systems of the universe. We are struggling to reorient social, economic, and political systems to know the boundaries and potential of nature. For as Thomas Berry noted, all human activities need to be "re-viewed" as a subsystem of the earth's system.[19] What does this mean in practical terms?

It means we need to seek out the deep, abiding patterns within things. From the wings of a butterfly to the veins of a leaf to the seeds of a fruit, there is a profound imprinting evident in nature. We can see it in the complex organizational structures of physics, chemistry, biology, and geology that have shaped this evolutionary process. This imprinting is part of the very structure of the universe that reveals its intelligibility, its luminosity, its energy. And it is to that patterning and energy that we need to respond for guidance and for survival. With enormous confidence in the mystery that has guided this process, we seek out the patterns that connect us to this web of life, knowing that deep in our own genetic coding are the links that bond us with other forms of life. What is imprinted in us is our cosmological heritage—our birthright—our own story. It is the threads of the story we are gathering here, it is the weaving we are beginning to do, but it is the patterning for which we are still searching.

The search for that patterning is part of the religious quest. From earliest times until the present day, humans have sought the means of orienting themselves to a universe of meaning and mystery through uncovering patterns that connect. This is essentially the function of myth and ritual in religion. These then become embedded in scriptures and in ethics, giving a meaningful context to daily action. It is the broader cosmological context of evolution we are absorbing now; it is the deeper ecological ethics we seek in relation to nature's patterns. It is the reading not only of written scriptures but also of the natural scriptures that we need to foster. This has implications for education, social systems, economics, design, and even politics.

Cosmology and Cultivation in the World's Scriptures

When we examine the early scriptures of many of the world's religions, we can see that they were inspired by the great cosmological movements of the universe—that nature was both teacher and guide. Even as religious traditions arose in distinctive geographic and cultural contexts, such as Judaism and Christianity in the Middle East, they were always cognizant of their relation to the larger dynamics of nature and seasonal cycles.

As we read these early scriptures, we see into the world of nature not simply as backdrop to human action but as inspiration and animator, as a vehicle for recognizing deeper truths, exploring greater mysteries. The natural world is not only that which has given humans birth and sustenance; it is that which sustains humans psychically and spiritually in very tangible ways. It becomes a source of symbol, myth, and ritual giving rise to the rhythm of transformation. Just as the natural world involves periods of change, so does the human world; just as the natural world embodies both pattern and chaos, so does the human world. Religion thus becomes a means of aligning the human world with the natural world.

So we return to these two fundamental directions of the religious experience—toward resonance with the universe, which lures us forward, and toward resilience within ourselves, which is manifest in ethical choices in the midst of constant change. We link ourselves, sometimes unwittingly, to an emerging, evolving universe, and yet we also draw back into the pulsations of the personal and the demands of the communal for creating sustainable societies. As we look at the scriptures of the world's religions, we sense this inner and outer dynamic joined by patterns. The Psalms in Israel, the Vedas in India, and the Book of Changes in China are some of the oldest written scriptures known to the human community, dating back to the first and second millennia B.C.E. They reflect a sense of longing for identification with a comprehensive cosmology, and at the same time they signal the needed component of personal cultivation or communal responsibility. They suggest that early river civilizations engaged in agriculture were concerned not just with dominion, as has often been suggested, but also with cooperation and harmony with nature.

At the heart of all these early scriptures is a profound sense of the dynamic flow of life in the midst of both change and continuity. It is harmonization with this life pattern, which is both within things and beyond, that characterizes these scriptures. How to effect reciprocal relations with the transformations of life is the challenge they present—and this is underscored by rituals that mitigate the unseen forces and call forth sustaining energy. To open up the transformative powers of the universe in the midst of change is part of the challenge of these early scriptures and the concurrent ritual practices for social organization. In this context, human history and culture fit into this great sweep of cosmological powers—not the other way around. In all this, we recall the role of religion in mediating human sensibilities toward transcendence and toward immanence, providing an activating dialectic for the great variety of symbols, rituals, and myths in the world's religions.

Convergence and Divergence of Attitudes toward Nature

This remarkable variety of approaches can be seen, for example, in the attitudes toward nature contained in the world's religions. For example, the world's religions would generally cohere in affirming that nature has a sacred element. At the same time, that affirmation would be based on quite different cosmologies and symbol systems. By the same token, if asked whether nature should be protected, the world's religions would generally answer affirmatively, but their environmental ethics would be distinctive in each case. For these reasons, if we are to move toward a global environmental ethic, as many suggest we should, it is crucial that we are attentive to this variegated perspective of religious and cultural particularity. Like a great stained glass window in which light shines through different colors, views of nature and environmental ethics appear in distinctive shades among the various world religions. However, the resulting mosaic of light may lend direction and inspiration for human endeavors toward a sustainable future.

Thus, in terms of the examples outlined in the paragraphs that follow, we might surmise there is an agreement that nature should be respected, but from different cosmological perspectives. For example, the Western biblical monotheistic tradition arises from an interactive cosmology of creator, creation, and creature. Creation is sacred because God created it. Creatures are valuable because they are created by God, and humans are particularly significant because they are formed in the image and likeness of God. From this cosmology, a stewardship model of environmental ethics arises in the Jewish and Christian traditions. Similarly, in Islam a model of vicegerency has arisen wherein humans act as vicegerents for Allah, the creator, in caring for creation.

In contrast to the Western biblical view of monotheism, Hindu Vedic cosmology is henotheistic, replete with a pantheon of gods. These gods inhabit the heavenly, atmospheric, and earthly realms. They are deeply involved with the elements that make up the universe—namely, air, water, and fire—as well as times of day such as dawn. The universe is said to have been created by the sacrifice of a Cosmic Person or Great Person (*Mahapurusha*). An environmental ethic in this cosmological framework evolves in relation to fulfilling one's dharmic duty to maintain order (*rta*) in the universe, which is both created by and inhabited with the gods. This duty is fulfilled through the offering of sacrifices, a giving back to the abundance of life and fecundity in nature.

Finally, the Chinese cosmological worldview is based not on a creation story, such as that which grounds Western religious traditions, nor on gods mingled with nature, as in Vedic Hinduism. Rather, it arises from a dynamic sense of ongoing creativity in the universe within the triad of heaven, earth, and humans. This vitalistic, dynamic sense of creativity at the heart of nature is what humans respond to in cultivating themselves. It becomes a basis for an environmental ethic of relational resonance, an alignment of oneself and harmonization of one's society with the patterns of change and transformation in nature. This gives rise to modes of living embedded in ecological design, such as *feng shui*. Let us turn, then, to a closer examination of these varied cosmologies and ethics of cultivation.

Cosmology and Stewardship—Israel

The Book of Psalms contains 150 prayer-poems probably intended to be sung or accompanied by music. In Hebrew, *Book of Psalms* means "Praises" (*tehillin*), reflecting affirmation or trust in God even in the midst of sorrow. Although these psalms were most likely compiled in the postexilic period (550 B.C.E.) for temple rituals, many of the themes stretch back much further.

As we look at the Psalms, we see these songs of nature worshipping, praising, and invoking the creator and his creation. These profoundly linked concepts go beyond constructed dualisms of Western monotheism that divide God and humans. Instead, there is in the Psalms a dynamic interchange of creator, creation, and creatures. There is a sense of the creatures' dependence on both creation and creator. This is more than simply a static monotheism within a historical trajectory. It is a worldview showing us a God of care and compassion as well as one of omnipotence and justice. But it is a God deeply engaged in creation, not simply directing it from afar. This is a God involved in both cosmos and history. It is a God who offers justice to his chosen people, and they in turn yearn for affirmation, mercy, and forgiveness. Thus, there is a sense of Israel's history as woven into a "coexistence with God," as the Jewish scholar Abraham Heschel suggests. For the Israelites, history was seen as revealing God's purpose and Israel was chosen for "converse" with Yahweh.[20] All this is set against the background of Yahweh as cosmic king and creator, enthroned over all of creation yet intimately connected with it. Indeed, this is celebrated in the enthronement psalms, which were part of the cult establishing a throne ascension festival. This was held each New Year, when Yahweh's rule over Israel, over other nations, and over the cosmos was celebrated with hymns and rituals.

The Psalms are divided into hymns of praise, of lament, and of thanksgiving. In the psalms of praise, we have a striking depiction of the creator and creation as deserving utmost respect, wonder, and awe:

to the One who alone does great wonders,

who by understanding made the heavens,

who spread out the earth upon the waters,

who made the great lights,

the sun to rule over the day,

the moon and stars to rule over the night.

—*Psalm 136:4–9*[21]

The order of creation is celebrated, and the power and majesty of the creator are underscored. Yet God's continual creativity in history is noted:

All of them [animals and humans] look to you

to give them their food in its season.

When you give to them, they gather up,

when you open your hand, they are satisfied to the full.

When you hide your face, they are disturbed,

When you take away their breath, they expire
> and return to their dust.

When you send forth your spirit, they are [re]created,
> and you renew the surface of the soil.

—*Psalm 104:27–30*[22]

The psalms of lamentation and thanksgiving might be seen as part of the cultivation side of the dyad. As injustice occurs, there is a call for deliverance, and as blessings are received, thanksgiving pours forth. Justice and mercy are reasserted against the forces of oppression and sorrow.

In short, the cosmological world of the interaction of creator, creation, and creatures is the container of the history of the chosen people. As the people cultivate their relationship with the creator of the cosmos, they also cultivate care for creation expressed in stewardship. While in this model history becomes a key element, nonetheless, maintaining a proper relationship to creation and the cosmic order of creation is the container for all the history of the chosen people.

Cosmology and Sacrifice—India

In India, this cosmological container is present in the Vedas, ancient hymns that celebrate the gods of nature. Here, we have a richly textured universe presided over by a variety of gods. This is not a model of monotheism, as seen in the Psalms, but rather henotheism, as described by Max Müller. This term describes a worldview in which there is a pantheon of gods with no strict hierarchy.[23] While there is more emphasis on cosmos than on history, still there is a sense that the gods are involved in human concerns and need sacrifices in order to maintain order in the universe and support human action. The sense of the awesome powers of nature as depicted in these Vedic hymns resonates to the present in India, where the hymns are still recited and Vedic sacrifices are still offered. In fact, sacrifice is the structured pattern of the universe itself.

The Vedic hymns were composed between 1600 and 600 B.C.E. and thus constitute the oldest written literature in India. They were transmitted orally for almost three thousand years, until some brahmins in Calcutta were reluctantly persuaded to write them down in the 1780s. There are four principal texts, the oldest of which is the Rig Veda, a collection of more than a thousand hymns. Although there are current historical debates about early Indian history, the Vedas are generally attributed to the Aryans, a nomadic and horse-riding people who moved into central Europe and India during the second millennium. As they settled in the Indus Valley region, they gradually took up agriculture. Thus, these hymns are a fascinating collection of a people moving from pastoral pursuits to farming.

In relation to our overarching theme of the interaction of cosmology and cultivation, we might say that there are two types of cosmological hymns in the Vedas, hymns of creation and hymns celebrating natural phenomena. But there is another type that, broadly speaking, deals with cultivation, in this case sacrificial rituals.

The first kinds of cosmological hymns deal with creation and origins; in other words, they are cosmogonic hymns. One of enormous importance is the Mahapurusha, which describes the birth of the universe from the sacrifice of a Great Person. This becomes a key link to modes of communal cultivation in sacrifice. The correspondence of the person to the universe provides the pattern for the relationship of all humans to the cosmos:

> When they divided the Man,
>> into how many parts did they divide him?
> What was his mouth, what was his arms,
>> what were his thighs and feet?

> The brahman was his mouth,
>> of his arms was made the warrior,
> his thighs became the vaisya [peasant]
>> of his feet the sudra [serf] was born.

> The moon arose from his mind,
>> from his eye was born the sun,
> from his mouth Indra and Agni,
>> from his breath the wind was born.

> From his navel came the air,
>> from his head there came the sky,
> from his feet the earth, the four quarters from his ear,
>> thus they fashioned the worlds.

> With Sacrifice the gods sacrificed to Sacrifice—
>> these were the first of the sacred laws.

These mighty beings reached the sky,
> where are the eternal spirits, the gods.[24]

Another, later, hymn reflects the universe as emerging from neither being
nor nonbeing. The power of this hymn is that it conveys a remarkable sense of
speculation, questioning, and wonder. Here again, we have a sense of the religious instinct resting in mystery, uncertainty, and awe:

Then even nothingness was not, nor existence.
> There was no air then, nor the heavens beyond it.
What covered it? Where was it? In whose keeping?
> Was there then cosmic water, in depths unfathomed?

Then there was neither death nor immortality,
> nor was there then the touch of night and day.
The One breathed windlessly and self-sustaining.
> There was that One then, and there was no other.

At first there was only darkness wrapped in darkness.
> All this was only unilluminated water.
That One which came to be, enclosed in nothing,
> arose at last, born of the power of heat.

In the beginning desire descended on it—
> that was the primal seed, born of the mind.
The sages who have searched their hearts with wisdom
> know that which is kin to that which is not.

And they have stretched their cord across the void,
> and know what was above, and what below.
Seminal powers made fertile mighty forces.
> Below was strength, and over it was impulse.

But, after all, who knows, and who can say
> whence it all came, and how creation happened?
The gods themselves are later than creation,
> so who knows truly whence it has arisen?

Whence all creation had its origin,

> he, whether he fashioned it or whether he did not,
>
> he who surveys it all from highest heaven,
>
> he knows—or maybe even he does not know.[25]

The figure outlines the cosmogonic origins of the universe that the Vedic hymns so vividly describe in the sacrifice of the Great Person (*Mahapurusha*). Surrounding this sacrifice, however, is always the unknown origin of everything, the mysterious beginnings as represented in the hymn just quoted.

The second kinds of cosmological hymns are those celebrating the power of natural phenomena. In these Vedic hymns, there are three kinds of deities: those of the heavenly, atmospheric, and earthly realms. These include Indra, the god of war and rain, who overcomes the evil serpent to release the waters for the benefit of humans, and Varuna, the sky deity, who restores and guards the order of the universe (*rta*). Also significant are the earthly deities of Agni, the god of fire, and Usas, the goddess of dawn, who brings refreshing hope and renewal to each day.

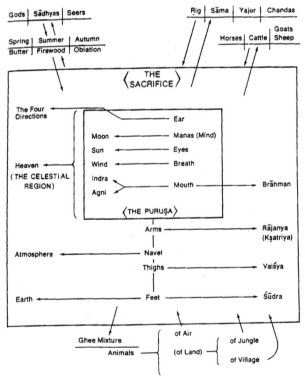

Source: T. J. Hopkins, *The Hindu Religious Tradition* (Belmont, Calif.: Wadsworth, 1971).

This light, most radiant of lights, has come; this gracious one who illumines all things, is born. As night is removed by the rising sun, so is this the birthplace of the dawn.

The fair-shining dawn has come, bringing forth the sun. The darkness of night has given up her domain. Related to each other, immortal, succeeding one another, mutually exchanging appearances, they move across the heavens.

Munificent dawn awakens men curled up asleep; one of enjoyment, another for devotion, another to seek for wealth; they who could scarcely see, now see clearly. All living beings are now awakened.

We behold her, daughter of the sky, youthful, robed in white, driving forth the darkness. Princess of limitless treasure, shine down upon us throughout the day.

—Rig Veda I, 113[26]

Finally, in terms of cultivation, there are hymns that define and celebrate ritual sacrifice as key to the maintenance of cosmological order in the natural and human realms. The power of ritual action is evident throughout these hymns. The early creation hymn of sacrifice previously mentioned sets the stage for the importance of ritual in this worldview. Prayers and offerings are key to placating the powers of the universe, such as wind and rain, thunder and lightning. Moreover, there is a need to maintain balance and order through correct speech, through the sacrifices of the present, through the consecration of the kings, through the great horse sacrifice, and through the offerings of *ghee* (clarified butter), of *soma* (hallucinogenic plant), and of fire itself.

To placate the powers of nature, to obtain material benefits, and to establish moral coherence—all these are reasons for the importance of ritual sacrifice in the Vedas. While this is true in many early societies, what takes on particular importance in India is the role of the sacrifices in maintaining order in the cosmos itself.

Cosmology and Harmony—China

Finally, in turning to the East Asian world of China, we see in the Book of Changes (I Ching) the dynamics of change and continuity in the universe celebrated not as gods of nature but as patterns, namely hexagrams, which can be read as symbols guiding human affairs. To discern correct action, humans must be in harmony with the movements of the universe. The first hexagram, the Creative, *Ch'ien,* illustrates this well:

Vast indeed is the sublime Creative Principle, the Source of All, co-extensive with the heavens! It causes the clouds to come forth, the rain to bestow its bounty and all objects to flow into their respective forms. Its dazzling brilliance permeates all things from first to last; its activities symbolized by the component lines, reach full completion, each at the proper time. (The Superior Man), mounting them when the time is ripe, is carried heavenwards as though six dragons were his steeds! The Creative Principle functions through Change; accordingly, when we rectify our way of life by conjoining it with the universal harmony, our firm persistence is richly rewarded. The ruler, towering above the multitudes, brings peace to all countries of the world.[27]

The creativity of the universe is manifest throughout the natural order. For a society deeply engaged with agriculture, as China was, the changes of the seasons were seen as key cyclical patterns mirroring transformation in human life. They were revelatory of the birth and death processes of nature and of humans. The constancy of the seasons gave guidance to human affairs. Indeed, it was often said that the seasons do not err and that therefore the great person takes them as a model for action and behavior.[28] Thus, the emperor, for example, was considered the polestar, the exemplar, for the entire society in this regard. He offered sacrifices at the great temples of heaven and earth in the capital city, Beijing. He ritually planted the rice in the fall and harvested it in late summer. (This symbolic planting and harvesting is still performed by the Japanese emperor in Tokyo.) Moreover, throughout Asia there are elaborate systems of *feng shui* that orient persons, houses, public buildings, even graves to the most auspicious direction and balance with nature.

In terms of the broad dialectic of cosmology and cultivation, Chinese religious thought concentrates on connecting biological processes of growth and transformation with particular virtues to be cultivated. The attributes of creativity are four, namely, sublimity, success, furtherance, and perseverance. These are metaphors for the life processes of beginning, duration, advantage, and flourishing. They are linked to the virtues of humaneness, faithfulness, righteousness, and wisdom. Thus, to be receptive to these cosmological processes of the life cycle, one must cultivate relational resonance in virtue. The result of this dynamic process of cosmological creativity finds its counterpoints in the receptive cultivation of the individual. The person is linked to the cosmos through life-generating patterns reflecting both order and change in the universe. A person can thus penetrate the tao of heaven and earth:

The Book of Changes contains the measure of heaven and earth; therefore it enables us to comprehend the tao of heaven and earth and its order.

Looking upward, we contemplate with its help the signs in the heavens; looking down, we examine the lines of the earth. Thus we come to know the circumstances of the dark and the light. Going back to the beginnings of things and pursuing them to the end, we come to know the lessons of birth and death. The union of seed and power produces all things; . . .

The result is not only the growth of knowledge but also the growth of virtue:

Since in this way man comes to resemble heaven and earth, he is not in conflict with them. His wisdom embraces all things, and his tao brings order into the whole world; therefore he does not err. He is active everywhere but does not let himself be carried away. He rejoices in heaven and has knowledge of fate; therefore he is free of care. He is content with his circumstances and genuine in his kindness; therefore he can practice love.[29]

The result of this penetration of the changes in the cosmos and the cultivation of virtue in the self is that humans are able to both cooperate and collaborate with heaven and earth. In this way, they form a triad with heaven and earth—completing their transforming and nourishing powers with relational resonance and practical programs.

Indeed, the sense of completing and harmonizing with the fecundity of life that underlies the I Ching is at the heart of this dynamic system of cosmology and cultivation. For what the I Ching aims at is how to release the transformative energies in nature so as to be resonant with the creativity of human energies. Here, the overflowing power of material force, or *ch'i,* comes into play.

Ch'i is that which unites all life, from atoms, plants, animals, and humans to the cosmos itself. This vitalistic principle of life holds within it the great transformative potential of life. These are the patterns that connect, buried deep within the storehouse of human knowing. Our genes contain these patterns of knowing that link us to all other atoms in the universe.

Conclusion

To reignite that link between our inner patterned genetic storehouse and that of the natural world is what is needed in all the major religious traditions. It is what is called for now in moving from the fire of chaotic groping toward patterns of order and meaning. These ancient scriptures exemplify how that linkage was fostered in earlier times and how the numinous encounter with nature was reaffirmed. Now we need to weave new linkages to both time and space within the context of the epic of evolution. If the epic is the warp, religions may be seen as the woof, as suggested by the theologian Philip Hefner. The patterns and design are still emerging. In terms of developmental time, we are seeking our place in this vast sweep of evolution. In particular, then, we need to examine the cosmological dimensions of the world's religions so that our efforts at moral self-cultivation will include reciprocity with the natural world as the relational field on which our life completely depends.

In terms of space, we are seeking appropriate modes of ecological design—how to live with the river patterns, how to tap into solar energy, how to flow with the rhythms of water, how to move with the currents of air.[30] All of this means harmonizing with the deep cosmological rhythms in nature—not controlling them or harnessing them in a manipulative way but learning once again nature's inner ordering principles, understanding the patterning imprinted in the cosmos and cultivated in ourselves. This is the way of religious inspiration—from its earliest pulsations to the present.

Can we listen, can we see, can we feel, can we touch anew with a feeling for the organism—with a deep resonance without and abiding reverence within?

If so, not only will we survive but the planet itself will flourish. And it will do so if we trust the transforming and nourishing powers of the cosmos.

It is this sense of relying on the larger cosmological unfolding of the universe that Thomas Berry invoked at the conclusion of his essay "The New Story":

> The basic mood of the future might well be one of confidence in the continuing revelation that takes place in and through the earth. If the dynamics of the universe from the beginning shaped the course of the heavens, lighted the sun, and formed the earth, if this same dynamism brought forth the continents and seas and atmosphere, if it awakened life in the primordial cell and then brought into being the unnumbered variety of living beings, and finally brought us into being and guided us safely through the turbulent centuries, there is reason to believe that this same guiding process is precisely what has awakened in us our present understanding of

ourselves and our relation to this stupendous process. Sensitized to such guidance from the very structure and functioning of the universe, we can have confidence in the future that awaits the human venture.[31]

Chapter 6

Gaia and the Ethical Abyss:
A Natural Ethic Is a G[o]od Thing

DORION SAGAN AND LYNN MARGULIS

Nature is intrinsically neither good nor evil; these, rather, are nature's human masks. French writer and political activist Simone de Beauvoir called the Marquis de Sade "a great moralist." By this she did not mean that he was highly moral, but rather that his writings, which attempted to disrupt the order of the bedroom with the same vigor with which the French Revolution had displaced the order of the state, force people to think about the foundations of what we consider good and evil. Masochists would hardly endure painful nonreproductive punishments if behavior were legislated simply by survival or genetic fitness. One cannot look fruitfully to "nature"—which, of course, is always perceived culturally—for unambiguous guidance regarding human behavior. Consider African bedbugs. Rambunctious males typically puncture not only females but also each other. They inject sperm through makeshift orifices, sperm that remains viable in the receiving male's body, only to be ejaculated though *his* intromittent (penile) organ to fertilize, with a decided lack of chivalry, similarly violated rapist-breeding female bedbugs.

Consider too the "evil" mites that Stephen Jay Gould tells us are born pregnant, inseminated by their incestuous brothers while still inside their mothers. The young eat through their mother's body from the inside to enter the world. We put "evil" in quotation marks because it seems clear that nature itself is neither moral nor immoral, but amoral—it simply is. And one cannot confine the would-be perversion of nature only to insects or other species, for humans also evolve and differ from culture to culture, sometimes radically, in what they consider right and wrong. An alien theologian, if God grants us the possibility of such a creature, would no doubt look upon cannibalism and virgin sacrifice as a mere ethnological stone's throw from animal sacrifice or the taking of the Eucharist. The Jain one-ups the vegetarian, placing a cloth filter over his mouth so that he does not inadvertently inhale insects; but even he occupies space that theoretically could be occupied by a more "worthy" being.

In writing the first draft of this essay, Dorion devoured a few spoonfuls of blueberry yogurt. But this seemingly wholesome and innocent snack contained active bacterial cultures, making him a kind of interspecies cannibal, a swallower-whole of living, breathing beings. Of course, so are you whenever you drink wine or eat yogurt, kefir, or cheese. You murder fungi and bacteria every time you clean your kitchen counter. You might protest that yogurt bacterial cultures are not sentient, but evidence suggests they are. Microbes seem to make choices; they detect and avoid acids and sugars, for example. We humans should not be too quick to absolve ourselves of micromurder. Knowledge of the innermost feelings of others is not directly accessible to us. Rather, we intuit their emotions and perceptions from their expressions. The executioner lowers a hood over the offending soon-to-be extirpated human victim—to dehumanize, de-face him. If we are not emotionally transparent—not privy to one another's feelings except through empathy, that is, the recognition of similar expressions, primarily facial expressions—we should not interpret the lack of obviousness of the feelings of the denizens of the nonhuman animal, plant, and microbial worlds to mean they don't exist.

In "Facing Nature," in *Biology, Ethics, and the Origins of Life*, we quoted outstanding Jewish philosopher Emmanuel Lévinas: "But what is produced here is not a reasoning, but the epiphany that occurs as a face."[1] And his commentator, Robert Bernasconi, had this to say:

> But it seems that the demand for an ethics can only be satisfied by denying the ethical relation. It is as though the thinker were to respond by offering tablets of stone. It is, of course, no better a response to issue the instruction which refers ethics to the truth of Being. And yet it is at least the case that to refuse the demand is not necessarily to deny the relation. . . . In other words, the ethical relation occurs in the face-to-face relation, as witnessed in the demand for an ethics itself, a demand which it is as impossible to satisfy as it is to refuse.[2]

The problem here is humankind's reluctance to admit that ethics is a construct, a mask whose arbitrariness we must conceal if we are to believe that goodness has a face. The dilemma is that we must deny the arbitrariness in order to trust one another, to continue to live as a community. In "Facing

Nature," we called the lack of morality at the heart of nature the "sun of ethical groundlessness." As with the sun, which we cannot stare at without going blind, the absence of any inner morality of nature is painful to face. So we face something more familiar—one another. Increasingly, we also face our electronic mail and voice proxies and develop for them codes of conduct and norms of behavior. Like everything else in this complex, sun-dependent system at Earth's surface, these codes and behaviors continue to evolve. In this chapter, we use the sun as a metaphor for a foundation we cannot face. It is, in fact, the solar provider and far more than a metaphor. The *o* that turns *God* into *Good* (or is it *Good* into *God?*) can be represented by the sun, the natural source of the planet's wealth. Our prodigious star begets the energy, intelligence, and activity we call life. According to renegade anthropologist Georges Bataille, the sun is the most abstract thing in our universe. Although it is always there, we cannot look directly at it. The sun—or rather its bounty of energy that we use, because it is sacrificed in the process we call life—presents this life with its greatest problems. Thermodynamically, the abundance, beauty, and complexity we detect in all life does not come from nowhere; rather, life's forms and activities are the result of a natural working out of a prior improbability. A universe divided into energy-poor space and energy-rich stars generates gradients that lead to self-organization.

On the basis of work by Montana thermodynamicist Eric D. Schneider, one can argue that improbable life and human intelligence—spirit, you might say—have their precursors in the improbable gradients of nature.[3] Nature tends to find complex ways to reach equilibrium and thus to reduce these gradients. A gradient is simply a difference across a distance, and nature abhors gradients, of which a vacuum is an example. A vacuum is a pressure gradient.

In our view, living matter is an evolving means of reducing a much larger gradient—that between the hot sun and cool space, the latter near absolute zero at $2.7°K$. Much of the ethical squalor of life derives from the fact that whereas life depends on the continuous squandering of the sun's energy for its growth, its materials are in limited supply and must be recycled. It is thus both intelligent and self-devouring, creating ideal conditions for the evolution of both anesthesia and self-deception. Furthermore, we believe that the human sense of ethics—of rightness and righteousness, wrongness and sin—itself is a natural evolutionary development, a recent phenomenon within the Gaian system of a "physiological" planetary surface—one in which atmospheric chemical composition and global mean temperature, for example, are regulated no less than the temperature and blood chemistry of a mammal. The roots of our preoccupation with good and evil lie squarely in our history as animals, warm-blooded social mammals that tended to overgrow their local resources throughout most of the Cenozoic era (65–0 million years ago).[4]

Science, in spite of its nefarious conformists and the unobservant activities of many self-proclaimed scientists, is "a way of knowing," as Professor John A. Moore of the University of California, Irvine, has insisted all his professional life.[5] Highly successful as an analytical tool when phenomena are studied and recorded as carefully as possible, scientific investigation has vastly expanded our awareness of the world. Think, for example, of quasars; the chaotic terrain beneath the sulfurous clouds of Venus; basalt extruded between the fleeing tectonic plates on either side of the Mid-Atlantic Ridge; the deep-sea pogonophoran tube worms, *Riftia pachyptila,* waving red, hemoglobin-filled gill extensions. Think about certain wasps, whose resident bacteria are essential for egg formation: Removal of the bacteria by antibiotic treatment causes the wasps to permanently lose their fertility. Regard the revelation of the electromagnetic spectrum, from X rays that expose the symmetrical structure of crystals to radio waves that open our garage doors and change our television channels; regard how we have put light to use. Scientific inquiry, furthermore, is a democratic and international activity that in principle, and unlike American television, can be engaged in by brilliant South Chinese male students able to learn English, hippie-adopted African American male adolescents enrolled in private schools, and computer-nerd Guatemalans brought to children's museums after school science class by both of their lesbian mothers. The entry fee to science participation is steep, but fewer intrinsic international barriers exist in science than in most other national, tribal, and local human endeavors. The results of three hundred years of science enlighten us. Science as a way of knowing may make us more aware and interesting people, but not necessarily better ones.

Our scientific knowledge of nature has nothing whatsoever to say directly about ethical behavior—how we live our lives and to whom we are faithful, which government, family member, or mate. Acts of science are intrinsically minuscule and slow. Obtaining information from nature and recording it as science is tedious, circuitous, and often repetitious and painful. Perseverance is required. People like to think of themselves as independent members of a superior species, but perhaps we are more like perceptual organs in a global nexus of life-forms that has attributes of a single organismic being.

The Gaia hypothesis is a new view of Earth as a live entity, a set of intertwined ecosystems with a global physiology. As minute components of Gaia, we individual humans are confronted every day by choices. We each have ample opportunity on a regular basis to tumble or falter, flail or collapse into the ethical abyss, where no relief is in sight. No one of us can successfully force the rest to abide by any absolute rule, whether it is to respect our elders or to feed our children. Each of us is deeply embedded in a pattern of metabolism, growth, reproduction, and survival, with an ancient history and a persistent minor direction that is a consequence of that history. All science can do is help illuminate the path we seek and inform us of our planet–people relations.[6]

The Gaia hypothesis is the intellectual brainchild of atmospheric chemist James E. Lovelock, nurtured since the womb of the international scientific space program (the National Aeronautics and Space Administration, the European Space Agency, and the Soviet space program).[7] It takes its name from the Greek goddess of Earth; etymologically, *gaia* is the origin of the English *geo,* as in *geo*metry, *geo*graphy, and *geo*logy. The Gaia hypothesis postulates that the estimated more than 30 million types of organisms in our biosphere that constitute the biota—flora, fauna, and microbes—are all descended from common ancestors, as Darwin taught. The biota provides the conditions for life on Earth, including a planetary physiology that regulates surface temperature, ocean acidity, and the flux of reactive gases of the atmosphere. Life and environment, in other words, form a single, interacting system. At the same time, this system is a response to the extraordinary astronomical environment of a highly improbabilistic energy gradient: an electromagnetic solar gradient converted—by, for, and as life—into the chemical gradients of a living planetary surface.

The space program has yielded a better understanding of Earth and its surface processes because of new information learned about our planetary neighbors, Mars and Venus. Photographs made from orbiting spacecraft provide evidence that at one time there was abundant water on Mars. Astronomer Toby Owen of the University of Hawaii remarked, "It rained really hard on Mars, but only once—perhaps for 100,000 years." He said he doubts it has rained there during the past 2,600 *million* years. Thus, although Mars's early history was presumably not so dissimilar from that of Earth, Mars is now a cold carbon dioxide planet, drier than any place on Earth.

If Mars circles the sun from an orbit outside that of Earth, Venus's orbit is inside it. Thanks to several Russian soft landings on the surface of Venus in the 1970s and 1980s, images and measurements confirm earlier telescope observations that Venus is very hot and very dry. Like Mars, Venus sustains no life. The atmosphere of both is more than 95 percent carbon dioxide.

So how can one explain the presence of living planet Earth between the two dead neighbors (or between the two planets that never lived at all)? First, perhaps our planet is misnamed; perhaps it should be called Water. Calling it

Water would bring people's attention to the major factor of the growth and evolution of life. Indeed, Earth, on average, has 3,000 meters of water over its surface—by contrast, Mars and Venus have less than a millimeter. This is one of the facts that led Lovelock to the Gaia hypothesis.

It is not only the presence of water that differentiates Earth from Mars and Venus. Earth's atmosphere is made up of many different highly reactive gases, very different from those of our neighboring planets. Why is this so? Because the gases that once existed on Mars and Venus have already reacted; their present dead, static carbon dioxide atmosphere is the result of this process. Earth's atmosphere, on the other hand, is an explosive mixture, with 79 percent nitrogen (which when energized reacts entirely with oxygen to make nitrates and other nitrogen oxides) and 21 percent oxygen. Carbon dioxide in Earth's air is reduced to 0.03 percent of the atmosphere because of the oxygen-producing and oxygen-removing phenomena of life. Moreover, it is life that retains the water on Earth, yielding the Gaian oceanic corollary that without life, photoautotrophic and chemoautotrophic bacteria, algae, and plants that remove CO_2, our atmospheric temperature would have been so high that we would have a planet with far less water.

The Gaia hypothesis thus holds that all living entities in the biosphere produce and remove gases and that this in itself is *a sign of life*. The joint metabolism and the tendency of organisms to grow exponentially and to interact in watery solutions have created a *physiology on a planetary scale,* which is not found on Venus, Mars, or any other extraterrestrial body. This physiology reflects Earth life's status as a complex system actively reducing the solar gradient, a fact supported by the satellite-observed coolness over the Amazon River basin and other complex, high-diversity ecosystems. Gaian physiology can also be viewed as the cycling of energy and matter to make a more complex gradient-reducing system, that is, one that exports entropy as heat into space, thereby augmenting the universal tendency for matter to achieve atomic chaos, randomization, and chemical equilibrium.

The atmosphere of our planetary neighbors, Mars and Venus, by contrast, reflects the absence of a complex gradient-reducing matter- and energy-cycling system and can, like the Gaia hypothesis, be explained by physics and chemistry. There is no planetary ethical mandate for life or death, although life has an edge in helping matter achieve chemical equilibrium. Without the complex gradient-reducing system we humans call life, Earth's temperature and acidity and the reactive gas composition of the atmosphere would be more predictable—but less effective at reducing the solar gradient.

Allow us now to bring you into the lives of the microbes via our Sciencewriters videotape, *Gaia to Microcosm,* where we see representatives of the earliest and smallest life-forms.[8] They provide a crucial key to comprehending—and perhaps even enjoying—Gaia, given that all living things on Earth are, in a manner of speaking, made up of bacteria. The history of life's continuing evolution can be documented in the fossil record of these very microorganisms over the past 3,500 million years, reaching back to the Archean eon of the oldest rocks and continuing to the present day. In fact, living communities of oxygen-producing bacteria structurally identical to the fossils are still found in a few places on Earth, such as Shark Bay, north of Perth in Western Australia, and Lee Stocking Island, in Exuma Sound in the Bahamas. What these bacteria, ancient and present, have in common is that they exist in communities that, by a process of photosynthesis, remove carbon dioxide from the air and precipitate limestone rocks while producing oxygen.

When this process first began, Earth's atmosphere was oxygen-poor. But that changed dramatically with the appearance of cyanobacteria (formerly called blue-green algae). The cyanobacteria recorded their presence in fossil structures known as stromatolites, "bacterial skyscrapers." The new bacteria were able to wrest hydrogen from water—that is, to change water chemically. Cyanobacteria break the chemical bonds between water's constituent elements, hydrogen (which they crave, and indeed demand) and oxygen (which they release into the air as waste). They use the hydrogen and cause it to react with the carbon dioxide in the atmosphere to make more of their kind. All life requires water and must be bathed in it, but only cyanobacteria seize the hydrogen from water in an act that releases oxygen as waste.[9]

Getting back to ethics, all living entities tend to display what German philosopher Friedrich Nietzsche called a "will to power"—the urge to grow and reproduce and make the world over in their image. This includes the microbial life-forms, as seen in the *Gaia to Microcosm* videotape. Their tendency, like ours, is to grow unceasingly. Their waste, like ours, creates selection pressures that prevent both their continual growth and the growth of other populations. Gaia is a selective agent, and even bacteria have an active social life, since they interact with their fellow bacteria: They travel in packs and, to reproduce, some prey upon others.

Bacterial life has endured, but about 2,000 million years ago it was joined by new kinds of life—nucleated organisms (protoctists), from which all larger living things more complex than bacteria evolved. With food, salts, and water, these organisms will divide and grow. Some members of the Kingdom Protoctista are as much as thirty meters long. Others fill the seawater off the Hebrides Islands of Scotland with their bodies—so abundant are they that they give a different color to the water in satellite imagery. These protoctists (*Emiliania huxleyi*), called coccolithophorids, grow as densely as 10 million to the teaspoon. Their elaborate coverings are made up of calcium carbonate buttons, ornate limestone scales. The calcium carbonate in the limestone came from the atmosphere, from which *Emiliania* removed carbon dioxide, after which it generated oxygen. Like all plants and algae, *Emiliania* can do this because its ancestors captured cyanobacteria and to this day it retains them inside its body.

The Gaia hypothesis helps us discern how the biosphere at or near the surface of Earth functions physiologically. However, since 1977 the concept of the biosphere has been expanded to include the mounds of calcium carbonate deep in shallow oceans created not by photosynthetic bacteria (since there is no light) but by bacterial metabolism that uses atmospheric or oceanic carbon dioxide along with the geothermal production of hydrogen gas and hydrogen sulfide gas as starting materials. These gases bubble up through the fissures in Earth's surface at the bottom of the sea. Thus, Earth's biosphere—containing the only life in the universe as far as we know—extends twelve kilometers or more into the watery abyss.

We in the West tend not to know of the contributions to environmental thinking made by Vladimir I. Vernadsky (1863–1945). This interdisciplinary Russian scientist, who popularized the term *biosphere,* discovered the Russian localities of radioactive fissionable elements, the Russian sources of uranium. Through his work, Vernadsky founded the international field of biogeochemistry, and his successors, students, and colleagues are honored in their homeland by numerous Vernadsky institutes. Vernadsky's face also appears on Russian air letters and postage stamps. Virtually unknown in the United States, his 1926 book *The Biosphere* was published in English translation only in 1999.[10] Vernadsky did for space what Charles Darwin did for time. Whereas Darwin asserted that all of us are connected through time by common ancestry (which molecular biology has shown to be incontrovertible), Vernadsky argued that all organisms are connected in space at Earth's surface. The waste material of one is the fresh food or respirable air of another. Not only does the fundamental rule of the Gaia hypothesis make biodiversity an imperative; the concept also reveals the shallow absurdity of any literal "declaration of independence." Independence from the carbon and hydrogen flow of this biosphere, to say nothing of its water, is tantamount to death in every case. Vernadsky recognized living matter as "animated water" and thought of life's transformations, expansions, chemical tenacity, and originality as Earth's most important geologic force.

From a Darwinian-Vernadskian view of nature, the entire biosphere looks like a single entity, an environment with all organisms having direct continuity through a 4,000 million–year history. As a single phenomenon motivated by radiation from the sun and the thermodynamic-genetic mandates of nature, its inhabitants, and their convoluted past, the biosphere is beyond the mores, morals, and delusions of the late Holocene upright ape whose destiny is incessant chatter and the physiological need for reassurance and community, a basic prerequisite to production of healthy offspring. Neither warm, wet, prattling mammalian humans nor any other individual can ever be independent from the biospheric environment. We can only gaze into the face of the abyss, the "mystery that pervades the well," as Emily Dickinson said. The abyss and the mountain peaks, both ethical and literal, become, from the view of "science as a way of knowing," profound and lofty objects of scrutiny and illumination. By themselves, they never prescribe what we should do or proscribe what we should not do. That is up to us.

We reassert that Earth and the phenomenon of life are both dominated by the genius of the microbial world, a motley assortment of bacteria and protoctists. Microbes have always been at the center of Gaian environmental regulation, and they will be until the sun's diameter extends to our orbit—that is, until Gaia ceases to exist. Gaian regulation is an absolute requirement of our existence, whether dissolute, righteous, ethical, or corrupt. One legitimate scientific goal might be to truly understand why humans tend to destroy the precise environment we need to sustain our kind of life. Australian environmentalist and photographer Reg Morrison, in his recent book about habitat holocaust, made an excellent start in the right direction. "Not the slightest scrap of hard evidence, either morphological or genetic," he noted in the preface,

> exists to suggest that *Homo sapiens* is not, like all other animals, a natural product of evolution. Therefore we, like they, are uncontaminated by supernatural influences, good, bad, or divine. We may well be excellent communicators and toolmakers, but overwhelming evidence shows that these distinctions are of degree, not of kind. The only irrefutable argument in favor of humanity's specialness is in fact purely mystical—and entirely circular. . . . I will argue that our peculiar genetic heritage purposefully blinds us to reality to make us malleable and compliant to its demands, and that our habit of assigning ourselves an imaginary specialness is the mechanism that delivers us into genetic servitude. Our purported spirituality is a consequence of two million years of painstaking Darwinian selection. I argue that our much-vaunted spirituality is a cultural illusion that became cemented into the foundations of

early human society by our potent combination of language and imagination; our obsessive urge to imbue our existence with mythical meaning was once the Excalibur of our species. It was the invincible weapon that carried our branch of the hominid line from the brink of extinction to the conquest of the planet. Since mystical beliefs of various kinds have also played a primary role in the catastrophic growth of the human population, the final chapters [of *The Spirit in the Gene*] are devoted to exploring mysticism's present and future impact on our already bruised and destabilized environment.[11]

Morrison went on to explain, with the use of wonderfully Australian examples, why people feel an affinity with the natural world that leads to respect, responsibility, and protection of its parts. Our empathy toward our food, beasts, and grasses lies deeply embedded in our natural history.

We agree that our "spiritual" relation to nature, our awe at nature's beauties and defense of nature's vast reality, is common to all people, apparently, at all places and times. From the ancient inhabitants of Africa's Kalahari Desert and Okavango Delta to the Inuit's far North and the hothouse plants in the penthouse suite of a corporation's chief executive officer, we humans surround ourselves by sunlight-bathed flowering plants whenever we can. What Morrison details, and we concur, is the accelerating tendency of our species to destroy the very world that supports us by incessant production of *Homo sapiens* babies. That is, Morrison elaborates the relation between spirit (religion, mythopoiesis, belief system, doctrine, dogma, philosophy, prejudice, preconception—call it what you will) and the habitat holocaust in which all of us now participate, whether or not we are aware of our actions and their consequences. Our behaviors, believe it or not, whether increasing our population or our pollution, are an integral part of Gaian environmental modulation.

Gaian regulation is necessary not only for the human future but for the continuity of *any* life-form. All require the flow of energy, carbon, nitrogen, sulfur, phosphorus, and water, although for each species the specific details vary. Climates change; water levels rise; predators evolve; plants are extinguished. Most of life preceded the appearance of humans, and most is likely to outlive our peculiar, manipulative species. Humankind's successors, like today's acid-loving sulfur bacteria or pressure-loving methane makers, would probably be unrecognizable to us even as living beings. We suspect that all of us humans are likely to continue to flounder in the ethical abyss until the end of Gaia. The end should come about 5,000 million years from now, when our star's diameter is scheduled to extend to the orbit of planet Earth (or, rather, Water). Before the sun's red giant stage, when we will suffer the cruel and final heat death, Gaia and all its intricate components (such as us, our descendants and pets, and food plants) will cease to exist in this place. And probably long before then, all talky-talky of "good and evil" will have been silenced forever, although perhaps some spacefaring theologians and ethicists will—in what form we do not know—have escaped to discuss eschatology among the stars.

Chapter 7

Religious Meanings
for Nature and Humanity

Margaret A. Farley

The question I have been asked to address is, Can religious and spiritual identity contribute to an understanding of nature and humanity? I will assume that
having a religious or spiritual "identity" means holding some religious beliefs
and in some way attempting to incorporate these into one's life and actions. So
the question becomes, Can we have religious beliefs that are relevant to our
understanding of nature and humanity, and are there spiritual practices that
produce, follow from, or expand such beliefs?

Since religion is a very complex phenomenon and spiritualities are numerous and diverse, I hope it will be useful if I narrow this question—focusing
primarily on Christianity as a religious tradition, but in a way that may provoke
analogous considerations of other religious traditions. Christianity is a likely
test case for the question—not because it offers the best answers but because
within it there have been many efforts to develop systematic theologies that
specifically address the meaning of nature and of the human person, and
because it has—for better or for worse—had a marked influence on Western
intellectual history as a whole. There are also, of course, many Christian traditions of theology and spirituality, so what I say will remain quite general and
will not necessarily apply to every individual or group that claims a Christian
identity. To some extent, my rendering of the Christian tradition will be more
recognizable by Roman Catholics than by Protestants, but it is not limited to
the Catholic tradition.

All major religious traditions become major in part because they have
something to say about the large questions human persons encounter—the
questions of suffering, of the grounds for human hope, of the meaning of per-

103

sonal maturity, of transcendence (historical, personal, communal). Religion, in fact, has a lot to do with meaning. It is generally experienced not as an irrational activity but rather as part of the effort of reason to make sense of what it confronts. Although its sources transcend what reason can gain access to by itself, its insights and convictions are believed to complement, not do violence to, what reason can understand. Religions include more than worldviews that appear to make sense, but they do include these. Hence, crises may occur within religious traditions when what once made sense is called into question, when dissonance is experienced between what a tradition has taught and what its adherents find emerging in their experience. This is what happened for many twentieth-century women, for example, when traditional—especially, but not only—religious understandings of themselves came into conflict with their own experience. This gave rise to widespread efforts on the part of women in almost every religious tradition to critique and to reconstrue traditional beliefs, an enterprise on which their continuing to stand within their traditions depended.

To some extent, a similar crisis has occurred for many religious believers, in particular Christians, when confronted not only by the threat (and the reality) of ecological devastation, and not only by the responsibility of humans in this regard, but also by the apparent contributions of their own religious tradition to the problem. Many forces, of course, have converged to create this problem—from economic exploitation and political competition to technological imperatives that all too often have exacerbated what we now refer to as the "rape of the earth." But among these forces has been the force of ideas—of convictions, beliefs, ideologies—that motivated or did not check the massive processes that have led to the devastation of life systems and even ecological collapse. The charge against Christianity in this regard is by now well known, and it has been taken seriously by thoughtful Christians, including many theologians. If Christian theology has not been the primary purveyor of ideas that account for our environmental problems, it has, at least, for a long time neglected questions of the meaning of nature and of humanity that might have countered them.[1]

The real question before us, therefore, is not just whether religion and spirituality can contribute to understandings of nature and the human person but also whether they can contribute in ways that will help now to protect, not destroy, the earth and all that dwells therein. To pursue this question, we must undertake three tasks—critique, retrieval, and reconstruction. The charges against Christian theology must be taken seriously, which means that construals of nature and humanity must be critically appraised. And if persons are to continue to stand within the Christian tradition, an effort must be made to retrieve neglected or forgotten elements in the tradition, elements that may now transform the dominant Christian understandings of nature and humanity. And finally, some reconstruction of these understandings must be undertaken in order for Christian theology to be part of the remedy, not the problem, in approaches to humanity and nature.

In this short chapter, I can only suggest some outlines for these three tasks. Christian theology is complex, and it appears in multiple strands of the Christian tradition. There are many theologies of nature and many theologies of the human person, not one univocal theology. Moreover, it is not sufficient simply to look at theologies of nature and humanity, since these are intertwined with, for example, theologies of God, creation, freedom, and sin.

Even the sources for Christian theology are multiple—standardly including scripture (the Hebrew Bible and the New Testament); tradition (the history and development of theologies, church teachings and practices); other disciplines of knowledge (e.g., philosophy, the natural and social sciences, history); and contemporary experience. Each of these sources requires interpretation, and when it comes to how the insights from these sources will work together and provide guidance for action, each requires decisions regarding how they will be used in the faith community. Hence, critique, retrieval, and reconstruction will need to be applied to all sources and to their uses in Christian theology and ethics. It becomes clear, then, why all I can do here is suggest what must be examined.

Critique of the Tradition

Every religious (and every Christian) understanding of the natural world and humanity is importantly connected with an understanding of God. The first critique that is relevant to our concerns, therefore, is a critique of some historical versions of a Christian theology of God. More centrally in some Christian traditions than in others, God has sometimes been seen primarily as transcendent, largely absent or hidden to human searching, the goal of human desiring but one that leads beyond this world and sometimes even in opposition to it. A transcendent God, sometimes further understood as requiring a submissive people, is a notion that has played itself out sociologically in human relations of dominance and subordination—God in relation to God's people, men in relation to women, parents in relation to children, teachers in relation to students, and so on. It is not difficult to believe that such a distant God might delegate governing authority to humans over the world of nonhumans and that such a God would have purposes so hidden that humans remain largely on their own in ruling the world. This view of God is in many respects a caricature of Christian beliefs about God, yet it has captured the imagination of theologians at times, and it has appeared often enough in popular belief. Its consequences have become unacceptable to many Christians, who search for better understanding of the God whom they experience and love.

Whether God is distant or near, uncaring or compassionate, the world that God created was for centuries in Christian theology looked upon as hierarchically ordered, static, a habitat of living beings but not itself living and dynamic. The second critique important for us today, then, is the one that has been made of doctrines of creation insofar as they are contradicted by the findings of modern science and insofar as they incorporate misleading dualisms between mind and matter, soul and body, rationality and emotion. Much of past Christian theology of nature was based on the physics, astronomy, and biology of its time. When these sciences changed drastically, theology, too, had to undergo Copernican-like revolutions, incorporating new insights about order amid disorder and chance; massive new information amid growing uncertainties; evolution and a human community derived from a common ancestry; challenges to human freedom from the neurosciences and psychology. For some, the dependence of old theologies of nature on old science appeared to be so great that everything heretofore believed about the natural world and the place of persons in it had to be rejected. Moreover, early church repression of theological adaptation to new science prevented much of the creativity that might have emerged in a theology of nature and an ethical understanding of the responsibilities of humans in the world.

The third area of critique important to our concerns focuses more centrally on theologies of the human person, on the relationship between humanity and nature, and on social and political theologies. In many ways, theology has not neglected the human person in the same manner in which it has neglected the cosmos. Centuries-long debates about human freedom are still instructive for contemporary efforts to understand human responsibility in the face of new forms of determinism. Theologies of human embodiment have moved far beyond, though still learn from, medieval notions of formed matter. Liberation and other political theologies have already introduced correctives that go beyond critiques of earlier social theories. New insights into power relations connect with long-standing concerns about limitless self-interest in fallen human beings. But with all this, further critiques are under way, offering special challenges to the anthropocentrism of much of Christian theology. Lynn White Jr.'s scathing critique of Christianity's role in the environmental crisis has been taken seriously (if sometimes only in arguing against it).[2] No theologian today is satisfied with Francis Bacon's (or White's, for that matter) interpretation of the Genesis texts wherein humans are given mastery over nature and ordered by God to subdue it. But if this so-called despotic interpretation of Genesis is no longer credible, newer stewardship interpretations are found wanting as well. There is more than one creation story in Genesis (and in other books of the Bible), and critical studies now extend to a search for more adequate understandings not only of the shared citizenship of humans and nonhumans but also of the coherence of scientific discoveries regarding evolution and biblical-theological interpretations of creation. This leads us to the question and the task of retrieval of lost insights, insights that can relativize, correct, or supplant elements in the tradition that are no longer credible to many of its adherents.

Retrieval of Theologies in the Tradition

It can be argued quite persuasively, I think, that deep within Christian traditions there lie quite other articulations of theologies of God and of the world that are both more central to the tradition throughout the centuries and more illuminative of the questions Christians and others raise today regarding nature and humanity. These need to be retrieved in a way that influences not only development of doctrine but also the life of faith in the popular Christian mind. What we are looking for are theological insights that do not justify (or, better, that forbid) human assault upon planet Earth, whether in terms of God's supposed command or of human interpretation of hierarchies of importance among the inhabitants of this planet.

Just as the creation stories in the book of Genesis provide us with more than directions regarding mastery over nature (indeed, quite other than these), so do the writings of key theologians in the history of Christianity offer us both bad and good news. The bad news—regarding an absent God, an instrumentalized nature, and God-ordered inequality in relations among human beings—needs critique. Much of the good news is still good and deserves to be retrieved.

For example, St. Augustine, who wrote in the fifth century C.E., is frequently blamed for the beginnings of Christian hierarchical thinking. It is true that Augustine, following Greek and Roman philosophers, did think of creation as hierarchically ordered. Yet his view of nature's order may challenge, not justify, our domination of the earth. In his massive work *The City of God,* Augustine noted (as he did elsewhere) the rankings among all creatures:

"Those that live are ranked higher than those that do not . . . sentient [beings] are superior to non-sentient . . . intelligent [beings] higher than non-intelligent."[3] These lines were oft quoted by Christian thinkers who followed Augustine. Not so often quoted were the lines that followed, in which Augustine, perhaps with tongue in cheek, nonetheless seriously critiqued the human tendency to value creatures not for what they are but solely for their utility to humans:

> Sometimes we so prefer certain non-sentient things to others that are sentient that, had we the power, we would annihilate these latter, reckless of the place they hold in the pattern of nature or wilfully sacrificing them to our own convenience. For who does not prefer to have food in his house rather than mice, money than fleas? This is less astonishing when we recall that, in spite of the great dignity of human nature, the price for a horse is often more than that for a slave and the price for a jewel more than that for a maid.[4]

It was Augustine, too, whose heart was restless for God but who nonetheless did not consider created beings as mere stepping-stones to God. What all beings *are* is related to God, but they *are* therefore of value in themselves. More than one lyrical passage such as this one in the *Confessions* sings of the worth of every creature:

> What is this God whom I love? I asked the earth and it answered, "I am not God." And all things that are on the earth confessed the same. I asked the sea and the deeps and the creeping things with living souls, and they replied, "We are not your God. . . ." I asked the blowing breezes, and the universal air with all its inhabitants answered: "Anaximenes was wrong. I am not God." I asked the heaven, the sun, the moon, the stars, and "no," they said, "we are not the God for whom you are looking." And I said to all these things. . . . "Tell me about my God, you who are not God. Tell me something about God." And they cried out in a loud voice: "God made us." My question was in my contemplation of them, and their answer was in their beauty.[5]

Important, too, among the elements of the Christian tradition are the twelfth- and thirteenth-century attempts at a theology that would integrate God, humanity, and the cosmos. Inspired by ancient Greek scientific works and the works of Jewish and Muslim scholars, Christian theologians sought to articulate a faith grounded in and nourished by two revelatory texts—the

Bible and creation. God revealed God's own self, and revealed the nature of humanity and of the world, in both of these "books." But this was a God who created ex nihilo, out of nothing, not in a long-ago beginning time but throughout the history of the world. This was a God who holds everything in creation, human and nonhuman, so that every being remains utterly contingent, utterly dependent for its very existence and for its activity, on the continuing—here and now—creative activity of God. This view takes nothing away from the work of created beings (nor would it later have to be at odds with theories of big bangs or of evolution), for God intended to share God's being and activity with all creatures—to share God's life and love and beauty. But a God who holds all in being is thereby intimately present to all—more intimate to every being than it is to itself. This is not a distant God, not an absent God—though profoundly hidden, yet gloriously revealed.

In the thirteenth century, Thomas Aquinas offered a theology and metaphysics of ontological participation, one that drew from Greek understandings but fit very well with understandings of a personal God who knows and loves all into being; a God who is all being, yet can create many beings; a God in whose being all other beings participate, indeed, in whom they "live and move and have their being."[6] Careful to avoid pantheism on the one hand and any shade of deism on the other (for the God he tried to understand was both immanent and transcendent), Aquinas offered a view of creation in which every being has its own worth. Every being is in some way instrumental in regard to others and to the whole (even humans are so), but every being is of value—of goodness and beauty—in itself as well. Such a theology yields what is sometimes called a sacramental view of the world and all that belongs to it. In the words of the twentieth-century scientist and theologian Pierre Teilhard de Chardin, "nothing is profane for those who know how to see."[7] God's presence is everywhere, and nothing falls outside God's embrace.

Understandings such as these were, of course, undermined when scientific advances discredited what there was in them that depended on an outmoded physics. Yet long after their losses to better science, they remain potential sources of insight, ready to be made compatible with contemporary findings. What begins in critique and is filled out through retrieval is now ripe for reconstruction.

Reconstruction of the Tradition

Deep in the Christian tradition is a view of human persons as created beings whose structure is complex: We are embodied spirits, enspirited bodies (embodied consciousnesses), with structures within structures—chemically, biologically, physiologically—and with capabilities for thinking and feeling, for planning and choosing. We are relational—not only social but also interpersonal, deeply dependent upon others for developing our own selves, open in relation to a transcendence that reaches all the way to the possibility of union with God. We are in the world—the world of nature and the world of historical, cultural, political, and economic systems and institutions. We have potentiality as well as actuality—possibilities for flourishing, but also vulnerabilities for diminishment. Each person is unique, yet we are all common sharers in the human community and in creation.

Ironically, what we may need to do with theological views such as this is, perhaps, for a time to turn away from ourselves and look around us. Only when we understand better what God is doing in the world of nature may we turn back to ourselves with greater wisdom about who we are. After all, we might have to admit that even though we are part of an ecosystem, we are in a sense misfits. We are the ones who worry about ecological disasters, and we are the ones who are responsible for them. We are profoundly interdependent with all other beings in nature, yet we are more dependent on the other beings than they are on us (or we would be, had we not already so modified nature that the future of all now depends on us). We think of the rest of nature as vastly inferior to us in achievement, but it possesses a harmony and rhythm that mock the restlessness and anxiety that are ours.[8]

What we need is to engage in a new de-centering—that is, to find a center beyond ourselves in order to find a center within ourselves. We have many sources in Christian theology for both understanding de-centering and helping to effect it. For example, we have strong resources for building a contemporary theology and an ethics of the common good, expanding our notions of solidarity with humanity and with all creation, learning what it means to stretch our hearts in a love of God that requires a love of neighbor and a love of the created universe. In fact, the Christian tradition has thought long and hard about certain forms of de-centering. It has cautioned against egocentricity, warned against solely self-centered love, offered judgments against the setting up of idols, especially the idol of one's own self. Christian theology since the nineteenth century has moved through major changes variously described as conversions (in focus) from the object to the subject, from the subject to the other, from the other to the community, from the community to those at its margins. Each of these has been a form of de-centering, of taking ourselves in an important way off center stage.

To turn now to the wider world will, as do other conversions, require whole new labors to enable us to see from a perspective heretofore not taken. Preliminarily, it will require new awakenings that take us out of ourselves and our business as usual. There is more than one way to begin: with fear (of ecological disaster), with repentance, or with new experiences of awe and joy in response to beauty. We no doubt need all these ways. Fear is easy to understand, if we take seriously what we know about the threats to our planet, and even terror can be salutary. Repentance may be easy to understand, too. This volume is about good or goodness, about the *bonum*. But implicit in our considerations is concern for the bad or evil, the *malum*. In the context of theological and ecological concerns, there may be evils we lament—conflicts and disruptions in the world of nature, animal suffering and human disease, deaths that may be part of nature but for which we mourn. In our context today, however, there are also evils for which we repent—evils *that do not have to be*. These are the evils of our own assaults on nature, intentional or unintentional, and the evils of our assaults on one another, because there is a link between our exploitation of the earth and our injustice to human beings. The poor suffer disproportionately from environmental destruction, and racism and sexism have ecologically distorted faces.[9] Conversion and repentance may come only when the face of suffering and loss becomes visible to us—in nature and in humanity—and it is in part the task of theology to make visible that face.

There is another way for conversion to begin: that is, with the beholding of beauty and its concomitant response of awe and unexpected joy. Perception of the good—if it is clear and full enough—awakens love. It reaches inside us and taps our capacity to love. Even more, the perception of what is beautiful awakens us, grasps us, and frees us, lifts us out of ourselves and makes possible the "Turning" of which the Jewish philosopher Martin Buber spoke.[10] Beauty taps our capacities both to know and to love, and it enables us to turn our gaze from preoccupation with ourselves toward the beholding of what is beyond us—of what is more than we are, even if we share in its being.

Neither terror nor repentance nor joy in beauty should be romanticized. Here is the possibility of life or death. For with the conversion that may come (or the de-centering) will come also the hard work of new ethical discernment and new moral choices. Just as working the land is not only a romantic idea but also an ongoing struggle (both for and against nature), so is there work to be done if we are to move the world of humans in the face of the moral imperatives that are ours.

My answer, then, to the question with which I began, is that a Christian theology of nature and humanity can contribute to our understanding, to our decisions, and to our hope. With all religious traditions, we may begin to see and experience (in the words of C. S. Lewis) that for all creation there is no center because all is at the center.[11]

Chapter 8

A Livable Future:
Linking Geology and Theology

GEORGE W. FISHER

As the world population doubled from 3 billion to 6 billion during the last half of the twentieth century, we began to wonder what limits there might be to growth. No clear answer has emerged. Despite early pessimistic projections,[1] global indices of human development and economic well-being have actually improved.[2] But at the same time, human domination of Earth's ecosystems has increased[3] and disparities between the very rich and the very poor have grown.[4] The limits to the number of people Earth can accommodate seem more elastic than first thought, but they depend critically upon how we choose to live.[5]

Most of the choices that define a livable future emerge from the need to balance competing goals—for example, satisfying the real needs of the world's poor while maintaining established consumption patterns in wealthy countries; preserving natural ecosystems while meeting human needs; and preserving meaningful options for future generations while meeting present needs. Each of these choices has scientific dimensions—we obviously need to know as much as we can about how the Earth system works, about how resources are produced, climate is controlled, disease transmitted, and so on. To be livable in any pragmatic sense, any future must be geologically sustainable. But each choice also has profound moral and ethical dimensions. Making these choices will require us to think deeply about what makes life really worthwhile, what gives life meaning beyond mere existence, and what it really means to be human. To be livable in a fully human sense, any future must be morally and ethically sustainable. And because moral reflection is for most of the world explicitly or implicitly grounded in religious traditions, we must

113

attempt to resolve these trade-offs in the unfamiliar terrain where geologic and religious reflection converge. In this chapter, I hope to show that there is more common ground between geology and theology than we might expect.

A Geological Perspective

The Project Apollo images of Earth as seen from space fundamentally changed our worldview. We began to sense that instead of facing an endless frontier, with new lands always beckoning just beyond the horizon, we live in a finite world, a lush oasis isolated in the emptiness of space. For the first time, we saw Earth as a complex system of soil, water, and air, home to billions of fellow creatures, large and small. And we began to see that all are linked by an intricate web of biogeochemical cycles in which the chemicals of life—carbon, water, calcium, nitrogen, phosphorus, potassium—cycle endlessly through a complex series of biological, chemical, and geologic processes, mostly powered by solar energy. We had understood most of this long before, but the photographs taken from the Apollo spacecraft burned that image into our consciousness in a way we could no longer ignore. We began to know in our hearts that we all depend upon that biogeochemical system and, so, upon one another.

To understand this system, we can start with the familiar food chain, more accurately known as a food web. Food webs tend to vary a lot from one ecosystem to another, but a few features are common to all. Surface ecosystems begin with plants that use solar energy to convert carbon dioxide into organic matter; those plants provide the energy needed by herbivores and, indirectly, by carnivores. But the food web doesn't end there. Animals produce waste products, and plants produce dead organic matter. If that detritus were allowed to accumulate, those of us living in eastern forest systems would soon be buried by leaves and other organic debris. The carbon and nutrients they contain would be lost, and eventually the whole system would grind to a halt. So a fourth part of the system—the fungi and bacteria known as decomposers—plays a key role by consuming that organic detritus and converting its carbon and nutrients into a form that can be used again by plants and some animals.

On the planetary scale, all ecosystems are linked by a global carbon cycle, in which carbon is cycled through the terrestrial and marine biospheres, and these are in turn linked to one another by the atmosphere and the river systems. Carbon isotopes from rocks in Greenland suggest that photosynthesis had already begun 3.85 billion years ago and therefore Earth had at least a primitive biogeochemical system virtually from the beginning.[6] The carbon cycle now regulates the level of atmospheric carbon dioxide, which, in concert with water vapor and other greenhouse gases, leads to an average surface temperature of 15°C, perfect for carbon-based life. Without that greenhouse effect, Earth's temperature would be −18°C. The oceans would be largely covered with sea ice, reflecting much incoming solar radiation and cooling Earth so drastically that life as we know it might never have developed. The greenhouse effect has served as a global thermostat for nearly 4 billion years, keeping Earth's surface temperature within the 40°C temperature range needed for life despite a 20 percent increase in solar radiation, despite a change from a reducing atmosphere to an oxidizing one, and despite five major extinctions in the past 500 million years, each of which radically transformed the mix of species that constitute the biosphere.

The requirements for a sustainable life system are pretty daunting. Earth must be close enough to the sun that its temperature is in the range that maintains liquid water. Its gravity field must be strong enough to retain an atmosphere that creates a surface pressure in the field of liquid water (unlike Mars or the moon). Its daily rotation must be fast enough that diurnal temperature variations are not too extreme (unlike Mercury or the moon). It must have a crust light enough to form large continental masses but thin enough to permit plate tectonics to operate (unlike Mars).

These last three requirements are pretty difficult to satisfy. They depend critically upon which planetesimals collided to form Earth, what the bulk composition of the resulting aggregate was, and what the dynamics of each collision were during the final stages of planetary accretion. Even small differences in the trajectories of the colliding bodies could have produced a different Earth, one unable to sustain life. But even an Earth perfectly attuned to nurturing carbon-based life might not have produced humans. Had a fluke meteorite impact 65 million years ago not eliminated most Mesozoic reptiles, the Cenozoic radiation of mammalian species that produced us might never have happened. And the fact that we are among the youngest of the mammals—modern humans appeared only 150,000 years ago—emphasizes the point that we are not essential to the presence of life on Earth. Only a few bacteria, viruses, and parasites that have learned to live at our expense, and some domestic species that we have bred into dependence, would miss us were we to disappear.

This geologic story can be read in two ways. The conventional reading is to admit that we are totally dependent on the continuing operation of the biogeochemical system and that the system is in no way dependent upon us. The other reading—less conventional but no less important—is simply to stand stunned by the beauty, intricacy, and incredible contingency of the story, the creativity of the system, the exuberance of life, and finally to stand in awe at the sheer privilege of being here, able to sense that exuberance and feel that awe. We scientists are privileged to see the delicacy and beauty of nature more clearly than most, and we should be less reticent about expressing this side of our work. In the end, helping to articulate our sense of that beauty and the feeling of privilege it can engender may be our most important contribution to understanding what it is to be human.

But the point I want to stress is that although these two ways of responding to the story are different, both point to the central importance of the life support system, and both suggest we must do all we can to nurture that system.

To respond intelligently to that mandate, we need a sense of how vulnerable the system is to our increasing influence and how urgently we need to reduce that influence. The system's vulnerability is difficult to assess. On one hand, it seems extraordinarily stable. It has continued to sustain life on Earth for nearly 4 billion years, despite the transition to an oxidizing atmosphere, the massive extinctions, the increased intensity of solar radiation, and so on. It will obviously be very difficult for us to destroy the system. But of course our concern is whether we might perturb the system so that it can no longer sustain us. The overall system has lasted a long time, but individual species have not. Ninety-seven percent of the species that have existed at one time or another have become extinct, most because they could not respond to changes in the system. Again, we sense our privilege at being here, and our vulnerability.

What confers survivability on a species is not precisely known, but there are some important clues. The relationship between individual species and their ecosystems is oddly mutual. No species can exist apart from a healthy ecosystem. Yet the health of the system depends critically upon the welfare of the species that constitute the system—the system exists only in that it is instantiated by a particular set of species. So the well-being of an ecosystem and that of its species are deeply intertwined, locked together by the biogeochemical processes they mutually support. At the same time, the classical idea of a "balance of nature," like that of a system in some fixed equilibrium configuration, is wrong.[7] Natural ecosystems tend to be distinctly patchy. Key processes change with the spatial and temporal scales at which we view them, and they seem to have multiple equilibrium configurations. Perhaps the best criterion of system health is adaptability, the ability to respond creatively to stress and to shift easily from one stable configuration to another as needed.

At the species level, generalists seem to be more successful than species adapted to very specific niches. Although humans are clearly generalists, we are beginning to limit our options as we try to adjust to a finite Earth. The risk is that we may do our job too well. If we succeed in identifying exactly what our needs are and adjusting our way of life to precisely that point at which Earth's capacity to meet those needs is maximized, we may become vulnerable to even small changes in climate or other properties of the global system.

The importance of adaptability makes ecosystem health difficult to measure. We can't just measure some parameter of the system today and compare it with a supposedly pristine state of the system. Healthy systems constantly change in response to the seasons, to climatic cycles, and to human forcing factors such as deforestation in the Amazon River basin or reforestation in New England. So change in itself is not necessarily an indication that something is wrong with the system.

Perhaps the best we can do is to compile a variety of indices designed to compare the human effects on different sectors of the global ecosystem with the capacities of those sectors. Stanford University biologist Peter M. Vitousek and colleagues[8] showed that we are using nearly half of the land's biological production and more than half of the available freshwater, that we account for more than half of the global nitrogen fixation, and so on. Their finding on marine fisheries is one of the most dramatic. As recently as the mid-twentieth century, we thought of the sea as an ultimate reservoir of food; we believed that if we ever outstripped the limits of terrestrial agriculture, the endless oceans stood ready to sustain us. More than half of the world's fisheries were then undeveloped. Today, yields in more than half of commercial fisheries either have plateaued or are declining. Our first real experiment in managing global sustainability seems to be going seriously awry. We could tick off other indices, such as urban air quality and infant mortality, and we could get involved in a prolonged debate about the importance of each. But that debate would miss the point.

The point is that geology has a message for us: We are utterly dependent upon the functioning of the global system, we are stressing that system in several critical ways, and we seem to be approaching some of the limits of what the system can provide. As the global population expands by another 3 billion or 4 billion in the twenty-first century, stresses on the system will increase, particularly if those who consume less adopt a Western level of consumption as their goal.

A Theological Perspective

This sense that we are approaching the limits of Earth's capacity to supply our needs brings us back to the points that began this essay—that limits to growth are likely to be experienced as the need to make increasingly difficult choices about how we live, rather than as rigid ceilings on resource availability,[9] and that for a future to be livable in a way that responds to our full humanity, it is therefore not enough for our choices to be geologically sustainable. They must be morally, or theologically, sustainable as well.

Until recently, post-Enlightenment theology saw nature as little more than a backdrop for the human drama in which the hand of God was to be discerned. In the twentieth century, however, nature again emerged as an important theme of theological reflection. Evolutionary thought provided the basis both for the work of the Jesuit Pierre Teilhard de Chardin[10] and for the emergence of process theology.[11] Religious scholars rediscovered rich traditional resources for understanding the ambiguity of our relationship to nature, with its elements of both transcendence and dependence.[12] That we are called to act as stewards of creation, caring deeply for and about the natural world, has become almost a truism for modern theologians and reinforces the geologic mandate to live in harmony with nature.

But theology challenges us to go beyond an ecological view of sustainability and to acknowledge that authentic human existence requires more than the basic physical needs that Earth can supply.[13] To be meaningful, life must include the opportunity to enjoy loving relationships with others and the freedom to seek fulfillment in rewarding work, done well. Theology insists that those goals can be widely achieved only in a society that values justice and equity.

Perhaps the most important message of theology is its constant reminder that humans are not the center of the universe and that the primary focus of theological ethics must always be on God, not on us.[14] Here, however, we encounter a problem. Imagining a livable future is a global issue and must engage a global community, including people who affirm any of some two hundred religions and people who acknowledge none. We need a way of thinking and speaking that can connect all segments of the global community and that can inform personal, communal, and global ways of thinking. The language of religion, however, tends to be particular to each faith tradition and therefore problematic for people outside that tradition. The problem is especially acute for those who espouse no religious tradition. Even the term *faith* has so many overtones that it has become problematic.

In his book *Dynamics of Faith,* theologian Paul Tillich proposes a way of thinking that I find helpful in opening a space for dialogue.[15] He suggests that instead of speaking in terms of faith, we speak in terms of what he calls our ultimate concern—whatever it is that ultimately grounds our value system: our ultimate basis for discernment, our ultimate criterion for deciding how to order our lives. As Tillich sees it, the truth of an ultimate concern can be assessed in two ways, one objective and one subjective. Objectively, he insists that we judge our ultimate concern on the basis of its ultimacy, the degree to which its content transcends personal or local interests. Subjectively, he suggests that we judge it on the basis of its power to move us, to impel us to respond from the very depths of our humanity, with all our heart, all our soul, and all our mind. For a concern to be truly ultimate for us, we must experience it as utterly compelling, even though it cannot be justified on the basis of reason alone.

Tillich's language is helpful in two respects. First, it challenges us to reflect deeply on exactly what it is we affirm as ultimate. Second, it makes room for both secular and religious thought systems and therefore provides a way of identifying areas of common ground and areas of complementarity between geology and theology. Geology would insist that our ultimate concern should include the continuing health of the global Earth system. Theology would agree that as Earth's stewards, we must be compelled by our ultimate concern to work toward a livable future, but it would insist on a notion of livability that goes beyond the mere functioning of the natural system to include an explicit dimension of justice. Theology would then go on to say that if we accept this broader notion of a livable future as our ultimate concern, we should feel a compulsion to work for it with all our heart, mind, and soul. Mere assent to the importance of livability is not enough; we are called to move beyond assent to an active commitment to work to bring that state into being. Religion is not about doctrine. It is about practice, and if our concern is truly ultimate, we are compelled to act on it.[16]

But here we encounter a problem with both geologic and theological dimensions of ultimacy. Although we sense that we are totally dependent upon the Earth system, we are also deeply aware that we don't fully understand the system, and that even when we agree on the need to act, we often disagree on what act is needed. The problem is even more acute when we confront the issues of justice. Here, theology has another message. It doesn't matter that we are uncertain about how to proceed or whether we can succeed. Doubt is a constant companion of concerns that are truly ultimate.[17] We must simply have the courage to do the best we can, in spite of our doubts. And again, that means we must mobilize more than just our minds. We need to engage our hearts and our souls as well. Theology invites us to act with care, energy, and deep joy at the almost incredible privilege of being called as partners in the continuing process of creation.[18] Those who affirm a religious tradition may find the courage to act in prayer, meditation, or some other spiritual practice capable of engaging them, heart and soul. People with a more secular orientation will follow different paths. Some may find the courage to act in a deep sense of commitment that emerges from their research. Others may act in a quiet sense of connectedness experienced while walking through nearby woods or cultivating a garden; still others, in the depth of their love for family and friends.

Wherever we find it, that sense of connectedness capable of engaging the whole person is what a theologian would call revelation.[19] Unfortunately, revelation is widely misunderstood. Many assume it is a process that abandons reason, but that's not it at all. Revelation is a process that involves the whole person—a confluence of reason with affective response, the experience of having all our cognitive tumblers fall into place at once, of suddenly seeing the world from a new and transforming perspective. Yale University theologian H. Richard Niebuhr put it well when he described revelation as an experience that makes all other experience intelligible, an event like falling in love, one that gives meaning to everything else.[20]

Revelation can emerge from either secular or religious insight. But every revelation, whether grounded in secular or religious experience, is always humanly distorted, always a partial image of reality. So although our commitment to an ultimate concern may give us the courage to act in spite of uncertainty, it must not be taken to confer certainty. Here, religion can learn a lot from science. Any meaningful way of imaging reality carries the risk of our becoming too committed to it. Our images can all too easily be taken to be reality rather than the meaningful but partial glimpses they are. And religious thought has proven all too vulnerable to that form of self-deception. Too rigid acceptance of any system of belief or image of reality is idolatry, of which religious history is full of glaring examples that have inhibited the growth of understanding instead of fostering it. Like science, religious thought must be willing to test its wisdom in light of human experience—to be, in the language of the Reformed tradition, "reformed and always reforming."

Conclusion

Finally, the point of this chapter is that as we try to imagine a livable future, we must explore the confluence of geology and theology or, more broadly, of science and religion. There is a surprising amount of common ground. Where differences remain, the two tend to be more complementary than contradictory, and we need to honor and take advantage of the differences as well as the commonalities. Both geology and theology suggest that a livable future must incorporate a concern for the health of the ecological system that supports us. Geology can help us understand that requirement more precisely and more fully. Theology can show us that a livable future must also incorporate a commitment to justice. Both help us to feel a sense of privilege at being here. Both rely on reasoned reflection on our experience. Geology serves as a model of the need to test, revise, and reshape our understanding of how the world works, at times rejecting our most cherished ideas. Theology encourages us to take seriously our affective response to the beauty of nature and life, and to allow the power of those emotions to give us the courage we need to live creatively.

We need to recognize that both science and religion are essential parts of what it is to be human and that if our vision of a livable future is to respond authentically to our humanity, it must be shaped by both. As we attempt to facilitate fruitful engagement between science and religion, we must have the humility to remember that each will be wrong perhaps much of the time. We must try to learn from our missteps and from one another. And we must do our best to judge one another for the best that we offer, not the worst. I'm not at all sure we can do all that. I'm sure only that we must try.

Chapter 9

Alma De'atei, "The World That Is Coming": Reflections on Power, Knowledge, Wisdom, and Progress

Jeremy Benstein

"More has been discovered in the last fifty years than in all of recorded history, and at the same time, more has been lost and destroyed— nature, cultures, on every level—than ever previously."

—Dr. Sylvia Earle, eminent oceanographer and resident explorer for *National Geographic*

"The secular, exploitative side of science must correspond to something in nature; otherwise it wouldn't be so efficacious in destroying the world. But at the same time, it must be missing something essential, for precisely the same reason."

—Prof. Seyyed Hossein Nasr, historian of science

As farmer-philosopher Wendell Berry pointedly observed, "the 'environmental crisis' is a misnomer, since it is a crisis of ourselves, not of the environment."[1] Most environmentalists would understand Berry's terms of reference and heartily agree with his striking and helpful reframing of a familiar issue. But most people are not environmentalists, and I'm afraid that much of the general public would not really know what on earth he is talking about. Those same people, particularly if they are of the newspaper-reading or even televised news–watching variety, would of course acknowledge the existence of

123

environmental problems, here and there, even serious ones. But a crisis? And of ourselves?

On the contrary: Conventional wisdom, at least the more optimistic versions, has it that human ingenuity, especially in its most omnipotent incarnation, technological development, surely is solving our problems as fast as they crop up. In fact, it is my impression that people (in this case, those in the middle and higher classes) enjoy the benefits of a comfortable lifestyle and the technology at its base while ignoring the increasingly heavy prices, the downside of those benefits and that lifestyle. They do not live with a personal consciousness of crisis (neither eco- nor ego-, i.e., self-, crisis); rather, they see themselves as the favored beneficiaries of one of the greatest boons known to humankind, the technological progress of the contemporary postindustrial West.

This chapter is an attempt to delve a little into the claim that we are indeed in the throes of a crisis and, although there are severe environmental repercussions, it is in fact a "crisis of ourselves," of our worldview and values, our spiritual "situ-ation" (literally, "placedness"). I write both as a concerned citizen, interested in the mutual relations of religion, science, environment, and the modern condition, and as a Jew trained in traditional textual exegesis and engaged in the application of those texts and values in our contemporary world. For instance, a traditional Jewish term for eternity or the afterlife is the Hebrew *olam haba'*, meaning "the next world," "the world to come," or, as the Aramaic version *alma de'atei* emphasizes, "the world that is coming." This spiritual world, of course, traditionally contrasts with the temporal reality in which we live. But there is another world that is coming (indeed, as some technology fans exuberantly claim, "the future is now!"), and one doesn't need to be a science fiction fan, conversant in branching futures or alternative worlds, to believe that this expression can very profitably be applied to *this* world, the reality we call home, the world we create and perpetuate (or not) through our actions—the world we will leave to our children.

Is progress truly progressing? Does increased technological prowess mean better lives and a better world? Can it be sustainable over time, and will it sustain us, in body and in spirit? What are the spiritual and cultural implications of a blind belief that everything is getting better all the time? Can knowledge be reconciled with wisdom, power with humility?

Progress (I): Promise and Peril

Let us begin with progress. The case for the amazing benefits that have accrued to recent generations as a result of technological development need hardly be made here. Witness only a partial listing of the breadth and depth of our "empowerment": the harnessing of natural sources of power for our needs, wants, and whims (from steam, via coal, oil, etc., to the atom); advances in medicine, warfare, and telecommunications (computers, telephone, television, Internet); a panoply of creature comforts; and, most recently, genetic engineering and the mapping of the human genome. Together these constitute a veritable miracle, whose transformations of personal quality of life possess an almost salvific character. The society that has inaugurated these achievements (the modern West), the people in that society who have been the pioneers in these fields (predominantly white male scientists and technocrats), and even the mental faculties that have motivated and enabled us to get this far (analytic reason and objectification of the world and its processes) are indeed all exalted and glorified in the light of these resounding accomplishments.

I can't and don't deny this—benefiting no less than others from the miracle—yet without overly indulging some deep Luddite sympathies, I'd like to accentuate the other, darker side. Sylvia Earle and Seyyed Hossein Nasr, quoted at the beginning of this chapter, eloquently express the highly ancipital, or double-headed, nature of the technological project—and so it has been, from fire on down. For all that has been gained, much has been lost, and growing piles of debris line the pathways of the technological motorcade. Moreover, the growing momentum of inventions and discoveries begetting more of the same has created an unstoppable juggernaut, which—along with all the undeniable benefits—comes with huge and growing social and environmental costs. When these costs are confronted at all, they are either overshadowed by or disassociated from the aforementioned advances, in the naive belief that we can have one without the other.

For some, there is also a price to the human spirit. As critics of technology continually inveigh, we spend more and more time, as individuals and as a society, contemplating the virtual belly button of our own technological prowess and marveling primarily at our own cleverness. What one can experience on the Internet seems far more amazing than what one can experience in a forest or a swamp—and this message is not lost on children growing up in the twenty-first century. This realization, however, does not depress everybody. For put another way, in the eyes of its most enthusiastic, optimistic proponents, the (hi)story of technology is the progressive revelation of the uniqueness of the human being—or at least the modern Western technocratic version—and our gradual elevation to a transcendent status over and above other creatures and nature as a whole. Transcending the physical limitations of our own bodies, we are getting ever closer to our apotheosis as pure consciousness.

Progress (II): Praxis and Politics

Interestingly, the history of scientific thought tells a strikingly different story. Sigmund Freud referred to a triad of "outrages upon our naive self love" when he grouped together Copernican heliocentrism, Darwinian evolutionary theory, and his own theory of the structure of the psyche and the centrality of the (irrational) unconscious mind. The social and intellectual history of the reception of these revolutions in society is not straightforward, but it is claimed, at least in theory, that these conceptual innovations have progressively unseated us, the human race (that is, the biblically inspired Western version), from our centrality in the cosmos and in the natural world and that they could be understood as undermining our calm self-confidence as purely rational agents. As paleontologist and historian of science Stephen Jay Gould put it, Nicolaus Copernicus changed "our abode from the immobile center of a limited universe to a small peripheral hunk of rock subordinate to one star among billions"; Darwin "cancelled our 'particular privilege of having been specially created' (in God's image, no less) and [propounded] our consequent 'relegation to descent from the animal world'"; and Freud altered "our view of mind from a logical and moral instrument to a largely non-rational device buffeted or controlled by an 'unconscious.'"[2]

How might this triple[3] "theoretical" assault on the underpinnings of human centrality, uniqueness, and supremacy have been received? One could at least imagine a great outpouring of human humility in light of these insights of literally cosmic import—for instance, post-Copernicus, a little Jobian self-abasement when confronted with parsecs, galaxy clusters, and light-years,[4] or perhaps some ecstatic *unio mystica* at our newfound Darwinian oneness with the natural world. After all, now we are no longer just dust and ashes, but also apes and peacocks.[5] And after Freud, why not a smidgen of tempering of rationalist scientism and its goal of understanding and controlling the world? If we indeed have such a justifiably hard time understanding and controlling *our own* psyches and behavior, then how can we ever hope to do the same, intelligently and sensitively, for the entire world? This brings us back to Berry's increasingly obvious comment about the contemporary crisis being of ourselves and not of the environment.

No—this was certainly a road not taken: Western society responded in no such way. These sobering realizations have had no discernible mitigating effect on human hubris as to our place in the world, on the progress of progress, or on the resultant snowballing technological development. On the face of it, in fact, news of these philosophical sea changes seems not to have reached most sectors of society at large, or, if it has, its less than conscious absorption might have had precisely the opposite effect. That is, rather than leading to a healthy humility, these conceptual reorientations, if they've sunk in at all, have become (subconscious) spiritual disorientations, fueling existential angst and insecurities that can be seen to underlie the scramble for material comforts, as discussed here later.

The sectors of society I refer to are (a) the mass of bourgeois citizenry leading their—our—daily lives, who through the enormous power of collective consumerism acquire, enjoy, or otherwise benefit from and therefore propagate technological developments; and (b) decision makers and policy shapers who, through the power of their (our?) influence, encourage, advance, publicly support, and finance similar and other developments, furthering and spreading more and more of said progress. In other words, for most, both "proles" and "pols," progress is indeed progress, technology works (and is, of course, only getting better), and theoretical scruples as to human self-understanding, or deconstructions of any ideological underpinnings, are just so much metaphysics, derogatory connotations intended.

Mystery and Mastery

So on the one hand, we have more technological power than ever before: Our actions affect far more of the world far more deeply, and far more adversely, than those of our forebears, both individually and collectively. But this techno-power does not translate into a sense of real personal, individual *empowerment*. For on the other hand, the worldwide spread of Weberian bureaucracy (the institutional structures of modernity), as well as globalization and the growing power of corporations over sovereign democracies, has led to a growing loss of control and to real *dis*empowerment: Citizens and face-to-face communities are dwarfed by the collective and its political and economic institutions. Ordinary people are losing their ability to democratically shape their societies and ensure the well-being of their environments.

These phenomena—growing technological and consumer power alongside spiritual malaise and political disempowerment—are linked. The central engine of globalization is worldwide consumer demand (fostered or invented by the corporations themselves): more people wanting more things[6] in more places. Globalized consumerism represents both the creation and the spread of a problem and a very particular, and highly problematic, response to something deeper. For arguably, the rampant materialism that characterizes Western society—both in the common sense of widespread consumerism and in the more philosophical sense of emphasis on matter and the physical over spiritual values and pursuits—is a result of the combined existential implications of the encroachments on our "metaphysical" well-being, including the aforementioned spiritual and political disorientation and disempowerment. Mass consumerism can be seen as a collective attempt to assuage the loss of our sense of personal significance, control, and satisfaction by gaining "power" over, and satisfaction from, *things*.

We have experienced a collective decontextualization of sorts, a "de-situation," a loss of sense of purpose or *telos,* an existential hollowing out, while at the same time gaining increasing physical control of the conditions of our lives in the here and now. In other words, we have been acquiring capabilities in the "what?" and "how?" departments while losing our grip on "why?" "to what end?" and "for whom?" Mystery has given way to mastery, with no guiding vision for its application.

So there is a deep dissonance between the "progress" of scientific theory, potentially decentralizing, even devaluing, the human project in the larger scheme of things, and the "progress" of technological praxis, loudly protesting nearly the opposite, that we are indeed godlike in our skills and abilities.[7] That dissonance has taken its toll.

But more significantly, there is something terrifying simply about the inner logic of progress itself as a belief system. Plainly put, if we think everything is always getting better, then (a) there is nothing of value to be learned from the past, for it is backward and primitive, and (b) we don't have to worry about the future, since it's going to be even better than this glorious age. Past and future and our connections to them and their residents (our progenitors and progeny) are devalued. The resultant overwhelming emphasis on the present creates a huge obstacle to identifying problems, especially those with long-term implications, and organizing ourselves to address and solve them. Sustainability, as a vision and as a goal, is stuffy and "retro": Why worry about the future when the future surely can take care of itself? We need to worry about ourselves above all.

Secularization and Its Discontents

Contrast this approach with the values of a traditional society.[8] For instance, biblical man (also woman, depending on one's interpretation) was rooted in the chain of intergenerational responsibility back to progenitors, revered ancestors, and on to progeny, future fulfillers of the covenant. They saw themselves as exalted, the beloved creatures of God: created in the divine image, the crowning glory of creation, yet humbled in the face of God and the awesomeness of that creation.[9] The earth itself, even if not worshiped or deified as in pagan cultures (or at least in environmentalist versions of them), was a sacred trust, never simply raw material.

Now, though, in the highly secularized present, we are alone in the void, the object of the affections of no one but ourselves (and with a sense of responsibility to no one else), and not at all humbled by a disenchanted nature that we apparently are increasingly learning to understand and control, at least in the short term, which has become our only frame of reference. Is it any wonder that we have lowered our sights, as it were, and sought our deepest satisfactions in this-worldly betterment?

A fascinating example of the implications of progress for worldview is the question of life expectancy. Advances in medicine are one of the most universally acknowledged, appreciated, and unassailable benefits of technological progress. We suffer less, we see fewer of our children die, and, whether or not this will be sustainable over the long term, we believe we have more control over disease than people had in previous eras. A very common response to any criticism of scientific development (and one given to me by a prominent Israeli philosopher) is that in the developed West, today's average life span is more than seventy years, twice that of previous generations or contemporary primitive cultures. We win hands down.

But is this so cut and dried? One of the most eye-opening comments I have come across on this topic, and on progress and its pitfalls in general, comes from a remarkable little book called *Lost Worlds: How Our European Ancestors Coped with Everyday Life and Why It Is So Hard Today,* by German social historian Arthur E. Imhof.[10] Imhof discusses several ways in which the experience of death is vastly different in our age from what it was in previous ones. In particular, he points out that although in fact our predecessors' chronological life span was much less, they believed in an eternal life after the temporal one; the same praxis that brought increased life expectancy wrought havoc on the religious worldview that included an unshakable belief in the afterlife. Imhof observes:

> We have shortened life tremendously. What does it mean to double or triple the life expectancy of one's physical existence when eternity has been lost? . . . We have completely eliminated the [incomparably larger] otherworldly part of life, secularizing it out

of existence. The only segment of life that remains for us is the earthly part, and for better or for worse, it has had to assume the role of the only important one.[11]

One might be forgiven for the quip that maybe progress—like nostalgia—ain't what it used to be.

Heaven: Pros and Cons

The idea of heaven—the ultimate otherworldly or next-worldly reward—bears a detailed "environmental" analysis. In the space of this chapter, I can offer only a bare outline. Heaven, it seems, has its pluses and minuses; it is part of one aspect of the problem while also fulfilling an important function in one configuration of a solution. On the one hand, otherworldliness is often anti-environmental: The temporal gives way before the eternal, with anything and everything physical and material treated as an impure vessel, a profane means to the sacred eternal end. And if the next world is the goal and this world is the means, then the means is inherently transcendable or even completely dispensable.[12]

And yet, emphasis on the hereafter also represents the ultimate in delayed gratification. The belief in an eternal reward was a mega-incentive, in the longest of long terms, against wrongdoing, ill-gotten gain and its enjoyment, and short-term materialism. One can accept suffering and hardship now, whether actual poverty or just the lack of fancy gadgetry, in the belief that one's just desserts eventually will accrue and will remain forever after.[13] Ethnobotanist and philosopher Gary Paul Nabhan has remarked, "It's hard to know whether there is or is not a God, but there sure are a lot of people walking around with a God-shaped hole in their hearts."[14] There are probably a lot of heaven-shaped holes in a lot of hearts, too. That is, we still need a bulwark against the quick fix, against our inability to curb our huge appetites for things, in order to help us impose limits on runaway consumption and breakneck technological development. But for most—for the predominantly secular society that needs it most—it will not be the dream of an otherworldly heaven. As Imhof pointed out, we have traded that in for progress.

Following seminal Jewish philosopher Franz Rosenzweig, we can discuss this question in terms of the relationship between God, Humankind, and World.[15] Previously, human arrogance and concomitant wrongdoing were mainly an affront to divinity or had repercussions for one's own person, whether spiritual, physical, or both. Humans needed to limit themselves for the purpose of currying divine favor (or avoiding divine wrath) or as part of a path of spiritual discipline—for the sake of the soul of the self. Now, though, with the ramifications of human hubris and destructive human behavior threatening global ecocide, we can add a new term to the equation, perhaps one that will possess more rhetorical suasion: We need to curb ourselves for the sake of the world[16] itself, for the ongoing perpetuation of creation, including, of course, ourselves within it.

Filling that heaven-shaped hole, then, needn't be so difficult. Heaven— *alma de'atei,* "the world that is coming," a dreamed-of better place—can be, *should be,* that all too real world our children and grandchildren will be inhabiting all too soon, not that other one that our deceased forebears might be in now. Here, a saying of environmental activist and thinker David Brower is in order. "Environmentalists may make meddlesome neighbors," he has often commented, "but they make great ancestors."

"Length of Days": An Environmentalist Reading of Some Biblical Passages

This new perspective, this expanded purview wherein we put the world at the center of our spiritual lives and seek heaven on this side of the rainbow, is well exemplified in a close reading of several biblical passages that include three seemingly unrelated commandments. They all deal with different realms, but they come with the same very large promise attached: Follow these commandments "in order that you may fare well and have length of days." This is the reward for honoring one's father and mother (Exodus 20:12, and again in Deuteronomy 5:16), for using honest weights and measures (Deuteronomy 25:15), and, most esoterically, for sending away a mother bird before taking her eggs or fledglings (Deuteronomy 22:6–7). This reward of living well and long has been traditionally understood in one of two ways: either instant, tangible rewards here and now or ultimate otherworldly satisfaction in the hereafter. There have been far-reaching theological disputes over how best to interpret the problematic promise.

A compelling illustration of these disputes is found in rabbinic literature. The Talmud[17] describes how Elisha ben Abuyah, the famous first-century rabbi-turned-heretic, might have lost his faith. It presents a scene in which a father instructs his son to gather some eggs from a nest but to be careful first to let the mother bird go. In fulfilling his father's request, the boy should be doubly rewarded with length of days: He is honoring his parents and fulfilling the divine command of sending off the mother bird. Yet he falls from the tree and dies. How could this be? Elisha may have witnessed just such a scene and—presuming that the biblical promise referred to the quality and length of life of the individual performing the commandments—concluded that the promise was false, that there was neither Judge nor justice in the world. Others, including his grandson, Rabbi Ya'akov ben Korshai,[18] have taken the opposite approach: We are to expect no reward whatsoever in this life for following any of the precepts. The rewards and punishments are all in the next life, heaven, the world to come.

The common denominator of these two seemingly contradictory interpretations is that they apply exclusively to the individual, whether the well-being referred to is temporal or eternal. A similar assumption underlies traditional commentators' differing views of the purpose of driving off the mother bird. The great twelfth-century commentator and philosopher Maimonides,[19] for instance, says it is for the sake of the (individual) animal—sparing the mother bird the pain of seeing her offspring taken. Others, such as Nachmanides,[20] claim that the commandment focuses on the individual person, in order to inculcate humane, compassionate behavior.

Yet why limit the discussion to the individual? The precept has a deep logic, and it becomes more provocatively palatable to contemporary sensibility when seen as relating to the health and well-being of the collective. All three of these commandments are in fact nothing less than prescriptions for sustaining human society and its place in the natural world.

Concerning the commandment to send off the mother bird, Wendell Berry has observed: "This [precept] obviously is a perfect paradigm of ecological and agricultural discipline, in which the idea of inheritance is necessarily paramount. The inflexible rule is that the source must be preserved. You may take the young, but you must save the breeding stock."[21] In short, by all means eat of the fruit, but take care not to destroy the fruitfulness.

This is not only a contemporary exegesis. Don Isaac Abravanel, a Jewish biblical commentator in fifteenth-century Spain and Italy, states it most clearly:

> The Torah's intention here is to prevent the possibility of untimely destruction and rather to encourage Creation to exist as fully as possible. . . . "In order that you may fare well and have length of days" means that it shall be good for humankind when Creation is perpetuated so that we will be able to partake of it again in the future . . . since if we are destined to live for many years on this earth, we are reliant upon Creation perpetuating itself so that we will always have sufficient resources.[22]

This is sustainability, or at least one aspect of it, for there are two distinct sides to sustainability that are often not explicitly differentiated. Usually, when environmentalists speak of sustainable development or, more generally, of sustainability, they are calling for an economic system of production and consumption that can sustain itself and its environmental context over the long term, enabling us to live up to our responsibilities to future generations. But again, following Berry, we need to sustain not only the physical environment and its products but also—perhaps primarily—ourselves, materially and spiritually. Sustainability then becomes intimately linked with the rejuvenation and preservation of sources of spiritual sustenance on every level.

Strikingly, the precise formulation of the biblical verses alludes to both sides: "quantity," a society's ability to sustain itself physically over time ("length of days"), not reaching or breaching the natural limits of the capacity of the earth, and "quality," a society's ability to nourish and sustain its members spiritually (to ensure that they "fare well"). Western society is far from this simple yet far-reaching ideal: For too long we have enjoyed the fruit and paid no heed to preserving the fruitfulness. One imperative, then, for long and good lives here on the earth, for us collectively as a society, is that we treat the natural world with reverence and self-restraint. Paul Gorman of the National Religious Partnership for the Environment put it this way: "Global warming isn't about carbon emissions; it's about intergenerational equity," and, quoting Deuteronomy 30:19, "Therefore choose life, that you *and your children* may live."[23]

Indeed, the social-environmental reading of this commandment stands in stark contrast to its individualistic interpretations. First, the dichotomous question of whether the commandment is for the sake of the animal or the human (in the short term) disappears, for it ignores the deep, long-term interdependence that exists between us all. Second, the expectation of instant material rewards, whether Calvinist or consumerist, has deep anti-environmental implications—it bespeaks short-term materialism, including "more is more" and instant gratification, and hinders thought of long-term effects. Likewise, as noted earlier, otherworldly spirituality usually privileges that which is considered eternal and spiritual and denigrates this world and its physicality.[24]

The idea of intergenerational sustainability is a response to both. It is a deeply religious response that resituates humankind in the flow of time and gives us perspective in the larger scheme of things. It is perhaps the most likely candidate to fill that heaven-shaped hole, for "the world that is coming" is best understood as this world, our world, which we are holding in trust and will shortly return to its rightful recipients, posterity.

This selfsame point is exemplified in the other two commandments that promise well-being and length of days. Honoring our father and mother, our progenitors, honors the idea of giving life and not just taking for ourselves. It rejects an inherently unsustainable throwaway culture in which even the elderly are disposable. Parents and our regard for them help situate us in a great intergenerational chain of being and are a strong statement against that sort of progress which would have us believe that the past has no value or meaning. Indeed, in a heavily knowledge-based culture, with the frontiers of that knowledge constantly being advanced, where parents thus find it increasingly difficult even to help their children with their homework, this is a vote for the importance of wisdom, which stems from tradition and experience, over cleverness and data.

Honest weights and measures, symbolic of fairness, justice, and equality, also represent a constitutive characteristic of a society that hopes to create well-being for all its members and to endure over the long term. Sustainability captures the two distinctive modes of justice that are becoming increasingly important in the growing mutual engagement of environment and society: the usual "horizontal" intragenerational justice and the "vertical" intergenerational variety, which demands fairness and equity beyond the quarterly report and the four-year term of office, extending to future generations.

To reemphasize, sustainability also means sustenance: We don't need just an economy that can sustain *itself,* important and imperiled as that is; we need a moral and spiritual life that can sustain and nourish *us.* This is the force of the promise in these precepts: not the long life of a single person, and not a pie-in-the-sky promise of bliss in the afterlife, but a life and a world of quality and meaning sustained for us and our children after us, and for all the world.

Conclusion: Power and Limits

Let us return to the present, to Berry's view of the crisis of self and the question of what is to be done. In light of the foregoing discussion, I would claim that we have, essentially, both too much and too little power. In terms of the crisis of environment, self, and society, the latter trope—political disempowerment in the face of immovable bureaucracy and bulldozer-like globalization—leads to one configuration. That is, if we the people have too little power, clearly someone or something else has too much; They are, or It is, the enemy. Our response, then, should focus on personal and political empowerment, public participation, decentralization, democratization of the marketplace, opposition to globalization, and the like. But the former aspect, each of us possessing too much of a different kind of power, but with too little guidance or wisdom, leads to a different configuration. Here again we meet the enemy, and also—clearly—he is Us. Here the answers must be framed in terms of lifestyle changes, personal awareness, simplicity, and self-limitation.

These two configurations of the crisis are related through the concepts of limits and limitations. Recognizing the world's physical limits is connected to recognizing, internalizing, adopting, and enforcing our own behavioral and spiritual self-limitations. We have reached the ecological limits of the global macrocosmos because we have not disciplined—set limits on—ourselves, the human microcosmos. The physical manifestations of the external crisis in the world—our having reached or breached systemic, ecological limits—reflect the essential spiritual responses called for in ourselves: the urgent imperative to (re)impose limits on our own appetites, lifestyles, and sense of self-importance.[25]

But that personal, spiritual lifestyle change is not enough. Politically, we also need to address the question of limits: We need to impose limits on those individuals and institutions that wield power for the benefit of the few and to the detriment of the many, and we need to burst the oppressive limits that have been imposed upon us by an impersonal system—that is, the driving force of a global society increasingly beyond our control.

And limits, when correctly understood and imposed, can lead to connections. Indeed, a solution can come only when we create the connections necessary to overcome the alienation that has led to this hollow, spiritless materialism. Returning to the Rosenzweigian triad, our age is characterized by distance, or downright estrangement, from the divine, the human (both self and society), and the natural. We need to religate,[26] bind, and bond not only spiritual connections with divinity (quite likely a possibility only for some) but also, perhaps more accessibly, social and personal connections in the form of nurturing relationships and communities and—not least—connections with the natural world as an ongoing source of sustenance.

Part II

Linking Spiritual and Scientific Perspectives with an Environmental Ethic

Part II of the book was written mainly by environmental and resource managers and users, who explore how through the integration of science and spirituality we may make wiser choices as consumers and exploiters of the natural world. In chapter 11, William Meadows, president of The Wilderness Society, introduces this part, urging a land ethic wherein advocacy based in moral passion leads us to land and resource use that honors and respects the sacredness of the earth.

Chapter 10, by Robert Perschel, once a forester who marked timber for harvest in the northern New England woods and now an environmental activist, combines personal and powerful stories that reflect on ways in which spirituality can be connected to the natural resource professions. He identifies four fundamental challenges for environmental professionals. First, he suggests, "we must become storytellers," unafraid to share with others the personal and spiritual experiences and relationships we have with the land. Perschel accomplishes this admirably in his chapter, reflecting on a childhood spent near an old swamp and, later in life, his work as a forester and conservationist. Second, he asks us to "integrate our spiritual lives with our work lives" and provides examples of how he has done this in his professional life as an employee of The Wilderness Society. Third, he emphasizes the need to express universal values invoking a common language that we all can use to speak to one another about faith and spirituality. Perschel suggests that we can find this language by exploring and expressing our passions and emotions. Finally, he suggests we must go beyond telling stories and integrate the spiritual into our everyday lives by seeking to express the universal. He exhorts us to act and apply all we know to resolve "the current environmental crisis we all have created." But he emphasizes that only by breaking down the barriers between work and worship can we identify our obligations to ourselves and to the natural world.

In chapter 11, Strachan Donnelley extends Perschel's theme of ethical obligation, leading us through an intellectually challenging discussion of values, spirit, and philosophy in the context of what he calls a "Leopoldian-Darwinian" worldview. Donnelley seeks to clarify the relationship between Aldo Leopold's land ethic and "fundamental Darwinian tenets" and, in so doing, delineate an evolutionary, ecological, and ethological perspective of the human relationship with nature. He initially builds this viewpoint through a detailed analysis of Leopold's understandings of reality, beauty, and goodness, all essential to articulating human ethical responsibilities to the natural world. Donnelley also invokes the ideas of Alfred North Whitehead, offering an "interim ethic" to help guide us through the struggle to understand our moral obligations to the land. He believes that our search for an enduring environmental ethic will be long and difficult but that we can achieve it by humbly basing ourselves in the context of a diverse and complex natural world and perceiving the multiple values, both spiritual and ecological, of the earth's evolutionary heritage so wondrously developed over eons of existence.

In chapter 12, Dave Preble and Carl Safina confront the challenge of integrating scientific, spiritual, and ethical perspectives with natural resource conservation in the difficult area of modern fisheries management. The authors identify common ground between traditional notions of faith and reason and their own secular humanism by emphasizing the importance of science and spirituality in building a firm ethical foundation. Preble and Safina, like Donnelley, invoke the perspectives of Aldo Leopold. Through two case studies— the decline of the pollock and bluefish fisheries off southern New England— they illustrate how Leopold's views can help us develop an ethic that guides our relationship with the sea as well as the land. The authors advance six "assumptions" they view as "starting points" for developing a practical moral standard for resource decision making. Central considerations include altruism and enlightened self-interest and a clearer understanding of the interdependence within the global ecosystem. Preble and Safina conclude that "shared assumptions and accepted ethical standards won't end our problems, but they will show us the way to solve those problems as they arise."

In chapter 13, David Petersen offers a provocative and personal essay on the spiritual dimensions of hunting, an issue likely to provoke conflicting moral reactions. For those who do not hunt and who value life above all else, purposefully killing another living creature and declaring it a spiritual experience can, as Petersen acknowledges, be at best an oxymoron. But, Petersen argues, the authentic or naturalistic hunter encounters life's sacred value through partaking "as an active participant in the most intimate workings of wild nature." Although Petersen accepts that one can assume many valid ethical positions toward nature, he asserts that being a moral hunter not only is ethically and philosophically defensible but also is a natural role for those who possess an "instinctive inclination" to themselves be part of the wild. Invoking the work of Paul Shepard, José Ortega y Gasset, Edward Abbey, and others, Petersen weaves together an artful discussion of the intense spirituality involved in the experience of being a hunter. He also critically examines the views of those who condemn hunting as a brutal anachronism and acknowledges that although "slob" hunters exist who deserve condemnation, the practices of these individuals should not be considered representative of all hunting.

In the final chapter in part II, Wendell Berry examines the ecological and spiritual implications of the global capitalist system, for which, Berry declares, nearly all of us, as consumers, bear responsibility. Berry argues that the very character of economic globalism, especially in the "developed" world, delegates most activities of basic living (e.g., provision of food, clothing, and shelter) to "proxies," typically large corporations and central governments. By delegating these practices, he suggests, we abrogate the responsibilities that accompany them, leaving the decisions that critically affect our food, our communities, and our environment—as well as perhaps our freedom and autonomy—in the hands of faceless others. Berry identifies the environmental crisis as not just a problem of damaged physical surroundings but also a global political and spiritual crisis, indicative of "our lives as individuals, as family members, as community members, and as citizens." He provides a rigorous critique of free market economics, industrial efficiency, competition, and the values encouraged by a system that demands low production costs and much higher sales prices. Berry argues that we must regain control over our economic choices as individuals and communities by developing and practicing "the idea of a local economy." This change would necessitate that we advance two principles—those of neighborhood and subsistence—that he believes necessary to facilitate a better understanding of where our goods originate and what kinds of people and practices produce them. Berry challenges us to take responsibility for an economy that often seems beyond our control and to consider carefully the values we wish to preserve and defend through our various modes of everyday living.

Introduction to Part II
The Search for Harmony

WILLIAM H. MEADOWS

Cannot the "good" in nature and humanity be defined by the relationship between land conservation and ethical behavior? If so, most of the credit must go to Aldo Leopold, a founder of The Wilderness Society and a graduate of Yale University and the Yale School of Forestry and Environmental Studies. It is his work—*A Sand County Almanac*[1]—that introduced many of us to this relationship between land conservation and ethical behavior. Leopold wrote, "There are two things that interest me; the relation of people to each other, and the relation of people to the land."[2] Is that not the focus of this volume?

He also wrote that "the individual is a member of a community of interdependent parts . . . the land ethic simply enlarges the boundaries of the community to include soils, water, plants, and animals, or collectively, the land." He wrote that "a land ethic changes the role of *Homo sapiens* from conqueror of the land-community to plain member and citizen of it."[3] This implies respect for his fellow members and also respect for the community. Leopold thought of conservation as a state of harmony between men and the land.

In considering chapter 1 of this book, I was struck by the comment that the contributors would be examining the "divide" between faith and reason that has been characteristic of Western and other civilizations. Perhaps. But aren't we really searching for the harmony between humanity and the land— the harmony about which Leopold wrote?

Creation of harmony between humanity and the land should be the desired outcome of our public policy debates on land conservation. But changes in public policy come painfully slow, especially when there are constant challenges from people promoting logging, mining, oil drilling, and access for dirt bikes and other off-road vehicles. The Wilderness Society is committed to protecting our country's last remaining wild places—our wilderness and our wildlife—our prime forests, parks, rivers, deserts, and shorelines. But we know that for these efforts to be successful, there must be a change in thinking about our relationship to the land.

One person good at thinking about our relationship to the land was Tom Watkins. Tom edited *Wilderness* magazine for almost twenty years. He recently died in Bozeman, Montana, where he had served at Montana State University as Wallace Stegner Distinguished Professor of Western American Studies. In Tom's book *Stone Time,* he wrote:

> We must learn, finally, that wilderness is not as our history has insisted, a threat to be conquered, but, in fact, a lesson to be embraced. For in wilderness, as in the eyes of the wild creatures that inhabit it, we find something that binds us firmly to the long history of life on earth, something that can teach us how to live in this place, how to accept our limitations, how to celebrate the love we feel when we let ourselves feel it for all other living creatures.[4]

Tom went on to tell about discovering the dancing image of Kokopelli, a flute-playing figure in Hopi legend, in a petroglyph in canyon country. He wrote:

> Whatever the precise message its maker wanted to pass along, I know that the antic figure speaks also of time, stone time. I look at it and know that I will return to this place again and again, a place that is as central to my knowledge—as all the memories of my life—and my family's life—all the history I have learned, all the books I may have read, or all the words I may have written. When I do, I will touch the stone and dream of the stars.[5]

Tom was speaking of a truly religious moment in his life.

◆ ◆ ◆

Let me admit to a personal struggle. I am still trying to find the confidence to feel safe bringing religious themes into my discussion about the environment.

Some have thought of the work of environmentalists and conservationists as being separate or distinct unto itself—segregated from other aspects of our lives. Some have separated the secular—and the political—from the spiritual. And we in the conservation community have allowed that to happen.

But we now realize that the approach to conservation issues must be holistic. Our efforts must include and acknowledge not only ecological, scientific, and economic values but also spiritual and religious values. In this holistic approach, there is no "divide" between faith and reason. The two, together, guide our ethical behavior; they create our land ethic.

By embracing our land ethic, we find common values with others, a recognition that we are interconnected—we are a community with common interests and common needs, in search of answers. The challenge is to understand these common values and how we are connected to a broader public, a public that includes hunters, anglers, farmers, ranchers, Native Americans—people who love the land—everyone.

So, the question for me is this: What does it mean to be a strong environmental advocate—in a political world—an advocate guided by moral passion? What is difficult for most of us, including me, is learning to talk about values, moral imperatives, spiritual themes, religion, God. And that is my principal message to you (and to me). Let us not be afraid to talk or write about religious themes, deeper values, moral beliefs, spirituality, and God.

We gained confidence when Patriarch Bartholomew spoke of "the abuse of nature as a sin."[6] However, we are still in search of the right language, the comfortable language. We are still trying to understand and define values, moral imperatives, a land ethic, care for creation, environmental stewardship, spirituality, the sacred.

I have found that rather than talking to people about values, the land ethic, or the sacred, it is more important to listen—to listen to what they say about their own experiences, their connections to special places: their own stories.

Two years ago, our regional conservation staff was in town for planning sessions, and we asked them to reserve an hour one afternoon to speak about "the land ethic." In order to get the discussion started, we had asked staff members who wished to speak to bring "sacred objects"—objects that reminded them of special places.

Well, the hour turned into three, with more than thirty staff members speaking about places that were important to them. Each spoke from the heart, with passion. What I found consistent in the stories were references to connections: connections to places, connections to people—to families, mothers, fathers, children.

In this case, it was people speaking about their values and beliefs, not discussing definitions of the land ethic but describing their connections to the land in very personal, heartfelt ways.

To me, that is the answer to my question of what it means to be a strong environmental advocate: The advocacy must be based on moral passion.

When I travel, I hear people from all backgrounds, interests, and political parties talk about their personal searches for connections: physical connections to the land; spiritual connections to nature—the trees, mountains, streams, wolves—and spiritual connections to one another—and to God.

There is a national search on for something that transcends our day-to-day, overworked, overstimulated, underrewarded lives. What I hear most often, what is common in these conversations, is the recognition of the sacred: the sacred nature of our connections and our responsibilities to the land and our community of life. I do not want to understate the political nature of our work, but I believe, as do many, that we are experiencing an ecological crisis that can be best understood as a spiritual crisis. And as we move into the twenty-first century, it is important that we recognize the need to move from a political campaign for the environment to a spiritual campaign.

Not long ago, The Wilderness Society sponsored a tribute in Boston to the late senator Paul Tsongas for the great work he had done in protecting Alaska's wilderness. It was a powerful evening for the three hundred people in attendance—leaders from the business, political, and conservation communities joining The Wilderness Society in tribute to Senator Tsongas. One special guest was Jonathan Solomon, a tribal elder of the Gwich'in, an Athabascan Indian community in Alaska. Jonathan spoke about the Gwich'in, whose name means "people of the caribou" because their culture and their life are tied to the caribou. The Gwich'in live immediately south of the Arctic National Wildlife Refuge, and Jonathan spoke about the importance of the refuge, a place Senator Tsongas tried to protect as wilderness, a place The Wilderness Society continues to try to protect.

The critical unprotected area in the refuge is the coastal plain, the home of the Porcupine caribou herd, numbering more than 150,000 caribou. The caribou go there each year for calving and the early months of feeding their young. The coastal plain is the biological heart of the refuge. I talked about my first trip to the refuge, but Jonathan told our friends in Boston that the refuge is so sacred to the Gwich'in that he and his people have never been there.

When we honor the sacredness of this earth, we will commit ourselves to a land ethic, an ethic that requires inquiry, knowledge, wisdom, and respect. Thus, we will become stronger advocates—advocates who believe in the power of knowledge and information guided by the principles of justice, fairness, and mutual respect. That will give us the confidence to speak as Jonathan speaks of the sacred, and we will have embarked on that twenty-first-century campaign—a spiritual campaign for the environment.

Chapter 10

Work, Worship, and the Natural World: A Challenge for the Land Use Professions

ROBERT PERSCHEL

When I was about nine years old, I had two experiences that defined my relationship with the natural world forever. One took place on a Long Island Sound salt marsh. I used to love to go into the marsh with my friends. But after I returned home one too many times soaking wet and covered with mud, my parents determined these excursions were too dangerous and forbade me from playing in the marsh with my friends. So, one beautiful spring morning when my buddies ran off, I discovered an old swamp maple tree that leaned over the water, and I climbed up the trunk and into the spreading branches. That was when I first became aware of the awesome beauty of the natural world and discovered a profound sense of being part of it. Every reed, every blade of grass, every bubble on the water was alive and perfectly connected.

I believe that in some way all of us share a common connection to such personal, intimate experiences of nature. For you, it probably was not a salt marsh on Long Island Sound. It may have happened for you in the deep woods of Maine, on the great prairies of the West, on the high peaks of the Rocky Mountains, or maybe in your own backyard or even within the walls of your home. I don't know where it happened, but I'm certain that it did happen. You have your own story of your intimate connection to the natural world. You've experienced the epiphany—that moment that elicits the "Ahhhhh." It may have been the glorious sunset that welcomed you at the top of your favorite mountain or the fury, power, and awesome beauty of a storm-tossed sea. Perhaps it was simply observing a squirrel in a neighborhood park and sensing the perfect, exquisite relationship the squirrel had with the tree, with the branch, with the acorn, and with the season of the year. Or it may have been the birth of a child—a wondrous act of nature all in itself.

These intimate connections to the land are critical to environmental professionals in meeting four important challenges in our work. First, we must begin to tell about these personal experiences with the land. We must become storytellers. Second, we must integrate our spiritual lives with our work lives; we serve as examples for others so that they, too, can live and work in concert with nature. Third, we must seek, find, and express values that are universal—for that is what will connect us with others. Fourth and finally, we must move beyond philosophy and apply ourselves to resolving the current environmental crisis we all have created.

Let's turn first to your story.

I know you have had these powerful experiences because countless people have related such stories with astounding depth and variety. It is the essence of these moments we've chased our entire lives—in our vacations and vacation dreams, in our photographs and paintings, in poems and songs, in beautiful dreams and memories, and in endless stories told in the attempt to capture and express—to hold—that which for one brief and compelling instant succeeded in capturing us for all time.

But why is it that every time we have an experience filled with the joy of being, we also have the complete dumbness of naming it as other than reality? Certainly, we think, it is not as real as balancing our checkbook, or paying the bills, or putting grain in the silo or timber in the mill, or keeping up with any of the hundreds of daily requirements and needs with which we have burdened ourselves. Those are the real things—so we tell ourselves. Those are the things that constitute the real world. The other stuff, the spiritual stuff—well, we are lucky if we experience that once or twice in our lives, and we may have to travel to Yellowstone National Park or the Serengeti Plain or read the latest book to experience it again.

The sheer joy of being—the pure thrill of knowing your place in the order of the natural world—that's something for a Henry David Thoreau or a John Muir, we say, or a monk or a hermit removed from the real world. We can't bring that into our daily lives. That would be too irresponsible, too unproductive, too wild. We can't bring that into our national policy decisions regarding the environment. We can't bring that into our jobs. We can't take that spirit with us when we lobby for the environment on Capitol Hill.

Or can we?

For almost fifteen years, I worked as a forester in the woods of New England. I spent long days marking timber sales. Alone. In the woods. I was there when the first snarls of snow fell out of the northern sky and softly filled up the woods. I was there when the first green shoots forced their way out of the wet mud and unfurled in a blanket of green. I was there when the first orange color etched itself on the edges of the maple leaves, and I watched the first leaves let loose their hold on life and flutter to the ground.

As a forester, you spend all day weaving your way back and forth through the hardwood forest, examining each tree in turn and deciding whether it should live or die. You repeat this each day, considering 30,000 or 40,000 trees and selecting about 300 of them to mark with a blue paint spot. Each decision involves factors such as age, size, health, soil, aspect, economic value, competition, potential growth, wildlife value, and so on. You calculate all these in your forestry-educated brain. You raise your paint gun to deliver the death sentence, and then something unnamable crawls up from your belly and asks, "Is this the right thing to do?"; "How well does this action fit into the natural flow of the forest?"; "What harm is this causing?"; "What does this have to do with me?"; "What does this have to do with that moment on the salt marsh?"; "What is your relationship with this entity you call a tree?"; "Is this a loving act, or a purely selfish one motivated by your need and the landowner's desire to earn money?"

You squeeze the trigger, or don't squeeze the trigger, and move on to repeat the process again and again, thousands of times each day, day after day, season after season, year after year. This is work that can change you—if you open yourself to the hard questions that are about your Self: Who are you as a human being, and what is your purpose, your responsibility, your role in and relationship with the natural world?

If you are willing to do that, I guarantee you that each step through the forest will change you. Each difficult and complicated decision to mark a tree and alter the forest will alter you as well, but only if you are willing to bring your spirit—the essence of who you are—with you into the forest when you mark timber. Or you can choose to live your professional life, and perhaps your personal life, in accordance with the satirical prescription once voiced by comic strip author Garry Trudeau: "I am trying to cultivate a lifestyle that does not require my presence."

During my time practicing forestry in New England, I had the opportunity to train several young foresters. I remember one particular day when I was in the woods marking timber with a young man just beginning his career. There were several inches of snow on the ground, and we were in a beautiful stand of oak. When two foresters mark timber together, they choose a line through the woods and the lead marker works his way along that line, marking trees in a swath perhaps 100–150 feet wide. The next marker follows alongside the first, using the last trees marked in the first swath as his or her line. So it is important for the lead marker to stay in front.

I took the lead marking position, but as we moved through the woods, I kept noticing my partner right on my shoulder. He was marking faster than I was and really pushing me to keep ahead. I watched him for a while, and he was really moving through the woods—marking one tree and then quickly moving on to select another. Finally, our marking paths intersected. I stopped him for a talk in the woods. Foresters do that once in a while—to talk about the work they are doing or any topic that might normally come up around the water cooler or coffee machine. In this case, we talked about marking timber.

I got right to the point, since I knew him well enough to take a risk. I asked him what he thought about when he marked timber. Did he see trees as just timber, board feet, dollar signs for him and the landowner? We stood in front of a large oak tree. I pointed to it and asked: "What is this in front of you? Is it just a tree? Is it only an object for you to mark and pass by? It's lived seventy years. What does that mean to you? What is your relationship with this entity?"

I put my hand on the tree. I slapped it hard and asked him, "What is this?" I had him put his hands on the tree, and then I gently pushed his head against the tree until his red beard was flush with the bark, and I said, "If you are going to do this job, it is important that you know what this is."

I stepped back and asked, "Do you know what I'm talking about?" When he turned to face me, there was a different look in his eyes. He simply said, "Yeah, I do." That was that. Our feet were growing cold and the light was fading, so we turned back to our work.

We continued marking along our lines, and soon I was aware that he was no longer on my shoulder. In fact, he was nowhere in sight. I came to the end of my line and turned to walk back through the snow in the now darkening woods. Finally, I came to a place where I could see him. He was standing motionless in front of a tree. He looked up and then down. He looked to the sides, to the adjacent trees, and then he explored the forest floor. He moved around to the other side of the tree and repeated the process. He was holding his marking stick in one hand and his paint gun in the other. Finally, he shifted the paint gun and tucked it in his armpit. With his free hand, he reached out in the dimming light to touch the tree.

I quickly turned and walked away because this experience belonged to him completely. This was his moment and his own way of learning his craft. This singular image is forever etched into my mind's eye. The darkening woods; the long, straight oak trunks; the covering of snow; the blue jeans, orange marking vest, plaid shirt, red beard, orange cap, and gray woolen gloves spattered with blue paint; the fingers splayed, reaching out to touch an oak tree.

I wanted that image burned in my mind so that on those days when things aren't going so well, when it seems as if we are losing ground and despair begins to creep in like a cold wind through a crack in the door, I can call up that image of that young man in the woods, reaching out.

And I'm sure that as I was trudging back to the truck, I was happily chuckling and whispering to myself, "That's one more for our side."

If we allow our work to bring us into intimate contact with the cycle of life and death, it will change us and welcome us into our place. As poet Mary Oliver indicates in her poem "Wild Geese," it

> calls to you like the wild geese, harsh and exciting—
>
> over and over announcing your place
>
> in the family of things.[1]

For most of human history, our work has kept us in contact with nature as we farmed the land, roamed the deserts, and fished the oceans. In fact, work was a form of wor(k)ship. In Hebrew, the word for worship, *avad,* also means "work." The Haftorah explains that the first mention of worship in the Scriptures occurs in Genesis 4:2, 3: "And Abel was a keeper of sheep, but Cain was a tiller of the ground. And in process it came to pass, that Cain brought of the fruit of the ground an offering (*avodah*) unto the Lord."

It is fascinating to find the same cross-reference of meaning in an entirely different language. The English words for work, worship, and world all come from the same Old English root (*weorc, weorth-ship, weorld*).

What if we return to an integration of work and worship? Might we then make different choices about the way we live in the world and the way we treat the land?

All of us—each individual who considers himself or herself an environmentalist, in each environmental profession and each environmental organization—are called upon to explore and refine the connection between our work and our deepest connections to the land.

At The Wilderness Society, we've looked long and hard at the challenge of fostering a new American land ethic—a challenge presented to us fifty years ago by one of our founders, Aldo Leopold. But how do environmental organizations, such as The Wilderness Society and others, go about making this happen? We clearly see that part of this new ethic will emanate from the mere existence of those wonderful places we seek to protect. A visit to the wilderness of the Grand Canyon, the Boundary Waters Canoe Area Wilderness, or the High Sierra will change you forever. Many have spoken and written eloquently about these experiences.

We wish it were possible for every American to have this contact with America's wilderness. But we also realize this is not possible.

Although The Wilderness Society will continue to be on the front lines in defending, restoring, and creating wilderness, we must accomplish something more. We need to find a way to bring spirit and values and ethics and religion into our lives, into our work, and into our contact with the entire landscape—not just those places that are protected forever as wilderness. We refuse to get caught in the trap of seeing this spiritual connection to the land only in relation to federally designated wilderness. We must find ways to help Americans recognize their connection to the land at all scales of the landscape, from the most remote wilderness areas to the most intimate urban green space. We hope to help establish a network of wildlands, with designated wilderness at its core, that will touch everyone's life and form the foundation for a connection to the natural world.

America is a welcoming place to work on such a great vision because it is a land that holds universal values in the highest regard. I believe there has always been interplay between these values we uphold and the land itself. The great forests and prairies, the raging rivers and lofty mountains and burning deserts, called out to the early people of this land, and our predecessors responded with what may be the most famous political statement in history, the Declaration of Independence. It identifies "certain unalienable Rights"—rights not granted by anyone and not to be taken away by anyone, anywhere, at any time.

These are examples of the kind of universal values, or principles, we now need to seek and find—ones that will elicit a response from each American citizen and redefine America's purpose in regard to the environment.

We responded once, and we are called to respond again. America is truly a state of universal principle—and it can be the fertile ground for developing and instituting a new relationship between humankind and the earth. We must make the most of what this land has given us. We must now give something back: a sense of our own identity, which includes our own intimate connection to the land.

A former Wilderness Society council member, Wallace Stegner, once wrote about these values. "Respect for nature is indivisible," he observed. "An old lady talking to her houseplants, a weekend gardener planting marigolds among his carrots and squash, and a backpacker exultantly surveying a wilderness to whose highest point he has just won, are all on the same wavelength.

In all of them, the religion of nature and the science of ecology meet."[2] Stegner later described this respect as an awareness of the bigness outside ourselves.

In a practical application of the science of ecology, ecologists at The Wilderness Society are mapping the relative degrees of wildness across the American landscape. But wouldn't it be fascinating to extend this analysis by one more step? After we map wildness across the landscape into your city and your backyard, wouldn't the next logical step be to map the wildness of the human heart? I'm speaking metaphorically, of course. I'm not calling for a representational map of spirit in the human heart. But our exercise of mapping wildness across the landscape does offer some interesting ways to talk about this. What do we mean by spirit? How can we encourage it if we don't have some handle on what it is? In a practical sense, how would you educate foresters to bring spirit to their work? How would you know if you were successful?

The word *wildness* comes laden with social and historical connotations. Roderick Nash, in his book *Wilderness and the American Mind*,[3] aptly described the reaction of the first Europeans to the American wilderness. To these newcomers, the wilderness was savage, full of terror. Wildness has a reputation as ungracious, wholly and innately dangerous, ravenous.[4]

We at The Wilderness Society are acutely aware of these burdensome connotations. After all, *wilderness* is our middle name. So we must meet the challenge of freeing our name from the negative connotations that burden it. Is it not the same for *religion* and *spirituality*? Even the term *values* has been corrupted and politicized. Undaunted, we accept the challenge and continue our exercise. We ask, What are the attributes that allow us to recognize wildness in the human heart?

When you are wild, you are . . . more natural. Well, that was fast. We're right back to the landscape-mapping attributes. In our wildness-mapping approach, we defined a wild landscape as having its characteristic composition unaltered by human creation and unpolluted. These are actually quite useful terms to consider when we map the human heart or psyche. What did we consist of before our social and familial environment altered us; before the world was explained to us and we were told what was important and how we should be; before we were bombarded by the unrelenting onslaught of twenty-first-century media, advertising, and propaganda? Do you realize that the loudest and most frequent messages most of us receive concerning joy come from advertising, which seems to say that we find joy when we drive a 5,000-pound vehicle very fast through a mountain stream?

Let's call up some different language to help in our search. *Innate, instinctual, hereditary, intuitive, original, knowing, natural, wild, free, fulfilling, joyful, wonderful, perfect. Aesthetic. In the moment. Present. Being. Connected, integrated, harmonious. In synch, centered, whole, aware, conscious. In the spirit* or *with the spirit. Spiritual, growing, flowering, blossoming, unfolding, becoming wild* and *wilder,* and— yes!—*it is good.*

The Latin root of *religion* means "to link back." We are linking back to our fundamental source of wisdom and knowledge. Wherever we look, there is the desire to link back—to find the source. It is in religion and poetry, and I see it in different forms within all our greatest teachings. We are always going back in order to move forward. We must go deeper in order to move outward. It is always so because what we seek is already there and available—if we choose to look.

I'm a New England forester, so of course I would find resonance in the poetry of Robert Frost. In his poem "Directive," he guides the reader through the regreening forests of New England, pocked with old stone walls and house foundations—monuments to farms and towns reverting to wildland. Frost points out the direction we need to take. He speaks of finding a guide who is interested only in getting you lost:

> The road there, if you'll let a guide direct you
>
> Who only has at heart your getting lost . . . [5]

Later, Frost indicates why we must get lost:

> And if you're lost enough to find yourself . . . [6]

So the directive tells us we must first get lost before we can find our way. The deeper wisdom will not come from the ephemeral works of our society and culture. In the woods, Frost advises us not to waste time with the old frame of the farmhouse, which is decomposing into the forest. He directs us beyond and below:

> Your destination and your destiny's
>
> A brook that was the water of the house
>
> Cold as a spring as yet so near its source
>
> Too lofty and original to rage.[7]

Cold water, near its source, lofty and original: This is a powerful symbol for what might inspire one to take a drink. But who will drink?

> I have kept hidden in the instep arch
>
> Of an old cedar at the waterside

A broken drinking goblet like the Grail

Under a spell so the wrong ones can't find it

So can't get saved, as Saint Mark says they mustn't.

(I stole the goblet from the children's playhouse.)[8]

Apparently the water from the source is not for everyone. Perhaps it is only for those who have truly lost themselves by this point, who are no longer encumbered by roads and maps and mediators—who, after drinking, cannot go out the same way they came in. If the cup were too easily found, those who were not yet really lost might find it and drink from the brook, thinking and telling others they had found the way.

Our challenge is clear. If we wish to connect science and religion and the natural world, if we wish to inspire a new land ethic in the American people, we must first find our source. We must drink deeply, and then—and this is important—we must carry this original, cold water with us deep in our bellies when we return to civilization. When we return to the "real world," we must always stay in contact with the brook that runs under the house, carry the water in our bellies or immerse ourselves every now and then.

Finding the source is challenge enough, but staying in touch with it while we go about our work and our lives is another matter. At The Wilderness Society, we are looking at how often we are in touch with this source as we go about our interactions with one another in the organization. How often are we able to express this deep connection when we write or speak about the environment? How often and how well do we express these deep feelings when we are lobbying on Capitol Hill for the bill that would protect the very forest where we took our drink from the source?

Not often enough, I must report. We aren't used to doing this. In some situations, there is an unspoken rule that this experience of the human condition must not be recognized. We really have to think about how well this would be received by our peers in certain situations. There is a palpable resistance. But if one person takes the plunge in a sensitive, articulate, and appropriate manner, then something remarkable begins to happen. It's as if the necessary permission has been granted, and suddenly there is a rush to join in.

I've seen this happen with large groups several times. A number of years ago, I was involved in a session for the Society of American Foresters regarding whether they should include a land ethic in their hundred-year-old code of ethics. Until that time, most of their canons had represented the appropriate relationship between professionals and their employers or their peers. These foresters were beginning the discussion of whether to write a canon regarding their relationship with and their ethical responsibility to the forest. This was new material, unlike other policy discussions they were accustomed to. My colleagues and I decided to open the session with my telling a story and then asking whether any of them had a story they would like to tell.

Mine was an unusual story because it had nothing to do with forests or the natural world. It was about universal values. I had determined that by involving these foresters, who were mostly older men, in such a story, I might change the dynamic of the meeting for the very important issue at hand.

Here's my story, of moving day.

My wife, Anne, and I were moving out of our second-floor apartment in Worcester, Massachusetts, to a new home. It was a warm morning in late spring, and two young moving contractors arrived at our house ready to load all our worldly possessions into their van and drive away. Right from the start, I didn't feel as if they were following directions particularly well or taking proper care of our belongings. I thought I smelled alcohol on their breath.

We were about an hour into the move, and I was on the second floor, packing boxes in the living room. The windows were open wide; one of the movers was on the stairs and the other was outside, in the van. Suddenly I heard someone yelling outside, but I couldn't make out what the person was saying. I stepped over to the window, and then I could hear a woman's voice down the block screaming, over and over, "My baby, my baby, my baby!" I saw the mover in the van bolt out the back and sprint down the street. I heard the guy on the stairs drop what he was carrying and pound across the porch. That's when I headed for the stairs.

I jumped down the front porch stairs, rounded the hedge, and hit the street. I could see down the block about 150 yards. A car was backed out into the street, and under the wheel of the car was a child's tricycle. The woman was standing next to it, screaming.

The three of us were now stretched out running down the street. The first mover was about three-quarters of the way down the block. The second guy was about halfway there. I started running as fast as I possibly could. My feet were pounding the pavement, and my arms were pumping. There we were, the three of us, all in a line, all running to the same place as fast as we could. We were totally focused and leaving no bit of energy unburned.

Time passes very slowly at moments like these. I remember watching the trees and houses move by, seeing my arms move up and down. I was trying to remember the last time I had sprinted at full speed and wondering whether I would have any strength left by the time I reached the car.

I saw the first mover reach the car and position himself at the back bumper.

He strained to lift the car but couldn't budge it. I dug down deeper, trying to will myself into a higher gear that I just didn't have. Then I saw the second mover reach the car and take up a position at the bumper next to his buddy. They both lifted but still couldn't make it move. I started concentrating on moving my arms and keeping my rhythm because it was obvious I wasn't going any faster. I finally reached the car, and they moved over to make room for me. I counted to three and we lifted together. The car shot up above our waists and the woman pulled a little girl out from under the tire.

Fortunately, the girl was fine. The car had backed over her as she passed the driveway, pinning her against the tire, but it hadn't crushed her. She didn't even seemed scared until the ambulance arrived and the emergency crew put her on a stretcher and secured her head, just to be safe. Only then did she really start to wail.

I have to laugh when I think about telling such a story, which had nothing directly to do with forestry or conservation, to this group of foresters. But it worked because it illustrated that there are times in our lives that are transcendent. These are moments when we are capable of going beyond all the arguments and fears and politics of the ongoing debate. This event was one of them. One moment I was very concerned about how well these movers were treating us, and the next moment I was lined up with them, the three of us running and lifting for our lives.

You would have been running, too. We all would have been running. Whatever your top speed is, you would have been using it. If you were using a wheelchair, you would have been rolling at top speed.

I have to tell you that the rest of the move went wonderfully. We all had pizza for lunch, and afterward Anne and I gave the movers the biggest tip we could afford. I've never forgotten them, and although I've never seen them since, we remain strangely connected in a moment in time—running—running forever.

When I finished this story at the forestry workshop, I asked the foresters whether any of them had a story they would like to tell about their first memories of the forest. A gentleman in his sixties or seventies immediately jumped up, walked to the front of the room, and commandeered the podium. He proceeded to tell us the story of how his father had first carried him into the Olympic rain forest when he was a small boy. He described their walk down the trail and the tree bough, laden with snow, that had brushed his face. He touched his cheek as he described it. We all felt the coolness. This guy was standing with both feet in Robert Frost's proverbial brook. When he had finished, all his colleagues jumped in, one after the other. We heard stories from all over this beautiful, sprawling country. It was an unforgettably moving experience. I still have my notes: Deer in the orchard on an Upper Peninsula farm. Deep snow in the hill country of Arkansas. Buttercups and blueberries for Mom in northern Minnesota. A poem about Gull Lake. The moon through a longleaf pine in Louisiana. Big trees near Grandmother's house in the Olympic Mountains. Lying in the grass in a hardwood forest in Wisconsin. Watching shooting stars in the Sierras. Logging with Father in Michigan. Bullfrogs at night in West Virginia. The pungent smell of the desert in Arizona.

When the last one had spoken, my colleagues and I turned the session to the matter at hand. We asked the foresters what they thought a land ethic should say, and someone offered a very bland descriptive statement. Suddenly, someone raised a hand and pointed out that the group had just left the place they had been a few minutes ago and were now back in the "real world," but they should write this from the connection of their hearts, not just from their brains. The Society of American Foresters did eventually adopt a land ethic canon, and although it was less than what some of us would have written, it was a first step. Let's hope that whenever the foresters revisit their land ethic, they make use of the cold, original source of water that's immediately available to them but that unfortunately tends to dry up much too rapidly. I often reflect on that meeting, and I believe it was that first forester's story of the Olympic rain forest that made all the difference.

We recently implemented a similar ritual in The Wilderness Society. Every year when the entire staff meets, we hold a sacred object session. Each employee gets a chance to bring in and talk about an object that has particular personal meaning. The sessions are always deeply moving, and what's best is that we learn so much about our colleagues that we probably wouldn't learn otherwise. We are trying to find ways to bring these deep connections into our daily work.

It is not easy to be the first one to speak. It is also not easy to find the right way to express what it is you experience. Poet W. S. Merwin wrote: "I want to tell you what the forests were like. I will have to speak in a forgotten language."[9]

I've already described the experience I had on a Long Island Sound salt marsh when I was nine. Not long before that, I had a dream that was troubling. I woke up in the middle of the night very disturbed, and my father asked me what I had dreamt. I could not tell him. I have never forgotten that dream, and I have never been able to describe it. It was disturbing in the sense that I could not explain it. I had a sensation of what it was I had seen, but there were no words big enough to fit around it and no words small enough to fit inside it.

Years later, I was told by someone who knew about these things that what I had experienced was not a dream at all. Remarkably, that was the moment when I finally understood its meaning, although I still don't have the words to describe it. But it was big. And it was timeless. I think I saw a bit of it when I was sitting in that old red maple near the marsh. And although I struggle to express myself to you, I don't feel the need to explain this particular dream that was not a dream. As Lao-Tzu advised in the Tao Te Ching:

The Tao that can be told

is not the eternal Tao.

The name that can be named

is not the eternal Name.[10]

Finding a way to express ourselves that strikes the same chord in others is always a challenge. There are some who do it well. Terry Tempest Williams makes contact with us in her beautiful prose; Barry Lopez, in his intricate and insightful stories of land and culture; and Paul Winter, in his evocative melodies and arrangements. Each is on the same wavelength and uses a different medium to hit the mark. Robert Frost hit the mark with his poetry. Wallace Stegner often hit the mark with his writing. When he referred to this perception as the "bigness outside of ourselves," I felt as if he were talking directly to me.

We are all relearning to speak this forgotten language, and the world needs more Williamses and Lopezes and Winters. And the world needs you to join them. You may not have the same skills in writing or storytelling or music, but you come fully equipped with your own wisdom and your own way of gaining access to it. We are all born with that gift. We make contact with the natural world most fully through our emotions.

The world needs your passion and your emotion, and it calls on you to find appropriate ways and appropriate situations to demonstrate that deep feeling that wells up within you.

The folks we refer to as land practitioners have a particularly select and honored place in any storytelling tradition. Although all of us share an intimate connection with the natural world, land practitioners are distinguished in three important ways: They enjoy a daily intimacy with the land, they earn their daily bread by their direct manipulation and use of the land, and the decisions they make on a daily basis affect the health of the land and are thus open to public scrutiny and criticism.

In essence, they are the people who have taken their love for and connection to the land and applied that to earning a living from the land. From this integration comes a different kind of intimacy and wisdom——one we all need to know more about if we are to forge a new kind of relationship with the land in this country. It is important to include and highlight the insights of people who work in such fields as forestry, agriculture, commercial fishing, architecture and landscape architecture, land development, and outdoor recreation. Some of them have successfully integrated their spiritual lives into their work, and we have much to learn from them.

Integrating spirit into work is a topic of growing interest that goes beyond the environment and the land use professions. People in all walks of life seek guidance on how to accomplish this. Their success in this endeavor is predicated on three factors. First, some work environments and subject matters lend themselves better to this integration. Simply because of the inherent nature of the work, one would think it easier for a wildlife biologist than for a contract attorney to find a spiritual aspect in his or her work. Second, it is much easier for those who have a supportive professional community that will help them find their way. The business community normally draws stricter lines of separation between business and spiritual life than does, say, the mental health care profession. Although each of these two factors is important, the third is most critical: the spiritual meaning the individual brings to the work. It is just as possible for a Manhattan lawyer to bring spirit to her work as it is for a Colorado River tour guide. It mostly depends on the personal experience one brings to the work.

The exploration of spirituality and work is critically important to life on this planet, including the quality of human life. Through our growing numbers and expanding technologies, humankind has wrought major changes on local, regional, and global environments. We have unintentionally embarked on great experiments regarding our relationship with the natural world. Over the first two decades of the new century, our success in gaining access to our deepest wisdom and bringing it to bear on environmental problems will truly dictate what life will be like for all future generations, human and nonhuman. We, the present generations, are the ones who engaged in these experiments and created these situations, and therefore we must bear moral responsibility for their consequences.

We are in the midst of the greatest extinction of species since the decline of the dinosaurs. We continue to lose habitat at an alarming rate, with no end in sight. It takes 10 million years of evolution to replenish lost biodiversity, and we are now destroying most of the habitats where evolution can occur. This is an endgame in which we are about to alter forever the natural world and our evolutionary place within it.

As if removing the habitat where evolution can occur were not enough, we are now speeding up the process of alienation from our evolutionary roots by engaging in genetic manipulation of plants and animals. We, the environmental community, are called upon to change the nature of the debate involving these decisions. They are about more than economic gain or the health of a single human organism; they are about creation and humankind's place within it, and as such, these experiments have deeply spiritual overtones. We are on a roll, making these decisions with too much rational thought and far too little spiritual wisdom.

W. S. Merwin, again, said it well:

Well they'd made up their minds to be everywhere because why not
Everywhere was theirs because they thought so. . . .
Well they cut everywhere because why not
Everything was theirs because they thought so.[11]

So much is happening so fast, and we are so far removed from a solution. What we need right now is a great shift in perception to support a major environmental policy shift. It usually takes decades or centuries for great transformations in perception to occur. The many years of social inquiry that preceded the end of slavery in the United States is an example. We don't have that much time anymore. It is time to cut to the chase, and do it now. We need to ask ourselves whether there is something that could unify the American people behind a single goal of protecting the environment.

This nation has accomplished great things in short periods of time. We made the commitment and went to the moon in less than ten years' time. We need to unite the American people behind a similarly broad-based initiative to protect the natural world. Right now, we are just playing around the margins with our environmental policy. What we really need to do is determine how much of a commitment is needed from the American people to truly protect our environment and leave a lasting legacy to all future generations. Then we need to unite the country behind it.

We have no hope unless we infuse the debate over the environment with the deep emotional and spiritual connections that it warrants and that will be required for a great social transformation. I think we can—and you who are engaged in environmental work are the women and men to do it. You will play a critical role in convincing the public that we can infuse spirit into our work and face our greatest challenges with a new and more encompassing wisdom.

As we continue our journey, we may find it helpful to keep in mind the words of David Wagner in his poem "Lost":

Stand still. The trees ahead and bushes beside you,

Are not lost. Wherever you are is called Here.

And you must treat it as a powerful stranger

Must ask permission to know it and be known.

The forest breathes. Listen. It answers,

I have made this place around you.

If you leave it you may come back again saying Here.

No two leaves are the same to Raven.

No two branches are the same to Wren.

If what a tree or a branch does is lost on you

You are surely lost. Stand still. The forest knows

Where you are. You must let it find you.[12]

In conclusion, as we move forward with our good work on and for the land, let us remember: We are all in this together. We are all on the same wavelength. We are all indivisible in our respect for and connection to the earth—reaching out in the gathering darkness, fingers spread wide to touch and understand our place in the family of things.

Chapter 11

Leopold's Darwin: Climbing Mountains, Developing Land

Strachan Donnelley

Land developers and consumers of natural resources, which directly or indirectly includes us all, find themselves in a complex moral predicament. We human beings inescapably and increasingly face long-term moral and civic (often inherently conflicted) responsibilities to both human communities and natural ecosystems and landscapes.

The Hastings Center's Humans and Nature Program is exploring these intertwined obligations in several regional planning projects, including one in the Chicago area. The project aims at the articulation of a regional (and global) "humans and nature" ethic adequate to our times and the human and natural future.

Nature, Polis, Ethics: Chicago Regional Planning, a project co-sponsored by The Hastings Center and the Chicago Academy of Sciences, was born out of a sense of regional loss and crisis as well as the lure of future regional opportunities and responsibilities. The project entails civic research and education involving several conservation, scientific, cultural, and planning organizations that are grappling with the juggernaut of Chicago's regional sprawl and its multifaceted systemic effects, from the ecological and natural landscape to the economic, social, and political and the cultural, aesthetic, ethical, and spiritual. Over a recent twenty-five-year period, the Chicago region's population grew by 4 percent while its land consumption grew by more than 40 percent, with platting raging like a wildfire.

With a sense of practical moral urgency and intellectual adventure, those of us involved in the project have spent six years exploring a new civic vision for the region (roughly southeastern Wisconsin, northeastern Illinois, and

161

northwestern Indiana); a new understanding of regional ecological and democratic citizenship; and a practical moral and civic consideration of a full range of human and natural values. We are deeply concerned with democratic community and social justice, but equally with the region's nature and the other, nonhuman inhabitants of its checkered, fragmented, but remanently beautiful prairie, farm, savanna, and lake landscapes. We are animated by a complex intellectual, philosophical, moral, and spiritual passion. We are determined to take Charles Darwin's evolutionary and ecological views of nature seriously. Similarly, we are inspired by the Midwest's conservationist patron saint, Aldo Leopold. We have struggled to bring an updated Darwinian and Leopoldian land ethic to the Chicago region. In short, we are philosophically, ethically, and civically committed to thinking of humans and nature together. We want to envision long-term moral and civic obligations to the region's future by framing a historical "humans and nature" moral landscape within which regionally concerned citizens can orient themselves. What natural landscapes were here after the last glaciation, some 13,000 years ago? How have humans and nature interacted and mutually transformed one another in the ensuing years? What is the present "humans and nature" landscape? What are the civic, moral, and natural possibilities for the future? Our questions come down to this: How do we get Darwin's nature into people's minds and hearts, and how do we get people to live well within the limits of Darwin's nature (in both senses of the phrase)?[1]

With respect to Chicago's land, I vividly recall growing up in Libertyville, Illinois, a farm town of 5,000 people some forty-five miles from Chicago, with 500 kids (both boys and girls) in baseball uniforms—bicycling on unpaved gravel roads, playing on prairie baseball fields, fishing for bullheads in the muddy Des Plaines River, our region's answer to the mighty Mississippi. At the age of eight, I came face to face with nature red in tooth and claw when I confronted a giant snapping turtle eating its way up the body of a recently caught bullhead that had been thrown back into the Des Plaines on a stringer. The turtle broke off, and for me the character of the Des Plaines forever changed. Sobered by the encounter, I rode my bike back home. I hayed in the summer heat and hunted for doves with my Labrador retriever, Si, in dry creek beds in the cooling evenings of fall. I only now begin to realize vividly that these were all deeply spiritual or spirited experiences, laced with multiple values stemming from the interfusion and interaction of the emerging human me and my home landscape.

Libertyville now is a Chicago suburb of 30,000 or more people, paved roads, and endless traffic replacing the gravel bike routes. We must struggle to save what land and farmscape values are left.

For me, not all has been lost. There have been some definite gains in the ensuing fifty-plus years. Darwin and Leopold, among many philosophical, scientific, and artistic others, have entered my mind and animated my body. Like Leopold and others, I, too, ponder flora and fauna—wildflowers, birds, trout, salmon, bullheads, and snapping turtles—which carry me back to our immemorial worldly origins. I, too, become overwhelmed with awe, gratitude, guilt, and a sense of responsibility to the world's past, present, and future.

Actually, I and the other participants in Nature, Polis, Ethics are only beginning to realize that spirit, the spirited, or the spiritual—pick your favorite term—is a mansion of many rooms: that perhaps there are as many forms of spirit, the spirited, and the spiritual as there are values, good and bad, human and natural. The complex historical interfusions and interactions of humans and nature are a rich mine that awaits further adventurous human exploration. There is more than enough food for thought about the good and the bad in nature and humanity.

In the remainder of this chapter, I will further explicate and add depth to my colleagues' and my regional civic explorations by revisiting Aldo Leopold and his *Sand County Almanac* and reflecting on the ethical and civic implications of Leopold's thought.

Climbing Leopold's Mountain

Aldo Leopold is the Alexander Pushkin of American environmental and conservation ethics. All Russian literature must trace its roots to Pushkin and *Eugene Onegin*. American environmentalists must find their origins in Leopold and *A Sand County Almanac*. As a guiding spirit of modern conservation, Leopold is by now well-covered ground.[2] Yet there remain good ongoing reasons for reconsidering *A Sand County Almanac*. First of all, Leopold, his work, and his "land ethic," however genuinely seminal, still are largely unknown to the general public, educators, and policy makers, public and private. Whatever can help spread Leopold's word and spirit is all to the good.

Further, there are important philosophical and ethical reasons to revisit Leopold. Trained formally as a forester and scientific ecologist, not as a philosopher or ethicist, Leopold nevertheless was a pioneering explorer in a terra incognita of practical ethics: our long-term moral responsibilities to humans and nature in the post-Darwin era—perhaps the looming issue of today, in Chicago and elsewhere. Indeed, it is arguably Leopold's conversion to a full-blooded Darwinian evolutionary and ecological worldview that accounts for his philosophical and ethical originality, subsumed cryptically under his land ethic, and his claim to our serious and critical attention.

Leopold's natural predilection and intellectual conversion to a naturalist's worldview and ethic take him outside or beyond characteristic modern philosophical and civic sensibilities, habits, and modes of thought. He was intellectually, emotionally, and spiritually attuned to what most American citizens are not: Darwin's revolutionary scientific theory and broader worldview of the historical evolution of all biotic life from a common origin via genetic and behavioral variation and natural selection. Darwin's theory of evolution, as brilliantly elucidated by Ernst Mayr, is complex, but certain crucial features constitute its philosophically revolutionary character.[3] First is the overthrow of *cosmic teleology*—nature's grand divine design and Designer. Nature dynamically authors its own forms and order, organic, ecological, ecosystemic, and biospheric. Second is the demise of ironclad *Newtonian determinism,* the hegemony of efficient causes ("billiard balls in motion") and eternal, unbreachable laws of nature. Nature and its constituents, biological if not also other, have multiple causes on multitemporal and multispatial scales. Historical contexts, dynamism, contingencies, and particularities rule the evolutionary scene. Third, perhaps the greatest shock of all, *typological* or *essentialist* thinking is superseded. Thought in terms of species types (horse, dog, rose, human being) is replaced by populational thinking. Individual organisms live in interacting and interbreeding populations, with each individual genetically and phenotypically different from all the others, no two exactly the same. This individuality and particularity hold for populations, communities, ecosystems, and bioregions as well—all levels of biotic nature. This multileveled diversity is absolutely crucial to evolutionary and ecological, if not also human cultural, processes.

Our task here is to explore and understand how Leopold gathered these fundamental Darwinian tenets into his own distinct midwestern naturalist's worldview and land ethic, which has become so suggestive for our times.

Leopold's land ethic is famously summarized by his defining of human moral good and bad in terms of positive or negative contributions to "the integrity, stability, and beauty" of the biotic community or the land. What we are meant to understand by *integrity, stability, beauty,* and *the land* remains a matter of ongoing debate, but I hope it will become reasonably clear as we go along.

Leopold's conversion to a Darwinian evolutionary, ecological, and biotic worldview is symbolically represented in his signature essay, "Thinking Like a Mountain."[4] Leopold had been professionally involved in game management in the Southwest, specifically the eradication of predators (wolves, bears, and mountain lions) for the sake of increasing deer populations for hunters, if not paving the way for cattle ranching. While on a mountain trip, Leopold and his companions came upon a she-wolf crossing a river to join her cubs. Following the dictates of what today would be called "wise use" game management, as well as the trigger-itch of young hunters, the group shot at the wolves, killing the she-wolf. As Leopold watched the "fierce green fire" dying in her eyes, he was taken up short. The mountain and the wolf knew something Leopold did not, and what they knew put him to shame. Predators and predation have an ultimate significance and a central role to play in evolutionary, ecological, and geologic time and in the ongoing well-being of ecosystemic nature and the humanly good life. Leopold had previously been thinking, feeling, and acting in a wrong frame of reference. He had not taken a long-range evolutionary, ecological, and ethological (animal behaviorist) perspective and thus did not have an appreciation for the roles that wolves and other large predators play in the overall health of specific ecosystems—keeping prey species at healthy levels, preventing the overcropping of plant resources, helping the ecosystemic whole maintain a dynamic balance or equilibrium. Henceforth, Leopold, if few others, knew better.[5]

To bring out the full moral and other human value dimensions of Leopold's conversion to an ethic that supports "the integrity, stability, and beauty" of the land, I will briefly travel far afield and situate Leopold's thought within a central drama of Western culture and philosophy: a fundamental quarrel over the final nature of the true, good, and beautiful of our world. With respect to ultimate value and significance, ever since the time of Plato and his pre-Socratic forebears, a battle has been raging between philosophical dualists, who claim two levels or realms of reality, and monists, who adhere to one worldly reality.[6]

On the one side are the dualists, with their interpretation of our world of historical change and becoming as an imperfect imitation or realization of a higher, unchanging, acosmic reality and perfection. We see this vividly in Plato (in some of his moods) and his doctrine of eternal and unchanging "forms," including the final Form of the Good, which are imperfectly reflected in our worldly reality and are the source of whatever order, goodness, and beauty that are realized. (Plato is one of the crucial forefathers of essentialist, typological thinking.) In *The Seventh Letter,* Plato speaks of knowledge of "the fifth entities" (the forms) as the highest form of human philosophical knowledge. In *The*

Republic, he relates the Allegory of the Cave, with shadows cast upon the cave's back wall (the appearances of the world we perceive or experience) and the blinding sun at the mouth of the cave (the Form of the Good), the latter which the philosopher perceives only after turning away from the "worldly" shadows and engaging in an arduous, dedicated struggle after final truth. In *The Symposium,* Socrates is instructed in the school of Eros (desire) and led through the various ascending stages of worldly beauty (the objects of Eros's desires)—sexual objects, friendships, political institutions, knowledge, and more—until the Mantinean priestess Diotima reveals to Socrates the final (aworldly) Form of the Beautiful (the Good and the Real), the consummation of Eros's and the Socratic philosopher's strivings.[7]

The search beyond the world of becoming and change to discover the truly real and the source of all order, beauty, goodness, and perfection did not start with Plato. He had pre-Socratic predecessors. Most notably, the Pythagoreans believed in an ultimate otherworldly, acosmic principle, *peras* (the "limited," that which provides definition), the perfect and untainted source of worldly harmonies—order, beauty, goodness—which are realized only by *peras* informing the *apeiron* (the "unlimited"), which is this-worldly, dynamic, itself formless, and thus deficient. The Pythagorean philosopher's salvation is in pursuing and apprehending *peras* in all its manifestations and final purity, in becoming assimilated to ultimate and unchanging harmony and order.

This early philosophical and religious dualism did not go unchallenged, and at the most fundamental levels. According to the contemporary pre-Socratic Heraclitus, such Pythagorean speculations are nonsense. In truth, he said, "it is wise to know that all [the world, the cosmos] is one, an Everliving Fire, kindling and extinguishing in measures." This dynamic *Logos* or *Arche* (that from which all originates and into which all returns) is the true and *internal* cosmic source of all order, goodness, and beauty, which are forever engendered out of worldly struggle and essential interactions among worldly constituents, including ourselves and all other organisms. Being or reality is born out of becoming and strife. War is the father of all. The world of dynamic, ever-changing harmony, beauty, and order is the philosopher's and our final home and salvation (realization of the good life).[8]

Here, in brief, is Heraclitus's monism, his single world that comprehends all of reality, which he staunchly opposes to Pythagorean and, by implication, Platonic dualism. The fundamental philosophical and cultural battle, as yet undecided, is joined. Significantly for our purposes, the convictions of Darwin and Leopold are decidedly more akin to the philosophy of Heraclitus than to that of Plato and the Pythagoreans.

Despite their differences, the philosophical wars between Plato, Heraclitus, and Leopold should not blind us to deep philosophical commonalities that are a clue to understanding Leopold and his abiding significance. All three thinkers dealt directly with ultimate reality (the real and the true), even if this reality cannot be fully or adequately grasped or articulated in thought or language. Moreover, fundamental reality is inextricably bound up with and expressed in beauty (beautiful objects and realities captured in human aesthetic and spiritual experience), which in turn expresses reality's ontological (relating to "being"), if not also moral, goodness—that which anchors and points the way to our deepest ethical responsibilities to the world.

Plato, Heraclitus, and Leopold were one in claiming that most of us humans are philosophically asleep, in a drunken stupor, or ignorant with respect to the real, the beautiful, and the good. Yet at least in the view of Leopold, if we do not wake up and get converted to the truth—get our heads screwed on right and our hearts in the right place—there is little lasting hope for us. Worldly reality, human and natural, will seriously degrade with respect to its realized and realizable beauty and goodness.

I will now leave the Greeks and attend more directly to Leopold's conception of reality, beauty, and goodness. We are exploring Leopold's worldview as decidedly Darwinian, forsaking atemporal, essential (Platonic) forms and norms as philosophical and moral resources. For Leopold, Darwin, and Mayr, reality was thoroughly temporal and historical—changing, becoming, evolving, building, and transfiguring itself over time.[9] This is our primary and final worldly and natural (evolutionary, ecological, geologic), if not cultural, home. Leopold wandered in a crane marsh and marveled at the bugling of the wildest of birds, the sandhill cranes, which over innumerable eons had interacted with their ecological community to build the marsh reality, laying the foundation for present and, it is hoped, future marsh life. The cranes are claimed to have a historically deep beauty and wisdom (whether genetic, phenotypic, or behavioral) that derive directly from their implication in evolutionary and ecological processes.[10] To destroy, undermine, or degrade this historical, time-engendered, and vulnerable reality is to commit an ultimate, cardinal sin. But that is precisely what we humans have been doing and continue to do in our ignorance of nature's engendering of mountains, crane marshes, and, more broadly, the land, which is the whole system of biotic and abiotic elements that together make up evolutionary, ecological reality—the only final reality (Plato and his followers notwithstanding) that we humans with any certainty know. We ignorant blunderers, transfixed by traditional, culturally inherited, and inadequate worldviews, aspirations, and commitments, have striven to be the conquerors of nature while setting up our own provincial human enclaves (cultural communities), whereas we should have become by now "plain members and citizens" of the natural community that includes ourselves and is called the land.[11]

Reality, Beauty, and Leopoldian Experience

We need further to unpack Leopold's worldview, since it still remains significantly foreign to our modern philosophical, moral, and civic ears, unschooled as most of us are in a full range of primary experiences of nature and in a thorough working knowledge, as well as fundamental conceptions, of evolutionary biology and the still newer sciences of modern ecology and ethology. In short, we need to work hard to approach Leopold's original vision, despite the evocative and well-crafted prose of *A Sand County Almanac*.

First of all, we should note that Leopold accepted philosophically, morally, and spiritually a fundamental Darwinian tenet. Human beings have emerged from and within nature, and it is sheer hubris and egotism to think otherwise, despite our special place or "difference" in the natural world—a significant human difference, which nevertheless is parasitic, as we shall see, on our being a part of nature. Honest recognition of our status in nature is a human and cultural boon rather than a curse. Humans have evolved along and in interaction with other forms of life. We have been and increasingly continue to be active agents, as well as "patients," in the earth's evolving reality and history, life's earthly cosmogony (coming into being). We are and forever will remain, directly or indirectly, part of complex food chains (energy flows and circuits) and biotic pyramids (soil and natural elements, flora, fauna—up to large, "crowning" predators), involved in ever-revolving rounds of ecological processes and predator–prey relations, despite our all too successful, if ultimately futile, efforts to "get out" of nature economically, socially, culturally, and spiritually.[12] Moreover, Leopold refused to shrink from the full consequences of recognizing our status in nature. He accepted and affirmed the hard Darwinian and Heraclitean truth that death, destruction, and disease are directly implicated in the creation of life's historical reality, beauty, and goodness.[13] Predation was only a primary example: "The only certain truth is that [the prairie's] creatures must suck hard, live fast, and die often, lest its losses exceed its gains."[14] The unwearied grebe reminds us that "if all are to survive, each must ceaselessly feed and fight, breed and die."[15]

Unambivalent acceptance of humanity's natural status in evolutionary, eco-logical nature accounted for Leopold's particular originality and the seeming, if not real, paradoxes of his thought. On one hand, Leopold believed all flora and fauna to be his communal brethren and neighbors—pine trees, wildflow-ers, chickadees, woodcocks, dogs, wolves, grizzly bears, and more. (We all inhabit the same tree of life and share a common origin.) Yet Leopold also accepted hunting and fishing for sport: human predation as an essentially atavistic, aesthetic, and spiritual experience, pursued under appropriate ethi-cal constraints.[16] He was passionately concerned with preserving rapidly van-ishing wilderness areas, wild flora and fauna, and human wilderness experi-ences (solitude, canoe and horse backpacking trips). Yet he also accepted and advocated active, enlightened management of the land.

The key to understanding, if not resolving, these paradoxes and Leopold's aesthetics and ethics is, again, Leopold's particular philosophical appropriation of Darwinian evolutionary biology, ecology, and ethology: the admixture or intermingling of science and his particular brand of human spirituality. The practical ethics of the *scientific* Leopold concerned the long-term well-being and health of ecosystems and evolutionary processes. This at times allows, if not demands, active human management of the land—for example, manage-ment of farmland in order concurrently to foster native flora and fauna (wild-flowers and prairie grasses, game and other animals).[17] Here is Leopold's sci-entifically informed stewardship or conservation ethic.

The "humanly spirited" Leopold's ethic grew out of and beyond his scien-tifically informed ethic. Here, in a characteristically modern fashion, he reap-propriated a Greek spirit, and that of Plato and Heraclitus in particular. Ecosystems and wild flora and fauna have a deep evolutionary history, within which Leopold the conservation actor and philosophical explorer dwelt. This is ultimate reality. To be directly in touch with cranes, grebes, wolves, cougars, and other fauna and flora within their natural habitats is to be directly in touch with historically evolved reality and natural and human origins—an ultimate spiritual or religious experience, laced with deep emotional and aesthetic valences, including a vivid sense of tragedy and loss. A mountain with its top predators—wolves, grizzly bears, mountain lions—is the real thing, deeply felt (fearfully, respectfully, or reverentially) as such. A mountain without its wolves; a marsh without its cranes; a field or wetland without its grebes, plovers, partridge, quail, or historical and characteristic wildflowers, grasses, or trees is a denuded and dispirited landscape, both ecologically and humanly—a loss felt keenly by those who know (the naturalist, the evolution-ary biologist, the ecologist, the ethologist, the "plain citizen" of the land). Here is the human experience of the ultimate real, beautiful, and good—or its absence.

There are definite and interesting Platonic and Heraclitean themes to all this. There are various levels of participation in the good, beautiful, and real, from an unknowing immediate engagement with its sensuous, emotional, and spiritual textures to a knowing, wide-awake, spiritually appreciative participation, an ultimate form of human existence, a pinnacle of the humanly good life. For Plato, it was awareness of the varying participation of all things in the eternal forms and the final Form of the Good. For Heraclitus, it was keen and knowing awareness of the Everliving Fire (the *Logos*) that underlies and informs all worldly becoming and achievement, including the "fiery," knowing philosopher himself or herself. For Leopold, it was the aesthetic and spiritual appreciation of natural reality, decidedly deepened by the knowledge gained from scientific evolutionary biology, ecology, and ethology and by the active, responsible stewardship that this experience and knowledge foster.[18] This is the cultural, aesthetic, and spiritual harvest to be gained from nature, as augmented by our exploring, questing minds and science's objectivity, its concern with facts and empirical truth. Here is humans' specific difference within nature. Only we can know, however imperfectly, and explicitly appreciate the fact of evolution, its history, and our active participation, for better or for worse, in the world's becoming. Only we can actively mourn evolution's historical losses (the extinction of species and ecosystemic life) and our ignorant, plundering participation in reality's degradation—for example, the demise of the passenger pigeon and more.[19]

The Leopoldian "Upshot"

On one crucial point, Leopold broke with Plato and Heraclitus. Although each interpreted or claimed a different reality in which we humans participate, Leopold's *A Sand County Almanac* and his land ethic, by his own admission, are not the final word. They do not carry the authoritative, dogmatic flavor of Heraclitus and (on occasion) Plato. As Leopold was keenly aware, evolutionary biology, and especially ecology and ethology, were (and are) in their infancy. We are largely ignorant of nature's complex facts and ways. There remains much room for further exploration and cultural harvest. In particular, our understanding of the "integrity, stability, and beauty" of the land needs ongoing reinterpretation in light of what we further learn about the dynamism of evolutionary, ecological, ethological nature—how much of nature's interactions is dynamic equilibrium and balance and how much is radical ecological and ecosystemic change. Upon this determination importantly rests the norms or criteria for pragmatically and morally judging the good, true, and beautiful of the land—its ongoing integrity, stability, and beauty. Ethically and ecologically, we still see through a glass darkly.

Yet despite this and more unfinished business, Leopold's pioneering efforts are of seminal worth. Leopold gave us a realistic moral purchase for critically questioning our cultural, economic, and technological progress, enterprises, and ongoing aspirations. What will they do in the long run to the health and integrity, organic and spiritual, of the land and ourselves? What will be the ongoing natural and cultural harvest? Are we, our human works, and a humanly transfigured nature sustainable or headed for disaster?

Moreover, Leopold importantly helped to wean us from extra-worldly moral norms, Platonic or other (the dualist's ethical, "perfectionist" vision). Leopold the naturalist, scientist, and cultural harvester delights in the spring mating flights and dances of woodcocks. Leopold the hunter is admonished to leave enough woodcocks in the fall so that there will be plenty of dancers in the next and following springs.[20] This is characteristically good conservation ethics, a land ethic that both rings true and allows for multiple human activities and values—various participations in the "really real" of evolutionary and humanly cultural life. Here is an ethic that is historically and contextually sensitive and deep and that stands in decided contrast to dominant, pre-Darwinian forms of normative ethics, utilitarian or Kantian, consequentialist or deontological, which largely leave time and historical becoming out of account, an ongoing influence of Pythagorean-Platonic (dualistic) tradition. Leopold's norms were creatively (interpretively) drawn from human and natural life as they have evolved and as they variously express biotic, including human, reality's beauty, goodness, and significance. What other ultimate philosophical and ethical resource can we have or need in this age of post-Darwinian "enlightenment"? As Leopold justly claimed, the cultural harvest from humans and nature is superabundantly there and sufficient for all who can see, hear, and think. We only have actively to appreciate and fulfill our land responsibilities.[21]

Leopold claimed that no important change in ethics comes about without an internal change in our intellectual emphases, loyalties, affections, and convictions. He was convinced that we needed a sea change in our current human and ethical valuations—new ethical contents, rights and wrongs, obligations, and sacrifices.[22] In trying to capture this sea change in values, I have largely aimed at revealing Leopold's new evolutionary, ecological worldview and its philosophical and ethical implications.

I want only to add a few further speculative reflections on the fundamental philosophical and moral importance of our being human biological organisms—speculations that, if persuasively argued for and embraced, would further Leopold's enterprise. Our organic mode of being, our fundamental status in reality, is our physical and experiential ticket into the great evolutionary and ecological drama of worldly life. We know life (and its opposite) and other living organisms only because we are instances of biological, animate life ourselves. Life provides us with the epistemic arsenal, or tools of knowing, by which we judge the quick from the dead as well as the various capacities and performances of life. Further, it is only because we humans are mortal, finite, and vulnerable—fundamental characteristics of organic life per se—that we can comprehend life's ways: its tragedies, triumphs, beauties, and goodness. All this is to say that we enjoy Leopold's "human difference" only because we ourselves are living organisms and not something more or other. Only life can know, appreciate, and value life in and for itself. Moreover, if all beauty and goodness—and evil—are direct or indirect manifestations of life, human and other, then we participate in a worldly realm of value (beauty, goodness, significance, and their opposites) only by virtue of our being complexly organized instances of life ourselves, that is, organisms. In short, organic life is fundamentally (ontologically) deeper or more comprehensive than mind or disembodied spirit. Our human souls are decidedly rooted in nature.

Philosophically and ethically, these reflections only tighten the Darwinian evolutionary and ecological knot. Perhaps Leopold's final brilliance is in sending us down the right path, in moving us into a Darwinian philosophical framework of thought that bridges organic life, spirit, and ethics. Yet even if this is true, we are far from arriving home. The path of understanding ourselves and nature is long, perhaps unending. (Heraclitus long ago said as much.) We, following Leopold, are just beginning. Yet Leopold has perhaps helped us to take the first halting steps in the right direction. This in itself counts as supreme philosophical and ethical service.

One final critical question or reflection does remain. Beyond Leopold's philosophical and scientific (Darwinian) strengths, the conservation philosophy and ethic of *A Sand County Almanac* seem particularly well suited to middle America and as an inspiration for the Nature, Polis, Ethics project in Chicago. Is this a good fit for all regions, not limited to Leopold's own midwestern prairie and plains landscape? Would or does he have the same pull for the citizens of the Hudson River, the Adirondacks, and New York City, or Charleston and South Carolina's coastal Lowcountry, among innumerable worldly "humans and nature" regions? Or does each region require its own philosopher-ethicist-scientist to move its citizens to fulfill their practical, long-term responsibilities to humans and nature? In the end, how universal is, or can, Leopold's appeal be? Does *A Sand County Almanac* have a requisite cosmopolitan flavor, or is it in the end "provincial," which paradoxically may account for its particular strength? Diversity and particularity, as we are coming increasingly to realize, are the spice, or rather the warp and woof, of life.

Managing Development and Land Use Responsibilities

The Darwin-inspired Aldo Leopold has set us off along the path of fundamental, perhaps unending, philosophical and ethical exploration. This is all to the good. Yet practical and urgent land use decisions cannot await endless quests, no matter how legitimate. Practice, by necessity, rears its often ugly head. We must decide upon an interim ethic, à la Leopold, at least as a rough guide for making crucial, perhaps fateful, decisions in the present.

Here, philosophical reflection can further help us. Alfred North Whitehead, early in the twentieth century, had a powerful conception and phrase: "the fallacy of misplaced concreteness."[23] Roughly, the idea that underlies the fallacy is that we humans live in a very richly complex world. Whether in science, philosophy, the arts, or practical life, we invariably are ruled by specific human interests, passions, and purposes. We abstract, "take out," or fasten upon specific features of the world's full concrete complexity. This is necessary and perfectly legitimate as long as we remember what we are doing. Mostly we do not. We take our abstractions, partial aspects of things, as the full, real, and concrete, which leads to distorted visions of the experienced world and ourselves. We repeatedly commit the pernicious fallacy of misplaced concreteness: taking the abstract (partial) for the concrete. Historically, this fateful misstep has led to all sorts of theoretical and practical human misadventures.

Whitehead's fallacy of misplaced concreteness and its presuppositions, when conjoined with a Leopoldian-Darwinian worldview, can help us to conceive an interim ethic for land developers and natural resource users (all of us).

Briefly, the reasoning goes as follows. Whitehead's fallacy and the philosophical reflections within which it is embedded imply that we human beings are variously situated within the world—as biological naturalists, economic entrepreneurs, political activists, artists of all stripes, recreationists and sportsmen, spiritual explorers, and more. Each such "worldly situated and interested" actor calls forth a particular potential or capacity of the naturally and culturally engendered human self. Each "takes account of" and values the (cultural and natural) world in a particular way without capturing or exhausting the world's complex, if vulnerable, concrete character. This is our endemic human situation and need not unduly plague us unless we forget ourselves, which, as we have seen, we characteristically, but not necessarily, do.

In short, we know that all our humanly cultural activities—whether economic, social, political, scientific, technological, recreational, artistic, or other—take place within particular and ongoing regional (and global) natural contexts and processes, evolutionary, ecological, and ethological. We must never forget this fundamental fact while pursuing our multifarious situations within, and "takings" and valuations of, the world. We must respectfully and practically attune our human activities to nature's dynamic historical ways. No doubt our various human takings and valuings spawn conflicts among themselves and with what is the ongoing natural good. Out of the crooked timber of humanity (and nature), nothing straight ever will be made, to paraphrase Immanuel Kant and Isaiah Berlin. No doubt this is true. This inherent limitation or finitude means that we require an "all things considered" ethic, an art of ethical and civic judgment that recognizes concrete situations of "moral ecology": that many things human and natural demand moral attention, that all important values (human and natural) require promotion, but that given particular concrete situations, priorities must be established and judicious trade-off decisions must be made, perhaps to be reconsidered at a later date. Such priorities and decisional compromises must seriously take into account the needs and goodness of historical evolutionary, ecological, and ethological nature as well as human beings and their ongoing cultural communities.

For developers and natural resource managers and users, what kind of an ethic is this? It is a time-honored "guide for the perplexed," particularly a guide for the Leopoldian perplexed. With genuine effort and humility, we can endeavor to avoid the fallacy of misplaced concreteness and address concrete moral situations with our eyes (relatively) wide open, not blinded by special and parochial human interests. We can attempt to be guided by the complex, if conflicting, demands of our own humanity and our historical natural home, especially our obligations to the long-range human and natural future. We can be moved by broad, generous, and nuanced senses of moral care, fairness, and respect for the various forms and capacities of life, human and other. A Leopold or a Whitehead could ask for no more than such moral art and judgment.

Chapter 12

A Rising Tide for Ethics

DAVE PREBLE AND CARL SAFINA

If we can study a holy book, can we study a holy brook? If we can search for a holy grail, might we search for a holy snail? If we can honor a holy see, can we honor a holy sea? What is designated by this word *holiness*? Surely one can gaze at stars overhead or drift in quiet waters and feel somehow spiritual; one can sense the power of a larger purpose and the inspiration of great mysteries. This can be true even without thought of the divine. Or, devotion to faith in divine power and divine communication might provide a life with framework and meaning. What indeed do we mean by the word *spiritual*? What becomes "holy"?

We might conceive to work in at least two spirit worlds: the world of spirit entities such as angels and gods, and the world of the human spirit. If one remains unconvinced of the existence of spirit entities, or rejects the notion of the mind of God or supernatural powers, yet believes in the power and guiding force of compassion, curiosity, and hope, is one less than "spiritual"? Can one approach with "holiness" something perceived as strictly material?

If spirituality might be of these two types, what constitutes "religious"? A narrow definition of religion might include such things as immutable dogma, formal rituals, or belief in divine entities. Yet if one chooses to strive daily toward some ideals, to engage in some work toward a larger purpose born of the human spirit but without explicit reference or recourse to divine authority, is that less than religious? Indeed, must we worry about two ways of being spiritual, holy, or religious? Are faith and reason truly separate and incompatible?

History seems to have reached a point at which these questions are being honestly asked and honestly answered, and as a result the often bitter schism between faith and reason that began in Western culture with Roger Bacon seven centuries ago is finally being rejoined. Signs of this reconciliation abound. Within the recent past, there has been a profusion of books and articles on the new synthesis of the two worldviews. The conference that spawned this book was itself an event that would not have seemed possible, or even have been contemplated, just a generation ago. The world now seems ready to accept the simple fact that faith and reason are, and must always be, complementary forces in our lives because both are needed to build an ethical foundation sufficient to support a continuing, self-sustaining civilization. Understanding and accepting this allows us to seriously consider ethics as a basis for our relationships not just with one another and our society but also with our sustaining planet.

More than a half century ago, Aldo Leopold identified three historical steps in the development of ethics. In his essay "The Land Ethic," he stated:

> The first ethics dealt with the relation between individuals; the Mosaic Decalogue is an example. Later accretions dealt with the relation between the individual and society. The Golden Rule tries to integrate the individual to society; democracy to integrate social organization to the individual.
>
> There is as yet no ethic dealing with man's relation to land and to the animals and plants which grow upon it.
>
> The extension of ethics to this third element in human environment is, if I read the evidence correctly, an evolutionary possibility and an ecological necessity. It is the third step in a sequence. The first two have been already taken.[1]

Aldo Leopold's proposed third-step ethic must now become a reality in our relationship not only with the land but also with the sea. Our increasing ability to alter ocean ecosystems dictates this necessity. Without an ethical compass, we bumble, without direction, from crisis to crisis, pointing fingers at our favorite scapegoats, denying personal culpability, and winding up as impotent bystanders to the loss of our most precious assets.

One area in which examples of this kind of bumbling through an ethical void are apparent is ocean fisheries. Fisheries form an intersection between people and nature in which we have extensive experience. An example of the self-destruction that can fill an ethical void is the annihilation of the pollock fishery by charter boats in the waters off Block Island, Rhode Island, during the late 1970s and early 1980s. By the mid-1970s, through the use of improved gear and modern electronic fish-finding and navigating equipment, it had become possible to catch truly huge numbers of fish by hook and line. With the

addition of powerful, lightweight diesel engines and nearly invisible monofila-
ment line, the newly developed methods achieved a deadly efficiency that is
still largely unrecognized by those who think of angling as a quiet sport with
little chance of seriously degrading fish populations. A single six-passenger
charter boat operated by a competent captain had become capable of taking a
metric ton of fish in a single outing.

Each May, jumbo pollock (*Pollachius virens*) would school on the underwater ledges south of the island, and during the years it took to destroy the fishery, an average of fifty boats would catch an average of seventy-five fish weigh-
ing an average of thirty pounds for about thirty days. In other words, the total
catch in one rather small area for each of these years was more than 3 million
pounds, or 1,500 metric tons. No one ever argued whether six people had any
use for a ton of pollock, since it had become mostly a numbers game. The fish
were thrown into fish wells without proper care and brought in to the docks
to dazzle prospective new customers before being filleted. This practice may
have attracted new customers to the deadliest boats, but by the time the fish
were finally processed and iced, their table quality was low, and many were
certainly thrown away.

As a participant in this wanton abuse of a resource, one of the authors
(Preble) once suggested that the charter boats agree to a voluntary thirty-fish
limit. Other charter captains responded that it was a good idea as long as "you
go first," and that they shouldn't limit their catch because it was "a drop in the
bucket" compared with what the draggers (commercial trawlers) were killing.
When the pollock population inevitably crashed, the draggers were blamed,
which was at least partially true, or customers were told that the pollock (or
the baitfish that they fed upon) were on a natural down cycle, which was not
true.

These convenient ambiguities did not exist, however, when the charter
boat operators applied the same general methods to bluefish (*Pomatomus salta-
trix*) and produced average catches exceeding one-half metric ton per day per
boat. Again, the total numbers were staggering, amounting to annual catches
of more than 8 million pounds, around 4,000 metric tons, from the waters off
Rhode Island alone. The wastage was even worse than in the pollock fishery
because the bluefish season was longer and, because it was later in the year, the
water and air were warmer, leaving the fish in even worse shape when they
were finally filleted. Much of the catch wasn't even taken home, and it became
common to see bags of bluefish fillets and even whole fish in dumpsters
throughout the mid-Atlantic and southern New England seaports.

Environmental sins often lead to unintended negative consequences. The novelty of catching a half ton of fish on rod and reel quickly wore off, and customers themselves found the waste distasteful. As they drifted away, the customer base created by the numbers game crashed even before the bluefish population did. Also, the low quality of the improperly cared-for fish convinced a whole generation of customers that bluefish are poor table fare, even though prior generations back to colonial times had generally considered bluefish to be better than salmon[2] (and they still are better, when properly bled and iced). The bluefish population may once again be on the increase, but for southern New England's charter boats, bluefish customers have become hard to find, and, in contrast to the situation when the pollock were lost, so have scapegoats.

Those involved in these travesties were not evil people. They were generally ethical in their dealings with one another and with their society, yet there was clearly an ethical void in the conduct of the Block Island charter fishery during the years of abundant pollock and bluefish. And the result was disastrous. The charter boats wasted fish, which largely wound up being thrown away, and ultimately lost not just the fisheries but also a large part of their customer base.

The Block Island pollock and bluefish charter fisheries are two very small and local examples of a colossal and worldwide ongoing disaster. We highlight them here not to castigate those involved but because these examples are little known and do not carry the political baggage of an example from the more well-known and far more widely damaging ethical deserts of modern industrial fishing. By their mundane nature, they illustrate both the breadth and the depth of the problems that have arisen in our fisheries in the absence of a moral compass, and they illustrate the critical need to take Leopold's third step, toward an ethic for our relationship to the oceans as well as the land.

So how do we actually take that third step? All ethics are based on shared assumptions, and a resource ethic must be based on assumptions about humankind and about the earth that are arrived at through a conflation of faith and reason. We propose these six assumptions as a starting point:

1. The known universe was created at a specific time, has since then been changing, and will run a course.
2. The natural world is palpable to reason. It operates under natural laws that are knowable and consistent and that we are part of.
3. All living things alter their environment (e.g., the current high level of molecular oxygen in the atmosphere was caused by photosynthetic organisms), and there is nothing inherently evil in that simple fact.
4. Humans have free will, even within the creator's plan,[3] and are the only

organisms able to make conscious decisions to alter their environment. We do not possess the power to end life on the planet, but we could end our own tenure here.[4]

5. Humans have an aesthetic sense and a need to fulfill it. As Edward O. Wilson said, "An enduring environmental ethic will aim to preserve not only the health and freedom of our species, but access to the world in which the human spirit was born."[5]

6. All living things, humans included, act in their own perceived self-interest (the basis of natural selection).

As a group, these assumptions are derived from and supported by both faith and reason, although some may lean more in one way or the other. However, taken together, they appear to bear an internal conflict in that they can be seen to justify behavior that ranges across the spectrum from altruistic to selfish. The resolution of this conflict is in the realization that altruism and self-interest lie at the two poles of our moral compass, apparently opposite but in fact conjoined. An ethical decision is guided by elements of both.

But altruistic behavior is difficult to justify except through some larger purpose. Is there a glimpse of such a larger purpose in the creation and evolution of the universe, presumed by ancient faith and now affirmed by modern cosmology? Certainly the continuous operation of all we can observe by consistent laws that are understandable to us would argue that there is. The two previously disparate worldviews, one derived from faith and the other derived from reason, no longer seem quite so incompatible. It may not yet be a comfortable marriage, but at least both now agree that we are an integral part of something far larger than ourselves. And it is now possible to answer the questions that began this essay in the affirmative without a sense of condescension.

Altruism may seem the more noble pole of our ethical compass, but taken by itself, altruism will lead us as far astray as will unrestrained self-interest. The so-called radical environmentalists fall into this error. They quixotically reject human-caused environmental alteration while ignoring the natural role of self-interest in the interactions of all living things, humans included, with one another and with their environments. Simply put, whatever our motives, our activities will be beneficial to some species and detrimental to others and will have an effect upon the planet. On the other hand, we possess the power to exert some level of control over many, if not most, of these effects through our ethical choices.

In the real world of political infighting for conflicting resource management goals, self-interest is the crux, the north-pointing pole, of our ethical compass, since altruism, unlike self-interest, is an insufficient source of motivation for most people. Leopold said, "One must make shift with things as they are," and self-interest is what ultimately must be appealed to if a third-step ethic is to be widely accepted and successfully applied to the task of preserving Wilson's "world in which the human spirit was born."

More than a half century ago, Leopold understood the interlocking nature of altruism and self-interest in ethics. He had also come to understand that a third-step ethic, relating humankind to the planet, would require practical knowledge of how the relationship works:

> All ethics so far evolved rest upon a single premise: that the individual is a member of a community of interdependent parts. His instincts prompt him to compete for his place in that community, but his ethics prompt him also to cooperate (perhaps in order that there may be a place to compete for).[6]

The key to a successful third-step ethic is truly knowing the interdependent parts, and therein lies the highest value of good science that is well done.

Knowledge, however, is of little practical importance unless others also know. The conclusions of our best science must be available and accessible and understandable. You may be on the side of the angels, but your small contribution to conserving our most precious resources is of little use if the forces of immorality are able to overwhelm your efforts through an appeal to ignorance. We must all be teachers and activists and even missionaries, though we must always guard against the arrogance of false certitude that ruins the efforts of so many present-day environmentalists and conservation organizations. It is important to be right, but it is essential also to win.

Competing self-interests can be complex, and human motivation is changeable, but wherever one's individual self-interest lies or whatever the source of one's particular motivation, an ethical compass based upon shared assumptions will generally lead to the same place. A younger fisherman whose self-interest is in building his business will make the same ethical choices as an older one whose self-interest is in making certain that his grandchildren are able to experience the sea as he has. An ethical compass based upon our six assumptions would have pointed toward decisions that could have constrained the resource-destructive and self-destructive conduct of the Block Island charter fisheries of the late 1970s and early 1980s.

The destruction of our ocean fisheries by hyperefficient industrial methods continues on a worldwide basis, with little progress toward abatement of even its worst excesses. What we now lack in the management of our ocean resources is a widely embraced ethical compass with its opposite but linked poles of altruism and self-interest. To escape this morass, we must take Leopold's third step. Shared assumptions and accepted ethical standards won't end our problems, but they will show us the way to solve those problems as they arise. With faith and reason, altruism and self-interest, finally joined we can accomplish what Leopold called our "job . . . of building receptivity into the still unlovely human mind."[7]

Chapter 13

Hunting for Spirituality: An Oxymoron?

DAVID PETERSEN

"[*Spiritual* and *sacred* are terms that refer] to those inexplicable relationships and processes that govern existence. There is no reason
sacredness cannot be manifest in *any* circumstances whatever, or in all
circumstances, even if some are more numinous than others."

—Paul Shepard

As one who makes an earnest (if not always successful) effort to think (if not
always act) objectively, I've never faced a more emotionally contentious challenge than substantiating and articulating the deep personal spirituality inherent to authentic hunting. So personal, complex, and troubling is this topic that
few hunters feel comfortable even talking about it. And to strident, moralistic
anti-hunters, any mention of spirituality in hunting elicits outraged howls of
"Oxymoron!"

Further complicating the discussion is that so many people today are
uneasy with the lexicon of secular spirituality and feel reluctant to discuss or
even think about spiritual issues outside the culturally codified bounds of a
liturgical setting. Additionally, the current plagues of pathological evangelism
and New Age insipidae have tainted the very word *spirituality* with the stain of
muddled metaphysical mush. For these reasons and more, spirituality is not a
topic you often hear openly discussed around hunters' campfires . . . yet
there it often abides.

To sort out the truth, we must begin by recognizing that hunters are not a
species apart. Hunters are people—fathers and mothers, daughters and sons,
saints and sinners alike. If a person is a slob hunter, he's predictably a slob in
every regard: work, family, community, traffic, even what passes in his life for

183

spirituality. There's nothing in the act of hunting that promotes moral erosion or incites blood-lust, as hunting's harshest critics, wishing to believe the worst, choose to believe. Rather than creating personalities and worldviews, hunting merely reflects them, good and bad, as shaped by the overarching human environment. In the end, everything turns on attitude and expectation: What you bring to the hunt shapes not only how you hunt but also what you take away.

What I bring to the hunt is a visceral desire to play my naturally evolved, ecologically sound, and (therefore) naturally moral role as an active participant in the most intimate workings of wild nature. I want to live, so far as possible, the way humans are meant to live. I want to nourish my body with clean, lean, wild meat, the food that made us human. And I want the palpably spiritual bonding with Earth and the great round of life and death and sacramental (as opposed to commercial) trophism that, for myself and so many others, only hunting can provide. When I get out there and get slowed down and tuned in enough to perceive and appreciate even the subtlest elements of natural creation—a warm mosaic of lichen on cold granite, a velvety fuzz of moss on a rotting log, the symphonic purling of a mountain stream, the sight and sound of one leaf falling—when I've got that good old "savage" connection going, I'm absolutely aglow with the joy of life, and unafraid of death. Without the intercession of clergy, shaman, or psychotropic drug, I have stepped through the cultural wall and into a primordially sacred realm. I have entered heaven on Earth.

Indeed, any postmortem paradise that lacked bugling September elk, flame-gold aspens rattling in a crisp October breeze, scarlet-throated trout leaping for joy in swift, sparkling water, the wild, hungry howls of wolves and coyotes, the preternatural wailing of loons on a moon-mirrored lake, the shotgun slap of a beaver's tail on a secret mountain pond, the humbling aliveness that comes with the possibility of meeting a grizzly bear or mountain lion along some shadowed forest trail, the gritty ecstasy of love on the rocks—any so-called heaven lacking such distinctly earthly blessings as these would be pure hell for me.

Yet why—I'm sometimes asked, and fairly so—why can't thoughtful, nature-loving people attain this level of neo-animistic spirituality just by watching, or perhaps photographing, wildlife, without looking to kill? It's a good, hard question. And my instinctive answer is . . . instinct. To paraphrase English writer James Hamilton-Paterson, a camera gets in the way of the hunter's eye, which is to say that humans evolved as hunters and hunted, not spectators. In the pragmatically poetic words of preeminent human ecologist

Paul Shepard, "Wildness cannot be captured on film; wildness is what I kill and eat because I, too, am wild."

Wild, that is, by natural design and thus by instinctive inclination. In a word, biophilia—defined by Yale University sociobiologist Stephen R. Kellert as "an innate need to relate deeply and intimately with the vast spectrum of life about us."[1]

Toward explicating the seemingly counterintuitive connection between the innate human inclination toward biophilia and the innate human predilection for hunting, Ontario biologist and hunting ethicist Michael Buss calls our attention to the fact that authentic hunting "requires a concentrated searching and observing of the environment. To see the environment through the practiced eyes of a hunter is to identify not only the *characters* in nature, as a naturalist might, but also to experience the 'emotions' of those characters, without giving them unrealistic, human or Disneylike qualities."[2]

As restated by Stephen Kellert, among authentic hunters—whom he terms "naturalistic" hunters—in "pursuing the prey, not only [are] its habits and abilities learned, but a vicarious sense [is] achieved of how it [experiences] its environment."[3]

Moreover, authentic hunters *do* rejoice, as our critics so often urge, in "just watching without looking to kill." As we always have. "Foraging peoples," Paul Shepard tells us, "typically spend thousands of hours every year pondering and studying the animals around them." And modern naturalistic hunters are no different. I spend more than ten months of every twelve "just watching" wildlife, jubilantly "pondering and studying the animals around" me, never once thinking of killing. Like the seasonally prescribed ritual it is, hunting has its bounds. And even when hunting, I sneak and peek and watch in wonder for weeks, while the killing, if and when it comes, kills only moments. Nor am I anomalous. It's precisely this authentic hunter's "minding of the environment," says Shepard, "the fluid quality of his attention and the habits of alertness and acuity, that link him in participation with all of creation."

As put by Spanish philosopher José Ortega y Gasset and restated by Shepard, Kellert, and Buss, the authentic hunter is "the alert man."

Sniffing a bit further along this same trail of logic—suggesting that the authentic hunter is uncommonly comfortable and alert in nature, thus observing more, thus feeling more, thus self-facilitating a profoundly biophilic affection for wildness—Aldo Leopold cleverly points out: "The deer hunter habitually watches the next bend; the duck hunter watches the skyline; the bird hunter watches the dog; the nonhunter does not watch. When the deer hunter sits down he sits where he can see ahead, and with his back to something. The duck hunter sits where he can see overhead, and behind something. The non-hunter sits where he is comfortable."

Yet beyond activating our innate biophilic affection for nature, Shepard concludes that authentic hunting also facilitates authentic spirituality, since it "brings into play intense emotions and a sense of the mysteries of our existence, a cathartic and mediating transformation."

Just so: In wild nature, within and without, I regularly find a depth of spiritual solace and an invigorating reaffirmation of cosmic sanity that I rarely find in the human-made world, including especially Western culture's Messianic Spirituality, Inc. In sum, the fresh-air sanity of natural wildness is our best, perhaps our only, antidote to the suffocating cultural pathology we euphemize as civilization.

Certainly, hunting is not for everyone. As Dan Crockett, editor of *Bugle,* the publication of the Rocky Mountain Elk Foundation, acknowledges, "Choosing to hunt raises no one to higher ground. It merely opens a pathway into a different land."[4] Whether and how far that pathway is followed are private matters. Yet for those who choose to stalk this ancient trail, authentic hunting remains the surest and most natural possible path into the sacred primal grove of pragmatic, biophilic spirituality—because it's the same well-worn way we took to becoming human.

◆ ◆ ◆

Until recently, I never thought of myself as a "spiritual person," certainly not in any ecclesiastic or vernacular sense of the term. Like television commentator Bill Moyers, I'm firmly of a mind that "a lot of religion gives God a bad name," no matter the religion or god in question. But in the midst of my late middle years, a profound spirituality has bitten into my being. To put a name to it, I've become an "Earthiest" (Edward Abbey), in that I "stand *for* what I stand *on*" (Wendell Berry).

An Earthiest—an original Abbeyism, so far as I know—is nothing more or less than a pragmatic neo-animist. And animism, I propose, is the ultimate spiritual reality. While nature—and therefore animism—is palpable, logical, and utterly comprehendible on any number of levels, "God," by definition, is unknowable. Physicist Paul Davies addresses this critical distinction: "To invoke God as a blanket explanation of the unexplained, is to make God the friend of ignorance. If God is to be found, it must surely be through what we discover about the world, not what we fail to discover."[5]

In other words, messianic religion, because of its absolute self-certainty, is, a priori, a failure of the spirit. "If a man will begin with certainties," cautions Francis Bacon, ironically presaging what we now call the scientific method, "he shall end in doubts; but if he will be content to begin with doubts, he shall end in certainties."

"In our other-worldliness," says bio-philosopher C. H. D. Clarke (the Canadian Aldo Leopold), "we have lost the feeling of man's oneness with the Earth, which modern faiths do not deny, but which early chthonic [zoomorphic, animistic, Earth-centered, human-humbling] faiths saw most clearly."

"In indigenous cultures around the world," professes psychotherapist Ralph Metzner,

> the natural is regarded as the realm of spirit and the sacred; the natural *is* the spiritual. From this follows an attitude of respect, a desire to maintain a balanced relationship, and an instinctive understanding of the need for considering future generations and the future health of the ecosystem—in short, sustainability. Recognizing and respecting worldviews and spiritual practices different from our own is perhaps the best antidote to the West's fixation on the life-destroying dissociation between spirit and nature.[6]

Commenting on this same topic in his weirdly wonderful book *Bone Games,* Rob Schultheis notes that when humanity lost the hunter-gatherer lifestyle, we lost the deepest spirituality we've ever known: "Something in us died: mojo, obeah, mana, Buddhahood, audacious rapture . . . dead. Dead and buried in an unmarked grave somewhere back there. Our ancestors knew more than we do."[7]

Indeed, according to Paul Shepard, our hunter-gatherer ancestors not only knew more than we do but also were more fully human—which assertion, of course, demands a definition of humanity.

◆ ◆ ◆

According to ethnographic research, animism has always been the universal cosmology of unadulterated hunting-gathering peoples worldwide, and it remains so. Likewise, neo-animism—Earthiesm, if you will—plays actively in the cosmologies of all authentic hunters today, whether they acknowledge it or not. As Aldo Leopold points out:

> Hunting is not merely an acquired taste: the instinct that finds delight in the sight and pursuit of game is bred into the very fiber of the race. . . . The love of hunting is almost a psychological

characteristic. A man may not care for golf and still be human. But the man who does not like to see, hunt, photograph, or otherwise outwit birds or animals is hardly normal. He is supercivilized, and I for one do not know how to deal with him.

Unlike the swooning disciples of some sky-bound beliefs, I have never been elevated by nature hunting and its attendant Earthiesm to the hypnotic heights of "holy rolling" or babbling in tongues, night-tripping with space aliens, or perceiving the face of Jesus in a fried tortilla. Yet the intensely emotional spirituality of hunting as personal participation in wild nature—culminating necessarily, at least now and again, in the blood-sealed sacrament of killing and consuming corporeal wildness—often moves me to tears.

Which admission should lead thoughtful critics to ask, How can you claim to love the same lovely creatures you work so passionately, even joyfully, to kill?

Architect Siegfried Giedion, lecturing at Harvard University, tackled this touchy topic head-on when he asked rhetorically: How is it possible

> that primeval man both killed and venerated the animal? [To comprehend this apparent irony] we have to forget our present attitudes toward the sacred. With primitive men the sacred had a twofold meaning. It included both the holy and the profane [secular]. Animals were simultaneously objects of adoration, life-giving food, and hunted quarry. This two-fold significance of the animal as object of worship and source of nourishment is an outcome of a mentality which did not confine the sacred to the hereafter. For them the sacred and profane were inseparable.[8]

And among authentic or naturalistic hunters, they remain just so today— sacred and secular, love and longing, life and death and rebirth—joyously inseparable. From my intimate and long-considered perspective, it is those who stand on the outside, unwilling or unable to comprehend this sacred duality, who lack spirituality; not those who, through active participation, are consumed by it. Does the wolf not love the caribou? And does she not undertake her hunts with joy? And does not the caribou, in his deepest phylogenetic heart and soul, love the wolf as well? It is the wolf that keeps the caribou strong, advises native wisdom, referring to the predatory mechanism of selective culling. This is not to say that wolves and other predators consciously select marginal or supernumerary members of a prey population for culling. Rather, they catch and kill those individuals that, for whatever reason, prove easiest to catch and kill. And what works for the wolf in the short run works for the caribou in the long. As Robinson Jeffers poetically declares:

> What but the wolf's tooth whittled so fine
> The fleet limbs of the antelope.

Without the selective genetic education of ongoing predation, wolf would not be wolf, caribou and antelope would be neither caribou nor antelope, and humans would still be apish fructivores. Indeed, without predation, nothing would even be.

◆ ◆ ◆

Current scientific knowledge suggests that humankind started down the long, winding path to sapience some 6 million years ago, when we and the chimps split from a common forebear. Across all that gaping void of time, we were gatherers and, increasingly, hunters: predatory omnivores, bipedal bears. By comparison, we've been farmers and herders for only 10,000 years—less than 1 percent of our species' tenure by even the most modest of informed estimates. And as genetics and comparative biology testify, 10,000 years is by no means long enough for a species-specific DNA pattern, or genome—which, according to informed consensus, changes in humans on average by only about 1 to 2 percent per 100,000 years—to have seriously begun adapting to the radically altered social and physical environment we've wrought for ourselves in that same brief interval. Were our ancient, instinctive needs for predatory omnivory (and the diet, exercise, lifeway, and cosmology those needs imply) not so deeply etched in our human being—were it merely something we once did along the road to becoming human, rather than what we *are*—hunting would have long ago been wholly abandoned and forgotten.

But such is not the case. As Shepard notes, "in defiance of mass culture, tribalism constantly resurfaces." And this despite centuries of agricultural civilization and sundry messianic religions' genocidal oppression of animistic tribalism via a concerted effort to bring about what novelist-philosopher Daniel Quinn (*Ishmael*) calls the "great forgetting."

While humanity's biophilic, animistic inclinations remain genetically resistant to cultural obliteration, such "innate tendencies" are not so much hardwired instinct as they are meat for what environmental psychologist Roger Ulrich terms "biologically prepared learning." Thus, although human infants across all cultures are born with a keen interest in animals and other natural life, those innate biophilic hungers must be culturally nourished in order to prosper and grow. Contrarily, in all urban civilizations, children's biophilic inclinations are largely ignored, neglected, sublimated, and increasingly supplanted by anthropocentrism (on Earth as it is in heaven) and by increasingly virtual replications of nature for commercial gain. Thus is the willful destruction of wild nature—which biophilic animism would never allow—recklessly ingrained in our children, culturally codified and morally sanctioned throughout the modern "civilized" world.

Meanwhile, those among us whose "biologically prepared learning" experiences have been rich enough to overcome cultural subversion, whose innate biophilic tendencies remain intact and thriving and who consequently fight to help protect natural wildness or, more daring yet, insist on remaining active players in wildness via authentic hunting—we who have not forgotten—are defiled by industrial culture as tree-huggers, elitists, and troublemakers in the first instance, barbarians, savages, and Bambi killers in the latter.

For my part, so be it. "To embrace the mass religions or ideologies of the present," advises Wyoming hunter and poet C. L. Rawlins, "we must first deny what we know in our very bones: how the world works." And how the world works is through an endless sacred cycle of digestion. All things born must die and, in one way or another, be consumed. To be or not to be is *not* the question, but *when*. The reality that life feeds on death is ineluctable, undeniable, even for the strictest of vegans, whom hunting ethicist Ted Kerasote exposes as well-meaning but hypocritical "fossil-fuel vegetarians."

To wit: Merely by purchasing vegetables grown on industrialized farms that have displaced former wildlife habitat—veggies that are chemically fertilized, plowed, planted, picked, packed, and transported long distances at great expense of fossil fuels while displacing more wildlife habitat with highways and other transport routes, and then sold in markets that devour more wildlife habitat yet—even the kindest-hearted vegans, exactly like the rest of us, must accept personal responsibility for the deaths of incalculable multitudes of life, large as well as small. Rodents and ground-nesting birds and even fawns—the iconic Bambi—are cut to bloody shreds by the diesel-belching machinery of industrial farming while elk and deer and myriad others, millions of wild lives annually, are smeared grotesquely across railroad tracks and runways and highways by vegetable-transport trains and planes, semitrailer trucks, and, occasionally, vegan-driven sport utility vehicles.

And, of course, we must consider the vegetables themselves—a wholly different tribe from our own, granted, but animate if not sentient beings no less: lives that end so that ours can continue. Thus the life-and-death dynamic persists even in veganism, if not so forthrightly. To trot out one of Paul Shepard's more colorfully cranky aphorisms:

The human digestive system and physiology cannot be fooled by squeezing a diet from a moral. We are omnivores: our intestines and teeth attest to this fact. . . . Vegetarianism, like creationism, simply reinvents human biology to suit an ideology. There is no phylogenetic felicity in it.

Phylogeny is the evolutionary history of a species, compressed into a common genome. Veganism is felicitous to the phylogeny of no omnivorous species, jutting like a bent spoke from the great, grinding wheel of biological life. In contrast, nothing could be more in tune with nature and thus more moral, sane, and, I argue, sacred than to follow our omnivorous instincts, needs, and "God-given" talents as human predators, openly and gratefully acknowledging, while personally participating in, the deaths that go to nourish our lives. In the attempt to accomplish such animistic humility, I propose, a far higher percentage of true hunters succeed than do vegans—while most among us, as supermarket carnivores, don't give a damn.

A bumper sticker piously proclaims, "If it has a face, I won't eat it." Yet if we look closely enough, *everything* has a face. As traditional Eskimo wisdom reminds us, all food consists of souls.

Nor is it merely a question of diet. As countrywoman, longtime vegetarian, and naturalist-philosopher Barbara Dean writes of her northern California rural environs:

> The interplay of life and death is everywhere here: in a post-season fly caught and eaten in a spider web above my desk; in the deer bones, freshly gnawed in the canyon across the stream; in the oak leaves, fallen and now decaying in a mat behind the house. I have been a vegetarian for more than twenty years, which I once thought exempted me from the violence that accompanies the securing of food. But a few weeks of working in the garden my first summer here . . . did away with that comforting illusion. . . . I soon grew uncomfortable with the notion that even a berry might not have a life. Each death is clearly part of sustaining another life, and, just as clearly, my own survival depends on being part of this chain every day in one way or another. Most of the time, I understand this inescapable reality well enough to justify my own role. But sometimes the darkness at the heart of that logic breaks through and I face what seems an intolerable truth. . . . I will never know enough about the profound complexities of life on

Earth to be sure that I perform this act—that I kill—with moral certainty. The conviction of my human inadequacy expands within me. And then, somehow, from somewhere, another emotion sweeps over me, and I am enveloped by a sweet and transforming humility, a feeling so unexpected that the experience can only be called a moment of grace. This feeling, which transcends the hunt and yet is utterly rooted in its essence, brings a sense of resolution to the impossible dilemmas with which I have been wrestling. I finally understand that humility is the key. Only through humility can the soul make peace with the terrible necessity of survival.

Viewed in this eloquently insightful light, we're morally and logically led to ask: Who is the more admirable? The naturalistic hunter who feels a deep and sincere (biophilic, neo-animistic) sense of gratitude for the lives she takes? (And what can we call this but humility?) Or the man who wears his veganism as a mask of detached aloofness from his own wild human nature?

Vegetarianism, arguably to the ascetic extreme of veganism, is a valid moral choice—and certainly a healthy choice when measured against our culture's gluttonous consumption of cruelly produced, environmentally destructive, cholesterol-larded, hormone-poisoned domestic meat "product." Yet—and here's my beef with evangelical veganism—vegetarianism is not the *only* morally valid choice for spiritual and physical health. For vegans to pretend otherwise, viewing themselves as hovering, angel-like, above and beyond the bloody sea of death-dealing life, is self-deluded hypocrisy. Vegans are merely strict vegetarians; they are not saints. (Hitler, you know, was a "gentle" vegetarian.)

No body rides for free. No thing gets out alive.

And when you get at it right, it's a perfectly sublime arrangement.

Says Pulitzer Prize–winning poet and roadkill hunter Gary Snyder: "To acknowledge that each of us at the table will eventually be part of the meal is not just being 'realistic.' It is allowing the sacred to enter and accepting the sacramental aspect of our shaky temporary personal being."

"Primitive" peoples knew this. Wild animals know this. And so do authentic, naturalistic hunters.

One of the most significant, if potentially baffling, scenes in Alaskan anthropologist Richard Nelson's award-winning memoir *The Island Within* comes when a Koyukon subsistence hunter voices the animistic conundrum, "Remember, each animal knows way more than you do." In addition to instinct—that magical ability to interpret and utilize the finest intricacies of landscape, weather, fellow creatures, and more—what every animal "knows" is its place in the great web of life. For millions of years, humans knew this, too. A few still do.

"We be of one blood, ye and I," Mowgli calls in greeting to his fellow jungle creatures—even as they busy themselves (politely off-camera) killing and devouring one another, even as many among them would hungrily kill and devour yummy young Mowgli, given the literary license to do so—with Bambi for dessert.

This is the real world. And in operating therein, I have been helped by authentic, naturalistic, spiritual hunting not only to accept the biological necessity of life-giving death, my own especially included, but also to applaud its practicality and embrace it as sacred.

♦ ♦ ♦

Each September, after I have hunted hard for as long as a month, finally, at some perfectly unpredictable moment, an animal appears—heart-poundingly close, uncharacteristically calm, insouciant. At such magical moments, it's easy to understand why traditional foragers worldwide believe animals sometimes "give themselves" to hunters who respect them. This animistic concept of cooperative, altruistic all-life unity is expressed beautifully in Native American poet Leslie Marmon Silko's "Deer Song":

> I will go with you
>
> because you love me
>
> while I die.

In words less lyrical yet movingly poignant in their bio-spiritual insight, José Ortega y Gasset suggests that "the hunt is not something which happens to the animal by chance; rather, in the instinctive depths of his nature [the prey] has already foreseen the hunter."[9]

I do not know. Yet here before me now stands the wapiti. Suddenly, all the weeks of effort—all the hours of sleep missed, all the miles hiked and mountains climbed, all the rain and hail and cold endured, all the elements that combine to make an authentic hunt—merge toward the ancient, inescapable denouement. As I reenact the essential drama of human history, my universe shrinks to a single hair, low and forward on the huge auburn chest. Arm and shoulder muscles flex, bending the bow. When all feels right, fingers relax and arrow leaps away.

The elk, unaware of its lurking predator, reacts as if stung by a wasp, bolting off a few steps—and then it stops and gazes calmly about, flicking its ears at flies. Does it even know?

I know. And like a man too long underwater, I think my chest must soon explode with the passion of it all. "Please," I whisper, "die fast." As if granting my plea, the great deer sways, stumbles, and falls. Soon comes the susurrous release of a final breath: breath, anima, soul—spirit leaping away from flesh.

After waiting and watching for a while, I ease up close and touch the still form with my bow—it does not react. Dropping to my knees, I peer into the dark, inscrutable eyes. And in those mirrored orbs is reflected my own fragility, my own impermanence, my own death looming. To not feel such unity of all life and all death in such a circumstance as this, one would have to be spiritually numb—as, tragically, far too many modern, make-believe, so-called hunters in fact are. Although many people, hunters among them, do not understand, this *is* a sacred moment.

"Life," says Ortega y Gasset, "is a terrible conflict, a grandiose and atrocious confluence. Hunting submerges [us] deliberately in that formidable mystery and therefore contains something of religious rite and emotion in which homage is paid to what is divine, transcendent in the laws of Nature."

Barbara Dean concurs, noting that

> in the moment of the kill, the hunter stands at the intersection of the most profound of opposites—life and death. He knows not only that those opposites are linked—indeed that one becomes the other—but also that his life depends on being part of the transformation, part of the ultimate, mysterious, ongoing communion of all life. There are other ways to experience life's Oneness, but I wonder if this truth is ever so immediate, so palpable, so full of feeling as in the hunter's act.

Distracting me from my moody musings, out in the silent woods and not so far away, a loud, shrill bugle sounds—followed by the brittle popping and cracking of heavy hooves crushing deadfall and the bemused, birdlike chirps of elk cows and calves. Life flows on. The cows among that little band are already pregnant, or soon will be. And if the winter is hard—I rationalize, beholding the dead bull before me—there'll be one fewer elk mouth competing for scarce winter browse . . .

. . . Down there in the valleys, where the byways bristle with buff young cyclists on toys "worth" many times the annual incomes of the Third World workers who made them . . . where the highways rumble with graying self-styled "outlaws" on Harleys "worth" more than my self-built cabin. . . . Down there in the valleys, where a fresh floodtide of urban refugees washes ashore each summer: searchers, seeking shelter from the raging human storm, many passionate anti-hunters among them—demolishing old-growth forests, bull-dozing new roads, building new homes, and fencing new hobbyhorse pastures; blindly displacing and potentially starving wapiti and other winter-weary wildlife in a desperate grab for "the good life" . . . even as they destroy the very values they pretend to have come in search of . . . even while condemn-ing "my kind" as knuckle-dragging anachronisms.

The little band of elk moves on. Silence returns to the forest and I return to the task at hand.

Like other natural predators, I suffer no simpering sympathy for my prey; I find no guilt, if no pleasure either, in the killing. Women's studies professor Mary Zeiss Stange writes:

> Far from being a mark of moral failure, this absence of guilt . . . suggests a highly developed moral consciousness, in tune with the realities of the life-death-life process of the natural world. The sim-plistic analogy of hunting to such forms of male aggression as rape and warfare breaks down at precisely this point, where a kinship is perceived between the hunter and the hunted.[10]

No guilt or sympathy indeed. But my empathy is gut-churning. As I gaze at this gorgeous wild beast I have so eagerly killed, my eyes cloud with tears, which I accept without shame. Yet at the same time I am positively electrified, buzzing with Ortega y Gasset's "mystical agitation." This too, I accept.

Nor am I alone. Such powerful polarities of emotion are common among authentic hunters, shaping a double-edged metaphor for the contradictions of life itself. Paul Shepard explains: "The successful hunt is a solemn event, and yet it is done in a spirit of joy. It puts modern man for a moment in vital rap-port with a universe from which civilization tends to separate him in an illu-sion of superiority and independence."

After thanking the fallen elk—note that I thank the *animal* for its life, not some cloud-riding Big Daddy who looks suspiciously like me—I hone my knife and begin the gritty work of making meat: unzip the heavy hide, open the bulging belly, plunge both arms in to the shoulders and struggle by Braille to free a hundred pounds of steaming organs, which, when exposed like some cosmic crossword puzzle, I ritually inspect and attempt to name, as if taking inventory of my own inner self. As always, I'm awed by the rock-hard muscu-larity of the great, heavy heart.

Elk heart . . . hart's blood . . . heart's blood . . . warm and wet on trembling hands.

As I work, I recall a story related to me by an Alaskan subsistence hunter of considerable experience. Recently, he said, a man who'd lived his entire young life along the ultra-urban California coast moved to bush Alaska. Although hunting had never been a part of his concreted life—in fact, without knowing anything of it, he thought he hated hunting—he now found it essential for physical survival, since the nearest market was two expensive hours away by air, with no roads. So, reluctantly resigned to necessity, the greenhorn set out one day to hunt for his winter's meat. By midday, he'd seen no moose and was tired and very hungry. When a hare appeared, he killed it, skinned it, built a fire, and cooked and ate it on the spot. Later, relating all this to my informant, the greenhorn stated solemnly, "It was the first *real* thing I've ever done in my life."

Just so.

By the time I'm finished—two hours it takes—darkness is threatening and I barely have strength enough left to stumble down the mountain and home. Before I go, I divide the quartered elk carcass between four huge cotton bags, which I've been lugging in my pack for weeks. By dragging the heavy bags a ways upwind of the odoriferous gut pile, I hope to hoard "my" meat from my fellow forest carnivores. They—the bears, coyotes, foxes, eagles, ravens, magpies, and more—will rejoice in the bounty of viscera and marrow-rich bones: the traditional offering.

Tomorrow, my hunting buddy Erica and I will make two slow trips up and down this mountain—a long and physically brutal day—to backpack out the two hundred pounds of deboned meat. A job of work it is, and I love it all: like building my own cabin, be it ever so humble; like getting in my winter's wood, all ten cords and more, winter after winter; like gathering wild mushrooms, berries, nuts, onions, and red clover flowers (the latter for a delicious and restful antioxidant tea). All such ancient, positively self-serving, inherently ritualistic chores are good work—"karma work," if you will—in that they exercise the spirit as well as the body. Unlike a city friend's five-year-old son, who recently felt compelled to ask, "Daddy, who killed this chicken we're eating?" I *know* where the meat on my plate comes from. In perfect parallel, I know as well where the radiant heat that winter-warms my cabin comes from, and in each and every case, at exactly what costs to all concerned—to me and my morality; to the elk, the tree, the ecology. Taken with an open-eyed attitude of gratitude, as it is by all authentic hunters, each meal of self-got wild meat, like each hand-split log fed to the hungry stove, is at once precious memory, animistic sacrament, and caloric consummation of the great endless round of life-giving death. As Colorado poet Art Goodtimes would have it:

Spirit leaping, from shape to shape.

In her insightful introduction to the most visually stunning book of 1998, *The Art of Thomas Aquinas Daly,* New York scholar Cassandra Langer reminds us: "Disguise the matter as we will, there is no question that throughout our history we have identified the spiritual with nature. [Traditional] rites of initiation teach the lesson of the essential oneness of the individual with the cosmos."[11]

Today we live in a human-made world of devastated wildness, monomaniacal materialism, unconscionable consumption, and weirdly *un*natural spiritual paradigms. Yet amid all this ugly ruin, for those to whom its multimillennial tradition still calls out, the hunt, pursued with an animistic, biophilic sense of unity, reverence, and humility, remains a meaningful rite of passage linking culture and nature, acknowledging and reconfirming the ancient "lesson of the essential oneness of the individual with the cosmos."

And that cosmos, our cosmos, for all palpable purposes, is our own sweet Earth. Indeed, to paraphrase Abbey, this world—of golden sunlight and eager flesh, of life and death and heart-cracking beauty—is the only world we can ever know. And plenty good enough. As Stephen Kellert so cleanly lays it out, "there's a greater richness of life right here on planet Earth, our planet, than in all the rest of the known universe combined."

As earthlings, ours is an ancient, blood-bonded synergy with natural wildness, forged across thousands of generations of eating and being eaten by wild animals, thinking and dreaming and praying wild animals, striving through art, dance, story, drama, song, mask, ritual, and the hunt to *be* wild animals. Thus, in the beginning and for so very long, were the human world and worldview universally, cosmically, zoomorphic.

Then came the Fall, as metaphorically chronicled in Genesis, from relatively paradisiacal (perhaps never quite noble, yet compared with today's agracultural paradigm, relatively paradisiacal) foraging in a nature-tended Garden of Eden—down, down—into the bottomless pit of sedentary, slave-making, increasingly smug and smoggy civilization. And with that tragic if inevitable Fall, more than 99 percent of human history, experience, and wisdom was discarded, purged, dogmatically disdained—if not wholly lost.

We cannot escape the succinct wisdom of poet e. e. cummings when he warns, "A world of made is not a world of born." All cultures are made. And ours is made to mindlessly worship technological efficiency: fast, easy, and certain. To transport this urban paradigm into what should be the challenging, meditative, and magically uncertain adventure of the hunt is to trivialize one of life's most profoundly beautiful and—for those blessed and burdened with hunters' hearts—spiritually invigorating endeavors.

Our prelapsarian ancestors all were hunters. And the comparatively gentle, infinitely sustainable lifeway these so-called savage forebears enjoyed for thousands of millennia was informed by the most positively pragmatic religion Earth has ever known—spontaneous, universal, ever adapting and reinventing itself in tribal foraging cultures everywhere. As defined by Richard Nelson, the animism of tribal hunters embraces and unites all of nature as "spiritual, conscious, and subject to rules of respectful behavior." In modern so-called sport of the type Stephen Kellert classifies as "dominionistic/sport hunting," as in modern so-called civilization, this ancient and honorable heritage is not only forgotten but openly mocked. For hunting and civilization to survive—for hunting and civilization to deserve to survive—this must change.

If all those posing so poorly as hunters today could only be awakened to the transcendent rewards of *true* hunting—the trip, not the destination; process, not product; reciprocity, not domination—all of hunting's actual and image problems would simply disappear, since no hunter would want to cheat or take shortcuts and all would be active ambassadors of biophilic responsibility. At the same time and consequently, all but the most implacable critics of hunting would be disarmed.

And, more broadly, if all those posing so poorly as humans today could somehow be awakened to the joyful spiritual rewards of simple, humble, Earth-centered spirituality—what a marvelous world this could be! As expressed in haiku by that footloose Buddhist sachem Layman P'ang:

> How wondrous, how mysterious!
> I carry fuel.
> I draw water.

In the end, we find spirituality only where we seek it. And only *if* we seek it. Authentic hunters seek and find living spirit in aspen grove and piney wood; in upland meadow and brushy bottom; in the musical murmur of mountain water and the glorious stench of rutting elk . . . and occasionally, ultimately, naturally, in bloodstained hands and hearts.

There is no oxymoron here.

Chapter 14

The Idea of a Local Economy

Wendell Berry

Let us begin by assuming what appears to be true: that the so-called environmental crisis is now pretty well established as a fact of our age. The problems of pollution, species extinction, loss of wilderness, loss of farmland, and loss of topsoil may still be ignored or scoffed at, but they are not denied. Concern for these problems has acquired a certain standing, a measure of discussability, in the media and in some scientific, academic, and religious institutions.

This is good, of course; obviously, we can't hope to solve these problems without an increase in public awareness and concern. But in an age burdened with publicity, we have to be aware also that as issues rise into popularity they rise also into the danger of oversimplification. To speak of this danger is especially necessary in confronting the destructiveness of our relationship with nature, which is the result, in the first place, of gross oversimplification.

The "environmental crisis" has happened because the human household or economy is in conflict at almost every point with the household of nature. We have built our household on the assumption that the natural household is simple and can be simply used. We have assumed increasingly over the past five hundred years that nature is merely a supply of "raw materials" and that we may safely possess those materials merely by taking them. This taking, as our technical means have increased, has involved always less reverence or respect, less gratitude, less local knowledge, and less skill. Our methodologies of land use have strayed from our old sympathetic attempts to imitate natural processes and have come more and more to resemble the methodology of mining, even as mining itself has become more technologically powerful and more brutal.

And so we will be wrong if we attempt to correct what we perceive as "environmental" problems without correcting the economic oversimplification that caused them. This oversimplification is now a matter either of corporate

199

behavior or of behavior under the influence of corporate behavior. This is sufficiently clear to many of us. What is not sufficiently clear, perhaps to any of us, is the extent of our complicity, as individuals and especially as individual consumers, in the behavior of the corporations.

What has happened is that most people in the United States, and apparently most people in the "developed" world, have given proxies to the corporations to produce and provide *all* their food, clothing, and shelter. Moreover, they are rapidly giving proxies to corporations or governments to provide entertainment, education, child care, care of the sick and the elderly, and many other kinds of "service" that once were carried on informally and inexpensively by individuals or households or communities. Our major economic practice, in short, is to delegate the practice to others.

The danger now is that those who are concerned will believe that the solution to the "environmental crisis" can be merely political—that the problems, being large, can be solved by large solutions generated by a few people to whom we will give our proxies to police the economic proxies that we have already given. The danger, in other words, is that people will think they have made a sufficient change if they have altered their "values," or had a "change of heart," or experienced a "spiritual awakening," and that such a change in passive consumers will necessarily cause appropriate changes in the public experts, politicians, and corporate executives to whom they have granted their political and economic proxies.

The trouble with this is that a proper concern for nature and our use of nature must be practiced not by our proxy-holders but by ourselves. A change of heart or of values without a practice is only another pointless luxury of a passively consumptive way of life. The "environmental crisis," in fact, can be solved only if people, individually and in their communities, recover responsibility for their thoughtlessly given proxies. If people begin the effort to take back into their own power a significant portion of their economic responsibility, then their inevitable first discovery will be that the "environmental crisis" is no such thing. It is not a crisis of our environs or surroundings; it is a crisis of our lives as individuals, as family members, as community members, and as citizens. We have an "environmental crisis" because *we* have consented to an economy in which by eating, drinking, working, resting, traveling, and enjoying ourselves we are destroying the natural, the God-given, world.

◆ ◆ ◆

We live, as we must sooner or later recognize, in an era of sentimental economics and, consequently, of sentimental politics. Sentimental communism holds, in effect, that everybody and everything should suffer for the good of "the many," who, though miserable in the present, will be happy in the future for exactly the same reasons that they are miserable in the present.

Sentimental capitalism is not so different from sentimental communism, as the corporate and political powers claim to suppose. Sentimental capitalism holds, in effect, that everything small, local, private, personal, natural, good, and beautiful must be sacrificed in the interest of the "free market" and the great corporations, which will bring unprecedented security and happiness to "the many"—in, of course, the future.

These forms of political economy may be described as sentimental because they depend absolutely upon a political faith for which there is no justification and because they issue a cold check on the virtue of political and economic rulers. They seek, that is, to preserve the gullibility of the people by appealing to a fund of political virtue that does not exist. Communism and "free-market" capitalism both are modern versions of oligarchy. In their propaganda, both justify violent means by good ends, which always are put beyond reach by the violence of the means. The trick is to define the end vaguely—"the greatest good of the greatest number" or "the benefit of the many"—and keep it at a distance. For example, the United States government's agricultural policy, or nonpolicy, since 1952 has mainly consented to the farmers' predicament of high costs and low prices; it has never envisioned or advocated in particular the prosperity of farmers or farmland but has only promised "cheap food" to consumers and "survival" to the "larger and more efficient" farmers who supposedly could adapt to and endure the attrition of high costs and low prices. And after each inevitable wave of farm failures and the inevitable enlargement of the destitution and degradation of the countryside, there have been the inevitable reassurances from government propagandists and university experts that American agriculture was now more efficient and that everybody would be better off in the future.

The fraudulence of these oligarchic forms of economy is in their principle of displacing whatever good they recognize (as well as their debts) from the present to the future. Their success depends upon persuading people, first, that whatever they have now is no good, and, second, that the promised good is certain to be achieved in the future. This obviously contradicts the principle— common, I believe, to all the religious traditions—that if ever we are going to do good to one another, then the time to do it is now; we are to receive no reward for promising to do it in the future. And both communism and capitalism have found such principles to be a great embarrassment. If you are presently occupied in destroying every good thing in sight in order to do good in the future, it is inconvenient to have people saying things like "Love thy neighbor as thyself" or "Sentient beings are numberless; I vow to save them." Communists and capitalists alike, "liberal" capitalists and "conservative" capitalists alike, have needed to replace religion with some form of determinism so that they can say to their victims: "I'm doing this because I can't do otherwise. It is not my fault. It is inevitable." The wonder is how often organized religion has gone along with this lie.

The idea of an economy based upon several kinds of ruin may seem a contradiction in terms, but in fact such an economy is possible, as we see. It is possible, however, on one implacable condition: The only future good that it assuredly leads to is that it will destroy itself. And how does it disguise this outcome from its subjects, its short-term beneficiaries, and its victims? It does so by false accounting. It substitutes for the real economy, by which we build and maintain (or do not maintain) our household, a symbolic economy of money, which in the long run, because of the self-interested manipulations of the "controlling interests," cannot symbolize or account for anything but itself. And so we have before us the spectacle of unprecedented "prosperity" and "economic growth" in a land of degraded farms, forests, ecosystems, and watersheds, of polluted air, failing families, and perishing communities.

◆ ◆ ◆

This moral and economic absurdity exists for the sake of the allegedly "free" market, the single principle of which is this: Commodities will be produced wherever they can be produced at the lowest cost, and consumed wherever they will bring the highest price. To make too cheap and sell too high has always been the program of industrial capitalism. The idea of the global "free market" is merely capitalism's so far successful attempt to enlarge the geographic scope of its greed and, moreover, to give to its greed the status of a "right" within its presumptive territory. The global "free market" is free to the corporations precisely because it dissolves the boundaries of the old national colonialisms and replaces them with a new colonialism without restraints or boundaries. It is pretty much as if all the rabbits have been forbidden to have holes, thereby "freeing" the hounds.

The "right" of a corporation to exercise its economic power without restraint is construed, by the partisans of the "free market," as a form of freedom, a political liberty implied presumably by the right of individual citizens to own and use property.

But the "free market" idea introduces into government a sanction of an inequality that is not implicit in any idea of democratic liberty: namely that the "free market" is freest to those who have the most money and is not free at all to those with little or no money. Wal-Mart, for example, as a large corporation "freely" competing against local, privately owned businesses, has virtually all the freedom, and its small competitors virtually none.

To make too cheap and sell too high, there are two requirements. One is that you must have a lot of consumers with surplus money and unlimited wants. For the time being, there are plenty of these consumers in the "developed" countries. The problem, for now easily solved, is simply to keep them relatively affluent and dependent on purchased supplies.

The other requirement is that the market for labor and raw materials should remain depressed relative to the market for retail commodities. This means that the supply of workers should exceed demand and that the land-using economy should be allowed or encouraged to overproduce.

To keep the cost of labor low, it is necessary first to entice or force country people everywhere in the world to move into the cities—in the manner prescribed by the United States' Committee for Economic Development after World War II—and, second, to continue to introduce labor-replacing technology.[1] In this way, it is possible to maintain a "pool" of people who are in the threatful position of being mere consumers, landless and also poor, and who therefore are eager to go to work for low wages—precisely the condition of migrant farmworkers in the United States.

To cause the land-using economies to overproduce is even simpler. The farmers and other workers in the world's land-using economies, by and large, are not organized. They are therefore unable to control production in order to secure just prices. Individual producers must go individually to the market and take for their produce simply whatever they are paid. They have no power to bargain or make demands. Increasingly, they must sell not to neighbors or neighboring towns and cities but to large and remote corporations. There is no competition among the buyers (supposing there is more than one), who *are* organized and are "free" to exploit the advantage of low prices. Low prices encourage overproduction as producers attempt to make up their losses "on volume," and overproduction inevitably makes for low prices. The land-using economies thus spiral downward as the money economy of the exploiters spirals upward. If economic attrition in the land-using population becomes so severe as to threaten production, then governments can subsidize production without production controls, which necessarily will encourage overproduction, which will lower prices—and so the subsidy to rural producers becomes, in effect, a subsidy to the purchasing corporations. In the land-using economies, production is further cheapened by destroying, with low prices and low standards of quality, the cultural imperatives for good work and land stewardship.

◆ ◆ ◆

This sort of exploitation, long familiar in the foreign and domestic colonialism of modern nations, has now become "the global economy," which is the property of a few supranational corporations. The economic theory used to justify the global economy in its "free market" version is, again, perfectly groundless and sentimental. The idea is that what is good for the corporations will sooner or later—though not, of course, immediately—be good for everybody.

That sentimentality is based, in turn, upon a fantasy: the proposition that the great corporations, in "freely" competing with one another for raw materials, labor, and market share, will drive each other indefinitely not only toward greater "efficiencies" of manufacture but also toward higher bids for raw materials and labor and lower prices to consumers. As a result, all the world's people will be economically secure—in the future. It would be hard to object to such a proposition if only it were true.

But one knows, in the first place, that "efficiency" in manufacture always means reducing labor costs by replacing workers with cheaper workers or with machines.

In the second place, the "law of competition" does *not* imply that many competitors will compete indefinitely. The law of competition is a simple paradox: Competition destroys competition. The law of competition implies that many competitors, competing on the "free market" without restraint, will ultimately and inevitably reduce the number of competitors to one. The law of competition, in short, is the law of war.

In the third place, the global economy is based upon cheap long-distance transportation, without which it is not possible to move goods from the point of cheapest origin to the point of highest sale. And cheap long-distance transportation is the basis of the idea that regions and countries should abandon any measure of economic self-sufficiency in order to specialize in production for export of the few commodities, or the single commodity, that can be most cheaply produced. Whatever may be said for the "efficiency" of such a system, its result (and, I assume, its purpose) is to destroy local production capacities, local diversity, and local economic independence.

This idea of a global "free market" economy, despite its obvious moral flaws and its dangerous practical weaknesses, is now the ruling orthodoxy of the age. Its propaganda is subscribed to and distributed by most political leaders, editorial writers, and other "opinion makers." The powers that be, while continuing to budget huge sums for "national defense," have apparently abandoned any idea of national or local self-sufficiency, even in food. They also have given up the idea that a national or local government might justly place restraints upon economic activity in order to protect its land and its people.

The global economy is now institutionalized in the World Trade Organization, which was set up, without election anywhere, to rule international trade on behalf of the "free market"—which is to say on behalf of the supranational corporations—and to *over*rule, in secret sessions, any national or regional law that conflicts with the "free market." The corporate program of global "free" trade and the presence of the World Trade Organization have legitimized extreme forms of expert thought. We are told confidently that if Kentucky loses its milk-producing capacity to Wisconsin (and if Wisconsin's is lost to California), that will be a "success story." Experts such as Steven C. Blank of the University of California, Davis, have proposed that "developed" countries such as the United States and the United Kingdom, where food can no longer be produced cheaply enough, should give up agriculture altogether.

The folly at the root of this foolish economy began with the idea that a corporation should be regarded, legally, as "a person." But the limitless destructiveness of this economy comes about precisely because a corporation is *not* a person. A corporation, essentially, is a pile of money to which a number of persons have sold their moral allegiance. As such, unlike a person, a corporation does not age. It does not arrive, as most persons finally do, at a realization of the shortness and smallness of human lives; it does not come to see the future as the lifetime of the children and grandchildren of anybody in particular. It can experience no personal hope or remorse, no change of heart. It cannot humble itself. It goes about its business as it if were immortal, with the single purpose of becoming a bigger pile of money. The stockholders essentially are usurers, people who "let their money work for them," expecting high pay in return for causing others to work for low pay. The World Trade Organization enlarges the old idea of the corporation-as-person by giving the global corporate economy the status of a supergovernment with the power to overrule nations.

I don't mean to say, of course, that all corporate executives and stockholders are bad people. I am saying only that all of them are very seriously implicated in a bad economy.

♦ ♦ ♦

Not surprisingly, among people who wish to preserve things other than money—for instance, every region's native capacity to produce essential goods—there is a growing perception that the global "free market" economy is inherently an enemy to the natural world, to human health and freedom, to industrial workers, and to farmers and others in the land-use economies, and, furthermore, that it is inherently an enemy to good work and good economic practice.

I believe that this perception is correct and that it can be shown to be correct merely by listing the assumptions implicit in the idea that corporations should be "free" to buy low and sell high in the world at large. These assumptions, so far as I can make them out, are as follows:

1. That stable and preserving relationships among people, places, and things do not matter and are of no worth.
2. That cultures and religions have no legitimate practical or economic concerns.
3. That there is no conflict between the "free market" and political freedom and no connection between political democracy and economic democracy.
4. That there can be no conflict between economic advantage and economic justice.
5. That there is no conflict between greed and ecological or bodily health.
6. That there is no conflict between self-interest and public service.
7. That the loss or destruction of the capacity anywhere to produce necessary goods does not matter and involves no cost.
8. That it is all right for a country's or a region's subsistence to be foreign-based, dependent on long-distance transport, and entirely controlled by corporations.
9. That, therefore, wars over commodities—the Persian Gulf War, for example—are legitimate and permanent economic functions.
10. That this sort of sanctioned violence is justified also by the predominance of centralized systems of production, supply, communications, and transportation, which are extremely vulnerable not only to acts of war between nations but also to sabotage and terrorism.
11. That there is no danger and no cost in the proliferation of exotic pests, vermin, weeds, and diseases that accompany international trade and, of course, increase with the volume of trade.
12. That an economy is a machine of which people are merely the interchangeable parts. One has no choice but to do the work (if any) that the economy prescribes and to accept the prescribed wage.
13. That, therefore, vocation is a dead issue. One does not do the work one chooses to do because one is called to it by Heaven or by one's natural or

God-given abilities, but does instead the work that is determined and imposed by the economy. Any work is all right as long as one gets paid for it. (This assumption explains the prevailing "liberal" and "conservative" indifference toward displaced farmers and small business people.)

These assumptions clearly prefigure a condition of total economy. A total economy is one in which everything—"life-forms," for instance, or the "right to pollute"—is "private property" and has a price and is for sale. In a total economy, significant and sometimes critical choices that once belonged to individuals or communities become the property of corporations. A total economy, operating internationally, necessarily shrinks the powers of local and national governments, not only because those governments have signed over significant powers to an international bureaucracy or because political leaders become the paid hacks of the corporations, but also because political processes—and especially democratic processes—are too slow to react to unrestrained economic and technological development on a global scale. And when state and national governments begin to act, in effect, as agents of the global economy, selling their people for low wages and their people's products for low prices, then the rights and liberties of citizenship must necessarily shrink. A total economy is an unrestrained taking of profits from the disintegration of nations, communities, households, landscapes, and ecosystems. It licenses symbolic or artificial wealth to "grow" by means of the destruction of the real wealth of all the world.

◆ ◆ ◆

Among the many costs of the total economy, the loss of the principle of vocation is probably the most symptomatic and, from a cultural standpoint, the most critical. It is by the replacement of vocation with economic determinism that the exterior workings of a total economy destroy human character and culture from the inside.

In an essay on the origin of civilization in traditional cultures, Ananda Coomaraswamy wrote that "the principle of justice is the same throughout . . . [it is] that each member of the community should perform the task for which he is fitted by nature." The two ideas, justice and vocation, are inseparable. That is why Coomaraswamy spoke of industrialism as "the mammon of injustice," incompatible with civilization.[2] It is by way of the principle and practice of vocation that sanctity and reverence enter into the human economy. It was thus possible for traditional cultures to conceive that "to work is to pray."

◆ ◆ ◆

Aware of industrialism's potential for destruction, as well as the considerable political danger of great concentrations of wealth and power in industrial corporations, American leaders developed, and for a while used, the means of limiting and restraining such concentrations and of somewhat equitably distributing wealth and property. The means were laws against trusts and monopolies, the principle of collective bargaining, the concept of 100 percent parity between the land-using and the manufacturing economies, and the progressive income tax. And to protect domestic producers and production capacities, it is possible for governments to impose tariffs on cheap imported goods. These means are justified by the government's obligation to protect the lives, livelihoods, and freedoms of its citizens. There is, then, no necessity or inevitability requiring our government to sacrifice the livelihoods of our small farmers, small business people, and workers, along with our domestic economic independence, to the global "free market." But now all these means are either weakened or in disuse. The global economy is intended as a means of subverting them.

In default of government protections against the total economy of the supranational corporations, people are where they have been many times before: in danger of losing their economic security and their freedom, both at once. But at the same time, the means of defending themselves belongs to them in the form of a venerable principle: Powers not exercised by government return to the people. If the government does not propose to protect the lives, the livelihoods, and the freedoms of its people, then the people must think about protecting themselves.

How are they to protect themselves? There seems, really, to be only one way, and that is to develop and put into practice the idea of a local economy— something that growing numbers of people are now doing. For several good reasons, they are beginning with the idea of a local food economy. People are trying to find ways to shorten the distance between producers and consumers, to make the connections between the two more direct, and to make this local economic activity a benefit to the local community. They are trying to learn to use the consumer economies of local towns and cities to preserve the livelihoods of local farm families and farm communities. They want to use the local economy to give consumers an influence over the kind and quality of their food and to preserve and enhance the local landscapes. They want to give everybody in the local community a direct, long-term interest in the prosperity, health, and beauty of their homeland. This is the only way presently available to make the total economy less total. It was once, I believe, the only way to make a national or a colonial economy less total, but now the necessity is greater.

I am assuming that there is a valid line of thought leading from the idea of the total economy to the idea of a local economy. I assume that the first thought may be a recognition of one's ignorance and vulnerability as a consumer in the total economy. As such a consumer, one does not know the history of the products one uses. Where, exactly, did they come from? Who produced them? What toxins were used in their production? What were the human and ecological costs of producing them and then of disposing of them? One sees that such questions cannot be answered easily, and perhaps not at all. Even though one is shopping amid an astonishing variety of products, one is denied certain significant choices. In such a state of economic ignorance, it is not possible to choose products that were produced locally or with reasonable kindness toward people and toward nature. Nor is it possible for such consumers to influence production for the better. Consumers who feel a prompting toward land stewardship find that in this economy they can have no stewardly practice. To be a consumer in the total economy, one must agree to be totally ignorant, totally passive, and totally dependent on distant supplies and self-interested suppliers.

And then, perhaps, one begins to *see* from a local point of view. One begins to ask, What is here, what is in me, that can lead to something better? From a local point of view, one can see that a global "free market" economy is possible only if nations and localities accept or ignore the inherent instability of a production economy based on exports and a consumer economy based on imports. An export economy is beyond local influence, and so is an import economy. And cheap long-distance transport is possible only if granted cheap fuel, international peace, control of terrorism, prevention of sabotage, and solvency of the international economy.

Perhaps also one begins to see the difference between a small local business that must share the fate of the local community and a large absentee corporation that is set up to escape the fate of the local community by ruining the local economy.

♦ ♦ ♦

So far as I can see, the idea of a local economy rests upon only two principles: neighborhood and subsistence.

In a viable neighborhood, neighbors ask themselves what they can do or provide for one another, and they find answers that they and their place can afford. This, and nothing else, is the *practice* of neighborhood. This practice must be, in part, charitable, but it must also be economic, and the economic part must be equitable; there is a significant charity in just prices.

Of course, everything needed locally cannot be produced locally. But a viable neighborhood is a community; and a viable community is made up of neighbors who cherish and protect what they have in common. This is the principle of subsistence. A viable community, like a viable farm, protects its own production capacities. It does not import products that it can produce for itself. And it does not export local products until local needs have been met. The economic products of a viable community are understood either as belonging to the community's subsistence or as surplus, and only the surplus is considered to be marketable abroad. A community, if it is to be viable, cannot think of producing solely for export, and it cannot permit importers to use cheaper labor and goods from other places to destroy the local capacity to produce goods that are needed locally. In charity, moreover, it must refuse to import goods that are produced at the cost of human or ecological degradation elsewhere. This principle of subsistence applies not just to localities but also to regions and countries.

The principles of neighborhood and subsistence will be disparaged by the globalists as "protectionism"—and that is exactly what it is. It is a protectionism that is just and sound because it protects local producers and is the best assurance of adequate supplies to local consumers. And the idea that local needs should be met first and only surpluses should be exported does *not* imply any prejudice against charity toward people in other places or trade with them. The principle of neighborhood at home always implies the principle of charity abroad. And the principle of subsistence is in fact the best guarantee of giveable or marketable surpluses. This kind of protection is not "isolationism."

Albert Schweitzer, who knew well the economic situation in the colonies of Africa, wrote some seventy years ago, "Whenever the timber trade is good, permanent famine reigns in the Ogowe region, because the villagers abandon their farms to fell as many trees as possible." We should notice especially that the goal of production was "as many . . . as possible." And Schweitzer made my point exactly: "These people could achieve true wealth if they could develop their agriculture and trade to meet their own needs." Instead, they produced timber for export to "the world market," which made them dependent upon imported goods, which they bought with money earned from their exports.[3] They gave up their local means of subsistence and imposed the false standard of a foreign demand ("as many trees as possible") upon their forests. They thus became helplessly dependent on an economy over which they had no control.

Such was the fate of the native people under the African colonialism of Schweitzer's time. Such is, and can only be, the fate of everybody under the global colonialism of our time. Schweitzer's description of the colonial economy of the Ogowe region is in principle not different from the rural economy of Kentucky or Iowa or Wyoming now. A total economy, for all practical purposes, is a total government. "Free trade," from the standpoint of the corporate economy, brings "unprecedented economic growth," but from the standpoint of the land and its local populations and ultimately from the standpoint of the cities, it brings destruction and slavery. Without prosperous local economies, the people have no power and the land no voice.

Part III

From the Perspective
of the Storyteller

The third and final part of the book offers a narrative understanding of the
links between science, spirit, and nature. Drawing on the particular insights of
the storyteller, part III includes the writing of two distinguished and widely
respected authors, Terry Tempest Williams and Barry Lopez. Williams, drawing from her recent and celebrated book *Leap,* chronicles the interactions of a
woman and a medieval painting. The powerful imagery of this story inspires
intense meditations and inspirational revelations about the human tenure on
earth and our relationship with the sacred. Lopez's story, "The Mappist,"
recounts a man's search for an elusive cartographer whose brilliant work
brings to life countless qualities and connections linking culture and landscape.
Both selections echo the many religious, spiritual, and scientific ideas of nature
and humanity advanced in other chapters of the book.

Chapter 15

The Garden of Delights:
A Reading from *Leap*

TERRY TEMPEST WILLIAMS

Paradise

I once lived near the shores of Great Salt Lake with no outlet to the sea.

I once lived in a fault-block basin where mountains made of granite sur-rounded me. These mountains in time were hollowed to house the genealogy of my people, Mormons. Our names, the dates of our births and deaths, are safe. We have records hidden in stone.

I once lived in a landscape where my ancestors sacrificed everything in the name of belief and they passed their belief on to me, a belief that we can be the creators of our own worlds.

I once lived in the City of Latter-day Saints.

I have moved.

I have moved because of a painting.

Over the course of seven years, I have been traveling in the landscape of Hieronymus Bosch. A secret I did not tell for fear of seeming mad. Let these pages be my interrogation of faith. My roots have been pleached with the wings of a medieval triptych, my soul intertwined with an artist's vision.

This painting lives in Spain. It resides in the Prado Museum. The Prado Museum is found in the heart of Old Madrid. I will tell you the name of the painting I love. Its name is *El jardín de las delicias*.

The doors to the triptych are closed. Now it opens like a great medieval butterfly flapping its wings through the centuries. Open and close. Open and close. Hieronymus Bosch has painted, as wings, Paradise and Hell. The body is a portrait of Earthly Delights. The wings close again. Open, now slowly, with each viewer's breath the butterfly quivers, Heaven and Hell quiver, the wings are wet and fragile, only the body remains stable. The legs hidden, six. The antennae, two. The eyes, infinite. The artist's brush with life, mysterious. Close the triptych. The outside colors are drab. Black, grey, olive blue. The organism is not dead. Hear its heart beating. After five hundred years, the heart is still beating inside the triptych. The wings open.

I step back.

Red. Blue. Yellow. Green. Black. Pink. Orange. White. Gold.

Paradise.   Hell.   Earthly Delights.

As a child, I grew up with Hieronymus Bosch hanging over my head. My grandmother had thumbtacked the wings of Paradise and Hell to the bulletin board above the bed where I slept. The prints were, in fact, part of the Metropolitan Museum of Art's series of discussions designed for home education. The Garden of Eden to the left with Christ taking Eve's pulse as Adam looks on—opposite—Hell, the bone-white face of a man looking over the shoulder of his eggshell body as the world burns: these were the images that framed the "oughts and shoulds" and "if you don'ts" of my religious upbringing.

Whenever my siblings and I stayed overnight, we fell asleep in "the grandchildren's room" beneath Truth and Evil.

Standing before *El jardín de las delicias* in the Prado Museum in Spain, now as a woman, I see the complete triptych for the first time. I am stunned. The center panel. The Garden of Earthly Delights. So little is hidden in the center panel, why was it hidden from me?

The body.

The body of the triptych.

My body.

The bodies of the center panel, this panel of play and discovery, of joyful curiosities cavorting with Eros, is not only a surprise to me, but a great mystery.

I stare at the painting. My eyes do not blink. They focus on the blue pool of bathers standing thigh-high in the middle of the triptych.

Bareback riders circle the black and white women bathing in the water, the black and white women who are balancing black and white birds on top of their heads. Cherries, too. Faster and faster, the bareback riders gallop their horses and goats and griffins; bareback riders, naked men, riding bulls, bears, lions, camels, deer, and pigs, faster and faster, circling the women.

The triptych begins to blur. My eyes begin to blur. I resist. Focus. I rein my eyes in from the pull of the bodies, the body of the triptych, the bodies bare, bareback on animals, circling, circling, circling them, circling me, black and white bodies, my body stands stoically inside the Prado determined to resist the galloping of my blood.

I feel faint. I turn from the painting and see a wooden chair shaped like a crescent leaning against the wall. The wall is white. I sit down, stare at the floor, the granite floor, and get my bearings.

I begin counting cherries in Bosch's Garden. I lose track, they are in such abundance. I stop at sixty. Cherries are flying in the air, dangling from poles, being passed from one person to the next, dropped into the mouths of lovers by birds, worn on women's heads as hats, and balanced on the feet as balls.

In Utah, my home, cherries are a love crop. They are also our state fruit. They grow in well-tended orchards along the Wasatch Front. Cherry picking was a large part of our childhood. Our parents, aunts, and uncles would load up their station wagons with kids and drop us off in one of the orchards alongside Great Salt Lake with empty buckets in hand. Sometimes we were paid by the pail or given bags to take home for our families. Once we were up in the trees, out of view, we could eat as many as we wanted.

One day, my great-uncle was standing on a ladder picking cherries with my cousin and me. We were perched on sturdy branches above him, ten-year-old girls unafraid of heights.

"What principle of the Gospel of Jesus Christ means the most to you?" he asked, filling his bucket.

Mormon children are used to these kinds of questions practiced on them by their elders, who consider this part of their religious training.

"Obedience," my cousin replied, pulling a cherry off its stem.

"Free agency," I answered, eating one.

———

"Bosch is rubbish," I hear a British guide say to her group. She is wearing a brown wool suit just below her knees. "He ate rye bread that was rotten, which most certainly brought on the cruelest of hallucinations."

My view of Paradise is often blocked by other visitors. I have no choice but to watch them interact with the painting.

"What we have here, ladies and gentlemen, is a massive orgy. It is rumored Hieronymus Bosch belonged to a religious sect that believed in purification through gratification."

Some of the visitors cluck their tongues.

"Notice the preponderance of strawberries and other fleshy fruits, symbols of lust. It is true God said, 'Go forth and multiply,' but we are not supposed to enjoy it like we see here. Bosch presents a perversion, ladies and gentlemen. I ask you to note the clear references to bestiality as men and animals prance around the pool in a state of arousal."

The guide points to the naked women cavorting in the pool that the cavalcade circles.

"And here, please witness Chaucer's 'Wife of Bath' who, as you recall, possessed a libido much too strong for her own good. '*A likerous mouth moste han a likerous tayl. In wommen vinolent is no defence, This knownen lecchours by experience.*'"

As the matron of arts begins to lose herself in Chaucer's tale, her group are showing their own signs of arousal. Suddenly aware of her own titillating vocabulary, she quickly shifts her analysis to Hell.

"I must say, I find great comfort in Bosch's depiction of Hell. We will pay for our bloody sins if we cannot control our bodily obsessions. Here we see the lovely, dreadful sophistications of the Middle Ages. Each sin has its appropriate payback. Rightfully so; if you are gluttonous, you will be eaten gluttonously."

A man who seemed to be preoccupied with one section of Hell in particular raises his hand and points to the panel. "Might these be vats of semen?"

She lifts her arm high over her head. "Follow me, please."

———

On this particular day in the Prado, I begin my observation of the triptych with binoculars. I want to see what birds inhabit the Paradise of Bosch.

The cradle chair in the corner of the gallery is empty. I sit down and begin bird-watching.

A mute swan floats gracefully in the pond behind Eve. It has an orange bill with a black knob. The knob is greatly enlarged in the male in the spring. This bird would have been familiar to Bosch in the Low Countries. This swan is not mute but makes a formidable hissing sound. In its wild state, it frequents remote wetlands. Why not Eden?

Mallards and shovelers float nearby as three white egrets stand in shallow water perfectly still, eyes intent on fish. Their long, sinuous necks and spearlike bills are mirrored in the pool alongside a unicorn bending down to drink. Their feathers form an elegant cloak easily unraveled by the wind.

Close to them is a spoonbill. I walk slowly toward this long-legged bird, a standing grace in the water. It swings its peculiar beak side to side in the white marl for crustaceans. The quivering nerve endings that line the interior of its mouth are feeling for clues and will send messages of what is below. Adam and Eve would do well to pay attention. Life is to be touched. The bill snaps shut, a crayfish struggles. It is decided: the crayfish becomes the spoonbill, who continues walking in Eden, seen or unseen, it does not matter.

North of the wading birds, flocks of swifts are swirling like smoke through a furnace-like mountain, transforming themselves from black to red to white, the colors of alchemy.

I sit down on the grassy hillside near the congregation of birds below the stone furnace. Wild geese fly in the formation of an arrow. If we follow their migrations will we better understand our own spiritual genesis?

As a child I remember believing that if I could ride on the backs of Canada geese they would deliver me to the future because they had arrived from the past. When I would bear my testimony before members of my own congregation, I would say I believed in God not because of what I had learned in church but because of the geese I watched each spring and fall, the fact that they knew their way, that they always returned. My parents said it was a sweet analogy. Not knowing what that word meant, I said, "No, they are not my analogy, they are my truth."

Rooks. Ravens. Crows. True conspirators. They converse in pairs while sitting on the rims of Bosch's canyons. One by one, they drop like stones only to recover in a joyous upswing. Back on the rim, they sit as bards disguised as birds and listen to everything being said. At night, they will enter Adam and Eve's dreams as subversive thoughts.

In Eden, I continue my search for birds.

Below Eve, there is a kingfisher with red legs, two toes forward, two toes back, syndactyl, speaking to a three-headed phoenix while a grey bee-eater fans its short broad wings and bows. Pheasants in courtship strut on the bottom margins of Paradise, a female opens herself to the approaching male, the spurs on her tarsi are exposed should she need to defend herself.

I turn around.

There, inside the eye of the pink fountain, sits a yellow-eyed owl, possibly Tengmalm's owl, distinguished by its round head, deep facial disks, and chocolate plumage. It nests in the cavities of trees. I kneel behind the thicket and watch. I have never seen this bird before. It scarcely moves. Were Hieronymus Bosch's acute skills as a naturalist appreciated? Were there medieval ornithologists who caught the painter's sardonic humor in Paradise, knowing this particular owl's call is a rapid, musical phrasing of *poo-poo-poo*?

I take down my binoculars and let them dangle around my neck. The guards are staring. I open my notebook and make a checklist of all the birds seen so far in *El jardín de las delicias*.

Swifts
Scarlet Ibis
Great White Egret
Little Egret
Wagtail
Blue Rock Thrush
Cuckoo
Spoonbill
White Pelican
Night Heron
Blue Heron
Stork
White Ibis

Jackdaw
Stonechat
Redstart
Rook
Brambling
Pheasant
Jay
Mallard
Gadwall
Hoopoe
Green Woodpecker
Kingfisher
Robin
Magpie
Goldfinch
Great Tit
Long-eared Owl
Tengmalm's Owl
Tawny Owl
Pygmy Owl
Little Owl
Widgeon

I look up. The guard nods. The Prado is closing. Who knows how much time has passed in the country of Bosch? I tuck my binoculars into my bag with my notebook and leave.

———

Hell

Open and close. Open and close. The wings of El Bosco's butterfly are fanning the fires, the fires of Hell. The flames blur, obscure, the view of Paradise.

Now I see El Bosco's masterpiece as a map of the human mind. On the left, the mind of the child, pure and innocent. We believe what we are told. We stay in Paradise as long as possible. On the right, the mind of the mad, dark and duplicitous. We are all manic-depressives with mood swings bashing against brass like the tongues of bells that erode our sense of equilibrium. Left hollow, our bodies are taken over by demons. My mind, out of my mind, I have abandoned Paradise.

———

I hide behind another human being. I can find no friends in Hell. I watch a game of solitaire where the last remaining cards are a two of hearts and a three of clubs.

Let the cards fall as they may, they say.

Must we?

Must we witness and watch and do nothing as roadcuts, clearcuts, the cut bodies of coyote, mountain lion, and deer are strung up by their hind legs as a warning to others that they are not welcome.

Must we witness and watch and do nothing as the peeled bodies of elders named Douglas Fir, Cedar, and Larch are chained to the flatbeds of trucks and hauled away on our highways, highways littered with roadkills, roadkills paving the way to dams, dammed rivers: the Colorado, the Columbia, the Snake and Mississippi; dammed canyons—Glen Canyon, Davis Gulch, Cathedral in the Desert—speak their names—remember their names—these places of beauty, these places of origin, toxic, toxic wastes, toxic deserts, bombed, battered, and betrayed in the name of national security—speak their names—remember their names—the Nevada Test Site in the Mojave, Hanford on the banks of the Columbia, Rocky Flats, Alamogordo, Dugway, the floodplains of eastern Idaho, the nuclear waste is simmering, shimmering, Coyote watches with burning eyes, burning eyes Bosch's owl with burning eyes in Paradise. There is a war raging within our own nation and it is not civil. Speak their names. Remember their names. They are going, going, the salmon, grizzly, tortoise, tiger beetle, bobcat and lynx, marbled murrelet, red-spotted frog, they are disappearing before our eyes, our own eyes. Find their eyes. Burning eyes. W e   a r e   s l o w l y   c o m m i t t i n g   s u i c i d e .

This is *The Natural History of the Dead.*

The land is being stripped. Strip-mined. Strip-searched. Gold-blooded murderers. There was a World War I sergeant investigating the teeth of the dead. He opened their mouths, pried out fillings, always the gold fillings, with a trench knife. He picked up a piece of pipe and broke out the other filled teeth and put them inside a gas mask tin for later, *who knows how much gold may be extracted from them?*

Let the cards fall where they may, they say.

I run to the corner of Bosch's Hell and pick up the cards; they no longer bear the two of hearts, the three of clubs. I turn them over. The cards burst into flames. I throw them on the ground. White salamanders scurry behind the table and hiss.

I am convinced that the twenty-first century will be the century of Noahs, when human beings will feel compelled to save the ecosystems and species dying around us in biological arks, since it will no longer be possible to save everything . . . The moral dilemma will reside in which and whom to choose, and on what knowledge, not to say wisdom, we should base our choice; and finally, who are we to decide on the right to exist of other life forms?

Novalis, in his "Legend of the Poet," evokes distant eras when there were poets who by making strange sounds on fantastical instruments, could awaken the secret life of forests and plants. I call on the women and men of science, on the environmentalists, and on the poets, so that together we can make it possible for the mythical Orpheus to sing again among us in the next millennium. Ecology, like poetry, should be practiced by everyone.

———

Hell is here, now, burning joyously, as millions stand in this City of Fire and bear witness to the transformation of their own communities. They are not voyeurs to change, but participants striking the match. Individual sparks emancipate from the flames in the Old World to the New World. Orange wings flapping in the darkness.

Monarch butterflies are migrating across North America, south to the creases in the mountains of Central Mexico. Michoacán. They fly fifteen thousand feet above the Earth to the Sierra Palone, an active transvolcanic range. Orange. Black. Monarchs wear the topography of flowing lava on their wings. The butterflies' final destination was a secret, not discovered by lepidopterists until 1974. Of course, the locals knew but they never told anyone that forty million monarchs were sitting on the mountaintops above their village opening and closing their wings in private conversations.

I am walking up a mountain along a steep, thin path. The path is dry and dusty. There are burning fields, cleared fields, and farms that appear as quilted squares on the steep hillsides. Gullies cut deep from rains expose red soil. A few monarchs are sipping nectar from roadside flowers, some called seneceo. *I have a guide. We pass men on the trail who remove monarchs from the path; they pick them up, blow the dust off their wings, and place them in sunlight safe from foot traffic. This is their job. This is their work.*

I stop. I think I hear rain. The guide smiles. We continue walking until the forest darkens, cools. Suddenly, we look up through a canopy of wings, wings fanning the air, creating the sound of rain, the sound of wind, the sound of wings, butterfly wings. The fir trees are laying down their arms. Here. Now. Millions of monarchs hang from the trees like frostbitten leaves, the underside of their wings exposed, burnished, and bronzed.

We are dressed in butterflies. The longer we stay inside the winged forest, the more we see and hear, the settling of peace, the rupture of peace. The sun appears from behind a cloud, there is a frenzy of flight.

Another voice speaks, "Here we stand inside the mind of God."

Why must we leave?

We walk back down the mountain. I trip on an exposed root, my foot falls on a butterfly. I have killed a butterfly. My guide bends down, picks up the still life with cradled hands, brings the monarch to his mouth and with one quick pop of his breath, blows it back to life.

In a miracle, it flies.

"Ciclo de vida," he says.

I want to believe. This is what I believe. In the middle of the road is a tiny vein of water crowded with monarchs. I continue walking down the mountain until the sound of wings is no longer audible. We stand outside the miraculous. Loneliness creeps down the hillside as I return to the smoke-filled clearing and the sounds of chain saws, the forest freshly felled.

Sparks are ascending and descending in the upper reaches of El Bosco's Hell.

I am in Spain. I am in Mexico. Old World. New World. It is the year 1500. It is the year 2000. Time is alive. Time is a lie. I am present to quivering wings. Monarch butterflies light on my hands and burst into flames.

Bouquets of fireworks are thrown to the sky. Valencia is burning. The masses are dancing arm in arm, in the streets they are dancing and singing. Across the bridge, the people dance, fireworks exploding in the river.

I stop and lean over the railing and make prayers to my gods, male and female, human and animal, recalling privately the vows I once made and burned.

Strike the match.
Protect the flame.
Ignite the hymns.

The spirit of God like a fire is burning. Start the city burning feel the stomach turning the ache that keeps returning *count your many blessings name them one by one* it is never enough give us our bread our daily bread more more slice the bread slice the wrist that's threatening to raise the hand against the hand who is destroying the Earth for the beauty of the Earth see the Earth see the servant Adam slumped in his damp Eden dead from words dead from Eve serenely drinking swallowing the sap of the dragon palm mistaking it for blood blood blood knowledge choking before she coughs up the seeds plant the seeds *we are all enlisted till the conflict is o'er: Happy are we! Happy are we!* Her health all health is as precarious as ladders raised against heaven up-down fall into hell the rungs of ladders are the frames of our own experience one step at a time how high do we dare to go how low do we dare to go these ladders in El Bosco's Hell stretch heights and depths until we fall free fall our souls travel without brakes no breaks no time no space or pause to feel or find or be true to anything but here we go to work and work and work and work eat work sleep work and work and work *put your shoulder to the wheel push along do your duty with a heart full of song we all have work let no one shirk put your shoulder to the wheel.* Clearcut. Cutthroat. Cut. Cut the road into the mountain. Cut. Take one. Take two. Take three. Take out the entire hillside for a house for a subdivision of the future. We are developing. See how we are developing. Six billion and rising. The rungs on the ladder, become the frames of our film. Speed them up. Run. The place where I was born is now a prison. Cut. Take four. The place where I was born is now a prison. Cut. Run the film again in El Bosco's Hell. Play my precious images of pain over and over again on the backs of the dead who lead me in Hell, who welcome me in Hell, my eyes watch as each frame rolls down their spines. Stop. A vertebra is exposed. My dying mother. Roll. Stop. My ghostly lover. Roll again. My own rapacious appetites play themselves one after the other for free, this is all free, free fall until images collapse in the boneyard of crimes and cruelties. Lay me down to sleep on fire and millstone. I cannot sleep. *Come, come, ye saints, no toil or labor fear but with joy wend your way.* The stakes are high. High on the ridge. Pull the stakes. One by one by one. *Count your many blessings see what God has done.* Take the wooden stakes out of the Earth into our hands one vertical the other horizontal tie them together with orange plastic tape turn them into crosses plant them in the soil see how rage grows see how rage flies dragonflies be calm they say sit at the table they say come to consensus they say with the power vested in them they say *oh say can you see* my body a clear-cut my voice a serpent wrapped around the tree the power vested in me *like a fire is burning.*

It is never enough.

Whataboutthecovenantswehavemadenottobebrokenwearebrokenwearebroken-
thisrecordofoursisbrokenisbrokenisbrokenwearebrokenthisrecordofours

God forbid. God forgive.

Earthly Delights

To open is not a sin.
To play is not a sin.
To imagine is not a sin.

Do you see the couple making love inside a mussel shell?

There is a traveler who walks beyond El Bosco's blue horizon. The town is Rib-
adesella, a northern port of Spain where deep caves hold the images of horses.
She walks along the beach. It is low tide. Among the rocks, she is aware of a
strange hissing. She stops, bends down, and locates the sound. It is the musings
of barnacles, creatures who stand on their heads with their feathered feet fil-
tering food as the sea overtakes them. Tiny armored shells protect the flesh
inside. She looks more closely. A double door whose sides disappear when
opened is tightly sealed. Only their voices whisper life. The traveler rises, looks
ahead, and finds mussels, saturated blue, also attached to the rocks. A herring
gull has pulled one of the bivalves from its base, breaks it open with its beak
and tears the orange body into sinewy strands and eats. Long, thick strands of
eel grass grow below, green.

The traveler stops at the Gran Hotel, where seventy-eight lanterns round
like the moon illuminate the beach. It has begun to rain. She takes a small room

with a balcony and sits on a pink plush chair until the sun sets. She enjoys a shower, slips into a chiffon dress, puts on her pearls, and walks down the spiral staircase noting the carved spindles in the shape of sea horses.

Inside the dining room, she asks for the table in the corner. It is still raining. The tide is rising. She orders paella. The waiter informs the traveler that it will take forty-five minutes to prepare. She says that is what she would expect from such a lavish dish. She relaxes and watches the waves reach, crest, and break in small elegant intervals. The traveler wonders why such harsh, direct lighting is used inside when everything outside is muted. She wishes for the light of candles to comfort the food.

It rains and rains.

While waiting for the paella, the traveler whispers to the waiter after he has filled her glass with wine that if a gentleman should walk into the dining room looking for a table and would like to join her she would be delighted to share the shellfish. The waiter nods. The traveler takes her first sip of wine. Rioja. Red. Black cherries. Plums. She reaches for the baguette, tears off the heel. There is a wedge of cabrales wrapped in leaves on the table. She spreads the cheese on the bread. As she takes it into her mouth the sound of bells through the high Áliva meadows in the Picos returns to her. Harebell, columbine, iris, lilies, ferns, penstemon, gilia, orchids—the transformed hayfields of Asturias are the florid backgrounds of medieval tapestries.

The waiter pardons himself and introduces a dinner companion to the traveler. She extends her hand to the man, who takes it generously and sits down across from her. The waiter pours him a glass of cabernet and refills hers. They both lift their glasses and then avert their eyes.

It rains and rains.

The paella arrives steaming.

The waiter, with two covered hands, carries the cast-iron pan sizzling and carefully places it on the table between the two eaters. As he moves away the traveler motions him forward one more time and whispers something in his ear. She returns her attention to her guest.

The City of Longing appears.

On her plate: mussels, barnacles, clams, squid, crab legs, and crayfish. Saffron rice: yellow-orange. Green olives stuffed with pimentos. Peas. Sliced hard-boiled eggs. Olive oil, some still simmering at the bottom of the pan.

On his plate: mussels, crab legs, clams, crayfish, barnacles, and squid. Saffron rice: orange. Perfectly sliced hard-boiled eggs. Black olives. Peas. White asparagus.

They lift their forks and begin to explore, to taste, to tease, to touch, to play, to romp, to knead, to court, to want, to do, to dare, to ride, to rock, to swim, to float, to fly, to feed, to toy, to try, to say, to hear, to see, to dare, to do, to break, to burn, to eat and be eaten. With saffron-stained fingers they break open the last mussels, blue-orange, and feed each other what is inside moving to the outside.

Explorar. Probar. Agitar. Palpar. Jugar. Retozar. Amasar. Cortejar. Querer. Hacer. Osar. Montar. Mecer. Nadar. Flotar. Volar. Nutrir. Juguetear. Intentar. Decir. Oír. Ver. Osar. Hacer. Romper. Incendiar. Comer y ser comida.

They drink coffee black with no cream. To be curious. To imagine. To question and be questioned. To desire. *Desear.*

The tide is rising to stand on one's head and feed.

Restoration

The restoration of nature, even our own, will require a reversal of our senses and sensibilities.

To see with our heart.

To touch with our mind.
To smell with our hands.
To taste with our eyes.
To hear with the soles of our feet.

———

Hieronymus Bosch put his finger on the wound.

What is the wound?

Our wound, separation from the Sacred, the pain of our isolation, may this be the open door that leads us to the table of restoration, may we sit around the table, may we break bread around the table, may we stand on top of the table, may we turn the table over and dance, leap, leap for joy, all this in the gesture of conserving a painting, conserving a landscape, conserving a spirit, our own restored spirits once lost, now found, Paradise found, right here on this beautiful blue planet called Earth.

Chapter 16

The Mappist

Barry Lopez

When I was an undergraduate at Brown I came across a book called *The City of Ascensions,* about Bogotá. I knew nothing of Bogotá, but I felt the author had captured its essence. My view was that Onesimo Peña had not written a travel book but a work about the soul of Bogotá. Even if I were to read it later in life, I thought, I would not be able to get all Peña meant in a single reading. I looked him up at the library but he had apparently written no other books, at least not any in English.

In my senior year I discovered a somewhat better known book, *The City of Trembling Leaves,* by Walter Van Tilburg Clark, about Reno, Nevada. I liked it, but it did not have the superior depth, the integration of Peña's work. Peña, you had the feeling, could walk you through the warrens of Bogotá without a map and put your hands directly on the vitality of any modern century—the baptismal registries of a particular cathedral, a cornerstone that had been taken from one building to be used in another, a London plane tree planted by Bolívar. He had such a command of the idiom of this city, and the book itself demonstrated such complex linkages, it was easy to believe Peña had no other subject, that he could have written nothing else. I believed this was so until I read *The City of Floating Sand* a year later, a book about Cape Town, and then a book about Djakarta, called *The City of Frangipani.* Though the former was by one Frans Haartman and the latter by a Jemboa Tran, each had the distinctive organic layering of the Peña book, and I felt certain they'd been written by the same man.

A national library search through the University of Michigan, where I had gone to work on a master's degree in geography, produced hundreds of books with titles similar to these. I had to know whether Peña had written any others and so read or skimmed perhaps thirty of those I got through interlibrary

231

loan. Some, though wretched, were strange enough to be engaging; others were brilliant but not in the way of Peña. I ended up ordering copies of five I believed Peña had written, books about Perth, Lagos, Tokyo, Venice, and Boston, the last a volume by William Smith Everett called *The City of Cod*.

Who Peña actually was I could not then determine. Letters to publishers eventually led me to a literary agency in New York where I was told that the author did not wish to be known. I pressed for information about what else he might have written, inquired whether he was still alive (the book about Venice had been published more than fifty years before), but got nowhere.

As a doctoral student at Duke I made the seven Peña books the basis of a dissertation. I wanted to show in a series of city maps, based on all the detail in Peña's descriptions, what a brilliant exegesis of the social dynamics of these cities he had achieved. My maps showed, for example, how water moved through Djakarta, not just municipal water but also trucked water and, street by street, the flow of rainwater. And how road building in Cape Town reflected the policy of apartheid.

I received quite a few compliments on the work, but I knew the maps did not make apparent the hard, translucent jewel of integration that was each Peña book. I had only created some illustrations, however well done. But had I known whether he was alive or where he lived, I would still have sent him a copy out of a sense of collegiality and respect.

◆ ◆ ◆

After I finished the dissertation I moved my wife and three young children to Brookline, a suburb of Boston, and set up a practice as a restoration geographer. Fifteen years later I embarked on my fourth or fifth trip to Tokyo as a consultant to a planning firm there, and one evening I took a train out to Chiyoda-ku to visit bookstores in an area called Jimbocho. Just down the street from a bridge over the Kanda River is the Sanseido Book Store, a regular haunt by then for me. Up on the fifth floor I bought two translations of books by Japanese writers on the Asian architectural response to topography in mountain cities. I was exiting the store on the ground floor, a level given over entirely to maps, closing my coat against the spring night, when I happened to spot the kanji for "Tokyo" on a tier of drawers. I opened one of them to browse. Toward the bottom of a second drawer, I came upon a set of maps that seemed vaguely familiar, though the entries were all in kanji. After a few minutes of leafing through, it dawned on me that they bore a resemblance to the maps I had done as a student at Duke. I was considering buying one of them as a memento when I caught a name in English in the corner—Corlis Benefideo. It appeared there on every map.

I stared at that name a long while, and I began to consider what you also may be thinking. I bought all thirteen maps. Even without language to identify information in the keys, even without titles, I could decipher what the mapmaker was up to. One designated areas prone to flooding as water from the Sumida River backed up through the city's storm drains. Another showed the location of all shops dealing in Edo Period manuscripts and artwork. Another, using small pink arrows, showed the point of view of each of Hiroshige's famous One Hundred Views. Yet another showed, in six time-sequenced panels, the rise and decline of horse barns in the city.

My office in Boston was fourteen hours behind me, so I had to leave a message for my assistant, asking him to look up Corlis Benefideo's name. I gave him some contacts at map libraries I used regularly, and asked him to call me back as soon as he had anything, no matter the hour. He called at three A.M. to say that Corlis Benefideo had worked as a mapmaker for the U.S. Coast and Geodetic Survey in Washington from 1932 until 1958, and that he was going to fax me some more information.

I dressed and went down to the hotel lobby to wait for the faxes and read them while I stood there. Benefideo was born in Fargo, North Dakota, in 1912. He went to work for the federal government straight out of Grinnell College during the Depression and by 1940 was traveling to various places—Venice, Bogotá, Lagos—in an exchange program. In 1958 he went into private practice as a cartographer in Chicago. His main source of income at that time appeared to be from the production of individualized site maps for large estate homes being built along the North Shore of Lake Michigan. The maps were bound in oversize books, twenty by thirty inches, and showed the vegetation, geology, hydrology, biology, and even archaeology of each site. They were subcontracted for under several architects.

Benefideo's Chicago practice closed in 1975. The fax said nothing more was known of his work history, and that he was not listed in any Chicago area phone books, nor with any professional organizations. I faxed back to my office, asking them to check phone books in Fargo, in Washington, D.C., and around Grinnell, Iowa—Des Moines and those towns. And asking them to try to find someone at what was now the National Geodetic Survey who might have known Benefideo or who could provide some detail.

When I came back to the hotel the following afternoon, there was another fax. No luck with the phone books, I read, but I could call a Maxwell Abert at the National Survey who'd worked with Benefideo. I waited the necessary few hours for the time change and called.

Abert said he had overlapped with Benefideo for one year, 1958, and though Benefideo had left voluntarily, it wasn't his idea.

"What you had to understand about Corlis," he said, "was that he was a patriot. Now, that word today, I don't know, means maybe nothing, but Corlis felt this very strong commitment to his country, and to a certain kind of map-making, and he and the Survey just ended up on a collision course. The way Corlis worked, you see, the way he approached things, slowed down the production of maps. That wasn't any good from a bureaucratic point of view. He couldn't give up being comprehensive, you understand, and they just didn't know what to do with him."

"What happened to him?"

"Well, the man spoke five or six languages, and he had both the drafting ability and the conceptual skill of a first-rate cartographer, so the government should have done something to keep the guy—and he was also very loyal—but they didn't. Oh, his last year they created a project for him, but it was temporary. He saw they didn't want him. He moved to Chicago—but you said you knew that."

"Mmm. Do you know where he went after Chicago?"

"I do. He went to Fargo. And that's the last I know. I wrote him there until about 1985—he'd have been in his seventies—and then the last letter came back 'no forwarding address.' So that's the last I heard. I believe he must have died. He'd be, what, eighty-eight now."

"What was the special project?"

"Well Corlis, you know, he was like something out of a WPA project, like Dorothea Lange, Walker Evans and James Agee and them, people that had this sense of America as a country under siege, undergoing a trial during the Depression, a society that needed its dignity back. Corlis believed that in order to effect any political or social change, you had to know exactly what you were talking about. You had to know what the country itself—the ground, the real thing, not some political abstraction—was all about. So he proposed this series of forty-eight sets of maps—this was just before Alaska and Hawaii came in— a series for each state that would show the geology and hydrology, where the water was, you know, and the botany and biology, and the history of the place from Native American times.

"Well, a hundred people working hundred-hour weeks for a decade might get it all down, you know—it was monumental, what he was proposing. But to keep him around, to have him in the office, the Survey created this pilot project so he could come up with an approach that might get it done in a reasonable amount of time—why, I don't know; the government works on most things forever—but that's what he did. I never saw the results, but if you ever wanted to see disillusionment in a man, you should have seen Corlis in those last months. He tried congressmen, he tried senators, he tried other people in Commerce, he tried everybody, but I think they all had the same sense of him, that he was an obstructionist. They'd eat a guy like that alive on the Hill today, the same way. He just wasn't very practical. But he was a good man."

I got the address in Fargo and thanked Mr. Abert. It turned out to be where Benefideo's parents had lived until they died. The house was sold in 1985. And that was that.

♦ ♦ ♦

When I returned to Boston I reread *The City of Ascensions*. It's a beautiful book, so tender toward the city, and proceeding on the assumption that Bogotá was the living idea of its inhabitants. I thought Benefideo's books would make an exceptional subject for a senior project in history or geography, and wanted to suggest it to my older daughter, Stephanie. How, I might ask her, do we cultivate people like Corlis Benefideo? Do they all finally return to the rural districts from which they come, unable or unwilling to fully adapt to the goals, the tone, of a progressive society? Was Corlis familiar with the work of Lewis Mumford? Would you call him a populist?

Stephanie, about to finish her junior year at Bryn Mawr, had an interest in cities and geography, but I didn't know how to follow up on this with her. Her interests were there in spite of my promotions.

One morning, several months after I got back from Tokyo, I walked into the office and saw a note in the center of my desk, a few words from my diligent assistant. It was Benefideo's address—Box 117, Garrison, North Dakota 58540. I got out the office atlas. Garrison is halfway between Minot and Bismarck, just north of Lake Sakakawea. No phone.

I wrote him a brief letter, saying I'd recently bought a set of his maps in Tokyo, asking if he was indeed the author of the books, and telling him how much I admired them and that I had based my Ph.D. dissertation on them. I praised the integrity of the work he had done, and said I was intrigued by his last Survey project, and would also like to see one of the Chicago publications sometime.

A week later I got a note. "Dear Mr. Trevino," it read.

> I appreciate your kind words about my work. I am still at it. Come for a visit if you wish. I will be back from a trip in late September,

so the first week of October would be fine. Sincerely, Corlis Benefideo.

I located a motel in Garrison, got plane tickets to Bismarck, arranged a
rental car, and then wrote Mr. Benefideo and told him I was coming, and that
if he would send me his street address I would be at his door at nine A.M. on
October second. The address he sent, 15088 State Highway 37, was a few
miles east of Garrison. A hand-rendered map in colored pencil, which made
tears well up in my eyes, showed how to get to the house, which lay a ways off
the road in a grove of ash trees he had sketched.

The days of waiting made me anxious and aware of my vulnerability. I
asked both my daughters and my son if they wanted to go. No, school was
starting, they wanted to be with their friends. My wife debated, then said no.
She thought this was something that would go best if I went alone.

♦ ♦ ♦

Corlis was straddling the sill of his door as I drove in to his yard. He wore a
pair of khaki trousers, a khaki shirt, and a khaki ball cap. He was about five foot
six and lean. Though spry, he showed evidence of arthritis and the other infir-
mities of age in his walk and handshake.

During breakfast I noticed a set of *The City of* books on his shelves. There
were eight, which meant I'd missed one. After breakfast he asked if I'd brought
any binoculars, and whether I'd be interested in visiting a wildlife refuge a few
miles away off the Bismarck highway, to watch ducks and geese coming in from
Canada. He made a picnic lunch and we drove over and had a fine time. I had
no binoculars with me, and little interest in the birds to start with, but with
his guidance and animation I came to appreciate the place. We saw more than
a million birds that day, he said.

When we got back to the house I asked if I could scan his bookshelves
while he fixed dinner. He had thousands of books, a significant number of them
in Spanish and French and some in Japanese. (The eighth book was called *The
City of Geraniums,* about Lima.) On the walls of a large room that incorporated
the kitchen and dining area was perhaps the most astonishing collection of
hand-drawn maps I had ever seen outside a library. Among them were two of
McKenzie's map sketches from his exploration of northern Canada; four of
FitzRoy's coastal elevations from Chile, made during the voyage with Darwin;
one of Humboldt's maps of the Orinoco; and a half-dozen sketches of the
Thames docks by Samuel Pepys.

Mr. Benefideo made us a dinner of canned soup, canned meat, and canned vegetables. For dessert he served fresh fruit, some store-bought cookies, and instant coffee. I studied him at the table. His forehead was high, and a prominent jaw and large nose further elongated his face. His eyes were pale blue, his skin burnished and dark, like a Palermo fisherman's. His ears flared slightly. His hair, still black on top, was close-cropped. There was little in the face but the alertness of the eyes to give you a sense of the importance of his work.

After dinner our conversation took a more satisfying turn. He had discouraged conversation while we were watching the birds, and he had seemed disinclined to talk while he was riding in the car. Our exchanges around dinner—which was quick—were broken up by its preparation and by clearing the table. A little to my surprise, he offered me Mexican tequila after the meal. I declined, noticing the bottle had no label, but sat with him on the porch while he drank.

Yes, he said, he'd used the pen names to keep the government from finding out what else he'd been up to in those cities. And yes, the experience with the Survey had made him a little bitter, but it had also opened the way to other things. His work in Chicago had satisfied him—the map sets for the estate architects and their wealthy clients, he made clear, were a minor thing; his real business in those years was in other countries, where hand-drawn and hand-colored maps still were welcome and enthused over. The estate map books, however, had allowed him to keep his hand in on the kind of work he wanted to pursue more fully one day. In 1975 he came back to Fargo to take care of his parents. When they died he sold the house and moved to Garrison. He had a government pension—when he said this he flicked his eyebrows, as though in the end he had gotten the best of the government. He had a small income from his books, he told me, mostly the foreign editions. And he had put some money away, so he'd been able to buy this place.

"What are you doing now?"

"The North Dakota series, the work I proposed in Washington in fifty-seven."

"The hydrological maps, the biological maps?"

"Yes. I subdivided the state into different sections, the actual number depending on whatever scale I needed for that subject. I've been doing them for fifteen years now, a thousand six hundred and fifty-one maps. I want to finish them, you know, so that if anyone ever wants to duplicate the work, they'll have a good idea of how to go about it."

He gazed at me in a slightly disturbing, almost accusatory way.

"Are you going to donate the maps, then, to a place where they can be studied?"

"North Dakota Museum of Art, in Grand Forks."

"Did you never marry, never have children?"

"I'm not sure, you know. No, I never married—I asked a few times, but was turned down. I didn't have the features, I think, and, early on, no money. Afterward, I developed a way of life that was really too much my own on a day-to-day basis. But, you know, I've been the beneficiary of great kindness in my life, and some of it has come from women who were, or are, very dear to me. Do you know what I mean?"

"Yes, I do."

"As for children, I think maybe there are one or two. In Bogotá. Venice. Does it shock you?"

"People are not shocked by things like this anymore, Mister Benefideo."

"That's too bad. I am. I have made my peace with it, though. Would you like to see the maps?"

"The Dakota series?"

Mr. Benefideo took me to a second large room with more stunning maps on the walls, six or eight tiers of large map drawers, and a worktable the perimeter of which was stained with hundreds of shades of watercolors surrounding a gleaming white area about three feet square. He turned on some track lighting, which made the room very bright, and pointed me to a swivel stool in front of an empty table, a smooth, broad surface of some waxed and dark wood.

From an adjacent drawer he pulled out a set of large maps, which he laid in front of me.

"As you go through, swing them to the side there. I'll restack them."

The first map was of ephemeral streams in the northeast quadrant of the state.

"These streams," he pointed out, "run only during wet periods, some but once in twenty years. Some don't have any names."

The information was strikingly presented and beautifully drawn. The instruction you needed to get oriented—where the Red River was, where the county lines were—was just enough, so it barely impinged on the actual subject matter of the map. The balance was perfect.

The next map showed fence lines, along the Missouri River in a central part of the state.

"These are done at twenty-year intervals, going back to eighteen forty. Fences are like roads, they proliferate. They're never completely removed."

The following map was a geological rendering of McIntosh County's bedrock geology. As I took in the shape and colors, the subdivided shades of purple and green and blue, Mr. Benefideo slid a large hand-colored transparency across the sheet, a soil map of the same area. You could imagine looking down through a variety of soil types to the bedrock below.

"Or," he said, and slid an opaque map with the same information across in front of me, the yellows and browns of a dozen silts, clays, and sands.

The next sheet was of eighteenth- and nineteenth-century foot trails in the western half of the state.

"But how did you compile this information?"

"Inspection and interviews. Close personal observation and talking with long-term residents. It's a hard thing, really, to erase a trail. A lot of information can be recovered if you stay at it."

When he placed the next map in front of me, the summer distribution of Swainson's hawks, and then slid in next to it a map showing the overlapping summer distribution of its main prey species, the Richardson ground squirrel, the precision and revelation were too much for me.

I turned to face him. "I've never seen anything that even approaches this, this"—my gesture across the surface of the table included everything. "It's not just the information, or the execution—I mean, the technique is flawless, the watercoloring, your choice of scale—but it's like the books, there's so much more."

"That's the idea, don't you think, Mister Trevino?"

"Of course, but nobody has the time for this kind of fieldwork anymore."

"That's unfortunate, because this information is what we need, you know. This shows history and how people fit the places they occupy. It's about what gets erased and what comes to replace it. These maps reveal the foundations beneath the ephemera."

"What about us, though?" I blurted, resisting his pronouncement. "In the books, in *City in Aspic* in particular, there is such a palpable love of human life in the cities, and here—"

"I do not have to live up to the history of Venice, Mister Trevino," he interrupted, "but I am obliged to shoulder the history of my own country. I could show you here the whole coming and going of the Mandan nation, wiped out in eighteen thirty-seven by a smallpox epidemic. I could show you how the arrival of German and Scandinavian farmers changed the composition of the topsoil, and the places where Charles Bodmer painted, and the evolution of red-light districts in Fargo—all that with pleasure. I've nothing against human passion, human longing. What I oppose is blind devotion to progress, and the venality of material wealth. If we're going to trade the priceless for the common, I want to know exactly what the terms are."

I had no response. His position was as difficult to assail as it would be to promote.

"You mean," I finally ventured, "that someone else will have to do the maps that show the spread of the Wal-Mart empire in North Dakota."

"I won't be doing those."

His tone was assertive but not testy. He wasn't even seeking my agreement.

"My daughter," I said, changing the subject, "wants to be an environmental historian. She has a good head for it, and I know she's interested—she wants to discover the kind of information you need to have to build a stable society. I'm sure it comes partly from looking at what's already there, as you suggest, like the birds this morning, how that movement, those movements, might determine the architecture of a society. I'm wondering—could I ever send her out? Maybe to help? Would you spend a few days with her?"

"I'd be glad to speak with her," he said, after considering the question. "I'd train her, if it came to that."

"Thank you."

He began squaring the maps up to place them back in the drawer.

"You know, Mister Trevino—Phillip, if I may, and you may call me Corlis—the question is about you, really." He shut the drawer and gestured me toward the door of the room, which he closed behind us.

"You represent a questing but lost generation of people. I think you know what I mean. You made it clear this morning, talking nostalgically about my books, that you think an elegant order has disappeared, something that shows the way." We were standing at the corner of the dining table with our hands on the chair backs. "It's wonderful, of course, that you brought your daughter into our conversation tonight, and certainly we're both going to have to depend on her, on her thinking. But the real question, now, is what will *you* do? Because you can't expect her to take up something you wish for yourself, a way of seeing the world. You send her here, if it turns out to be what she wants, but don't make the mistake of thinking you, or I or anyone, knows how the world is meant to work. The world is a miracle, unfolding in the pitch dark. We're lighting candles. Those maps—they are my candles. And I can't extinguish them for anyone."

He crossed to his shelves and took down his copy of *The City of Geraniums*. He handed it to me and we went to the door.

"If you want to come back in the morning for breakfast, please do. Or, there is a cafe, the Dogwood, next to the motel. It's good. However you wish."

We said good night and I moved out through pools of dark beneath the ash trees to where I'd parked the car. I set the book on the seat opposite and started the engine. The headlights swept the front of the house as I turned past it, catching the salute of his hand, and then he was gone.

I inverted the image of the map from his letter in my mind and began driving south to the highway. After a few moments I turned off the headlights and rolled down the window. I listened to the tires crushing gravel in the roadbed. The sound of it helped me hold the road, together with instinct and the memory of earlier having driven it. I felt the volume of space beneath the clear, star-ridden sky, and moved over the dark prairie like a barn-bound horse.

Notes

Chapter 1. Building the Bridge

1. *Oxford English Dictionary,* 2nd ed. (New York: Oxford University Press, 1989).
2. Ibid.
3. E. O. Wilson, *Biophilia* (Cambridge, Mass.: Harvard University Press, 1984), 48.
4. Ibid., 49.
5. R. Dubos, *The God Within* (New York: Charles Scribner's Sons, 1972), 255.
6. D. Takacs, *The Idea of Biodiversity: Philosophies of Paradise* (Baltimore: Johns Hopkins University Press, 1996).
7. Ibid., 259.
8. Ibid., 279.
9. Dubos, *God Within,* 42–43.

Introduction to Part I

1. R. M. Adams, *Finite and Infinite Goods: A Framework for Ethics* (New York: Oxford University Press, 1999), 148.
2. Ibid., 348.
3. I. Murdoch, *The Sovereignty of Good* (New York: Schocken Books, 1971), 66.

Chapter 2. The Contribution of Scientific Understandings of Nature to Moral, Spiritual, and Religious Wholeness and Well-Being

1. A. Leopold, *A Sand County Almanac, and Sketches Here and There* (New York: Oxford University Press, 1949), 209–210, 214.
2. U. W. Goodenough, "Reflections on Science and Technology," *Zygon* 35, no. 1 (March 2000): 5–12.
3. U. W. Goodenough, "Causality and Subjectivity in the Religious Quest," *Zygon* 35, no. 4 (December 2000): 725–734.

4. T. Berry, *The Dream of the Earth* (San Francisco: Sierra Club Books, 1988).

5. U. W. Goodenough, *The Sacred Depths of Nature* (New York: Oxford University Press, 1998), 59–60.

6. Ibid., 148–149.

7. Ibid., 151.

8. Ibid., 72–75.

9. M. Oliver, "Wild Geese," in *Dream Work* (New York: Atlantic Monthly Press, 1986).

10. Goodenough, *The Sacred Depths of Nature*, 75.

11. O. Lyons, address to delegates of the United Nations, 1977. Reprinted in A. Harvey, ed., *The Essential Mystics: Selections from the World's Great Wisdom Traditions* (San Francisco: HarperSanFrancisco, 1996), 14–15.

Chapter 3. Spiritual and Religious Perspectives of Creation and Scientific Understanding of Nature

Unless otherwise noted, biblical citations in this chapter are from *The Holy Bible: New International Version* (New York: New York International Bible Society, 1978).

1. A. Leopold, "The Land Ethic," in *A Sand County Almanac, and Sketches Here and There* (New York: Oxford University Press, 1949), 202.

2. Ibid., 203.

3. A. Leopold, "The Forestry of the Prophets," *Journal of Forestry* 18 (1920): 412–419.

4. *The Compact Edition of the Oxford English Dictionary*, s.v. "complement."

5. D. J. Hall, *Imaging God: Dominion as Stewardship* (Grand Rapids, Mich.: Eerdmans, 1986), 8. David Ehrenfeld defines a prophet as one "who describes the present" (personal communication, 1994).

6. "Declaration of the Mission to Washington: Joint Appeal by Religion and Science for the Environment," reprinted in R. S. Gottlieb, ed., *This Sacred Earth: Religion, Nature, Environment* (New York: Routledge, 1996), 640–642.

7. This assertion is based in large part on L. White Jr., "The Historical Roots of Our Ecological Crisis," *Science* 155 (10 March 1967): 1203–1207.

8. M. Oelschlaeger, *Caring for Creation* (New Haven, Conn.: Yale University Press, 1994), 1–2.

9. C. Pope, "Reaching beyond Ourselves: It's Time to Recognize Our Allies in the Faith Community," *Sierra* (November–December 1998): 16–17.

10. M. Planck, "On Religion and Science," 1937, reprinted in translation in A. Barth, *The Creation in the Light of Modern Science* (Jerusalem: Jerusalem Post Press, 1966).

11. This is Booth's restatement of Ernest Hocking: "If, to agree on a name we were to characterize the deepest impulse in us as a 'will to live,' religion also could be called a will to live, but with an accent on solicitude—an ambition to do one's living well. Or, more adequately, *religion is a passion for righteousness, and for the spread of righteousness, conceived as a cosmic demand.*" W. C. Booth, "Systematic Wonder: The

Rhetoric of Secular Religions," *Journal of the American Academy of Religion* 53 (1984): 677–702.

12. J. Carroll and K. Warner, eds., *Ecology and Religion: Scientists Speak* (Quincy, Ill.: Franciscan Press, 1998); P. M. Anderson, ed., *Professors Who Believe* (Downers Grove, Ill.: InterVarsity Press, 1998); R. J. Berry, ed., *Real Science, Real Faith* (Crowborough, East Sussex, England: Monarch Books, 1991).

13. See W. P. Brown, *The Ethos of the Cosmos* (Grand Rapids, Mich.: Eerdmans, 1999); G. J. Spykman, *Reformational Theology: A New Paradigm for Doing Dogmatics* (Grand Rapids, Mich.: Eerdmans, 1992); and H. Bavinck, *Christelijke Wereldbeschouwing* (Kampen, Netherlands: Kok, 1913). Spykman quotes Bavinck: "The Christian worldview holds that man is always and everywhere bound by laws set forth by God as the rule for life. Everywhere there are norms which stand above man. They find a unity among themselves and find their origin and continuation in the Creator and Lawgiver of the universe" (Bavinck, *Christelijke Wereldbeschouwing*, 90–91).

14. *Compact Oxford English Dictionary*, s.v. "religion," "ligate," "ligature," "religate," "religation."

15. World Wildlife Fund, *The Assisi Declarations: Messages on Man and Nature from Buddhism, Christianity, Hinduism, Islam, and Judaism* (Gland, Switzerland: World Wildlife Fund, 1986).

16. Alliance of Religions and Conservation, World Wildlife Fund, 2000. Available online at http://www.panda.org/livingplanet/sacred_gifts/assisi_2.html.

17. S. H. Nasr, "Islam and the Environmental Crisis," in *Spirit and Nature: Why the Environment Is a Religious Issue: An Interfaith Dialogue*, ed. S. C. Rockefeller and J. C. Elder (Boston: Beacon Press, 1992), 83–108; quote, 104.

18. Milford Muskett, University of Wisconsin–Madison, personal communication, November 2000.

19. This is the term used by Nasr in "Islam and the Environmental Crisis."

20. C. A. Russell, *The Earth, Humanity, and God: The Templeton Lectures, Cambridge 1993* (London: University College London Press, 1994).

21. Leopold wrote, "In closing, it may not be improper to add a word on the intensely interesting reading on a multitude of subjects to be found in the Old Testament. As Stevenson said about one of Hazlitt's essays, 'It is so good that there should be a tax levied on all who have not read it'" (Leopold, "Forestry of the Prophets," 419). Northrop Frye sees the Bible as necessary for understanding Western culture; see N. Frye, *The Great Code: The Bible and Literature* (New York: Harcourt Brace Jovanovich, 1982).

22. In that essay, Leopold quotes from R. G. Moulton, ed., *Moulton's Modern Reader's Bible* (New York: Macmillan, 1895): "Seemeth it a small thing unto you to have fed upon the good pasture, but ye must tread down with your feet the residue of your pasture? And to have drunk of the clear waters, but ye must foul the residue with your feet?"

23. I use *biosphere* as equivalent to *oikomene,* as in Psalm 24:1 in the Septuagint (translated from the Hebrew *tebel*) and in 1 Corinthians 10:26, 28.

24. From C. B. DeWitt, "Ecology and Ethics: Relation of Religious Belief to Ecological Practice in the Biblical Tradition," *Biodiversity and Conservation* 4 (1995): 838–848. Reprinted in N. S. Cooper and R. C. J. Carling, eds., *Ecologists and Ethical Judgements* (London: Chapman and Hall, 1996).

25. Compare these ethical principles with the content of G. T. Miller Jr., *Environmental Science: Working with the Earth,* 5th ed. (Pacific Grove, Calif.: Brooks/Cole, 2001), 23, which reviews statements by the National Academy of Sciences and the Royal Society of London.

26. Job 40:19 suggests that the Maker of creatures is the only one with license to destroy them. Therefore, past extinction events give no excuse for extinctions caused by human action.

27. R. Young, *Young's Literal Translation of the Holy Bible,* rev. ed. (Grand Rapids, Mich.: Baker Book House, 1898). Emphasis has been added to the word *serve* in this quote and the one from Joshua that follows.

28. Joshua 24:15.

29. Genesis 2:8.

30. See John 3:16, Psalm 104, and the hymn "O Worship the King" for illustrations of God's love and care for the world. Also see Colossians 1:15–20, 1 Corinthians 15:45, and Hebrews 1:3.

31. Published in J. B. Callicott, ed., *Companion to A Sand County Almanac: Interpretive and Critical Essays* (Madison: University of Wisconsin Press, 1987), 281.

32. T. Ends, "Tilling and Keeping: Christians Working to Promote Sustainable Agriculture" (paper presented to the Christian Environmental Council, Michael Fields Agricultural Institute, East Troy, Wis., 2000).

33. *The Revised English Bible with the Apocrypha* (Oxford, England: Oxford University Press, 1989), excerpts from Romans 7 and 8.

34. See Russell, *Earth, Humanity, and God,* especially pp. 136–137, "The Plight of Humanity."

35. These causes correspond with Colin Russell's "motivating springs for human action": human arrogance, ignorance, greed, and aggression. See also C. B. DeWitt, "Ideas of University of Wisconsin–Madison Students," appendix B in D. Lehmman, *What on Earth Can You Do: Making Your Church a Creation Awareness Center* (Scottdale, Penn., and Waterloo, Ontario, Canada: Herald Press, 1993), 192–195.

36. L. K. Caldwell, quoted in G. T. Miller Jr., *Living in the Environment: An Introduction to Environmental Science* (Belmont, Calif.: Wadsworth, 1988), iii.

37. P. H. Raven and G. B. Johnson, *Biology,* 3rd ed. (St. Louis: Mosby Year Book, 1992), 1216.

38. M. K. Gandhi to the Economic Society at Allahabad University, Uttar Pradesh, India, 1916. Quoted in H. E. Sri Krishna Kant, "Caste, Community, Conversion"

(inaugural speech at the conference "Main Streaming the Church for Nation Building," National Council of Churches of India, Hyderabad, India, June 7, 1991).

39. R. A. Guelich, "Sermon on the Mount," in B. M. Metzger and M. D. Coogan, eds., *The Oxford Companion to the Bible* (New York: Oxford University Press, 1993), 687–689.

40. Excerpts from Matthew 6:9–33 are from *The Holy Bible, King James Version* (New York: Thomas Nelson, 1972).

41. J. M. Keynes, *Essays in Persuasion* (1930; reprint, New York: Norton, 1963), 371–372.

42. Ibid.

43. C. Schultze, "The Public Use of Private Interest," *Harper's,* May 1977, 45–46.

44. J. Sittler, "Ecological Commitment as Theological Responsibility," in *Evocations of Grace: Writings on Ecology, Theology, and Ethics,* ed. S. Bouma-Prediger and P. Bakken (Grand Rapids, Mich.: Eerdmans, 2000), 76–86; quote, 79–80. First published in *Zygon* 5 (June 1970): 172–181.

45. Oelschlaeger wrote: "I think of religion, or more specifically the church . . . as being more important in the effort to conserve life on earth than all the politicians and experts put together. The church may be, in fact, our last, best chance." Oelschlaeger, *Caring for Creation,* 5.

46. See, e.g., W. P. Brown, *The Ethos of the Cosmos: The Genesis of Moral Imagination in the Bible* (Grand Rapids, Mich.: Eerdmans, 1999).

47. As an example of the taking up of this challenge, Ismar Schorsch wrote, "For my own part, I wish to offer a portrait of Judaism as a millennial effort to foster a religious culture of self-restraint that intuitively respects the value and integrity of its natural environment." I. Schorsch, "Learning to Live with Less," in *Spirit and Nature: Why the Environment Is a Religious Issue: An Interfaith Dialogue,* ed. S. C. Rockefeller and J. C. Elder (Boston: Beacon Press, 1992), 25–38.

Chapter 4. Values, Ethics, and Spiritual and Scientific Relations to Nature

1. R. Nash, *The Rights of Nature: A History of Environmental Ethics* (Madison: University of Wisconsin Press, 1989); J. Passmore, *Man's Responsibility for Nature: Ecological Problems and Western Traditions* (New York: Scribner, 1974); L. White Jr., "The Historical Roots of Our Ecological Crisis," *Science* 155 (10 March 1967): 1203–1207.

2. A. Leopold, *A Sand County Almanac, with Other Essays on Conservation from Round River* (New York: Oxford University Press, 1966), 217, 219, 230.

3. E. O. Wilson, "Biophilia and the Conservation Ethics," in *The Biophilia Hypothesis,* ed. S. Kellert and E. O. Wilson (Washington, D.C.: Island Press, 1993), 37.

4. S. Kellert, *Kinship to Mastery: Biophilia in Human Evolution and Development* (Wash-

ington, D.C.: Island Press, 1997); Kellert and Wilson, *Biophilia Hypothesis;* E. O. Wilson, *Biophilia* (Cambridge, Mass.: Harvard University Press, 1984).

5. R. Carson, *Silent Spring* (Boston: Houghton Mifflin, 1962).

6. Leopold, *Sand County Almanac.*

7. B. Elkin, *The Wisest Man in the World* (New York: Parents' Magazine Press, 1976).

8. A modified version of this story appears in the prologue to S. Kellert, *Kinship to Mastery.*

9. Kellert, *Kinship to Mastery.*

10. J. Appleton, *The Experience of Landscape* (London: Wiley, 1975); J. Heerwagen and G. Orians, "Humans, Habitats, and Aesthetics," in Kellert and Wilson, *Biophilia Hypothesis.*

11. Heerwagen and Orians, "Humans, Habitats, and Aesthetics"; G. Hildebrand, *The Origins of Architectural Pleasure* (Berkeley: University of California Press, 2000); R. Ulrich, "Biophilia, Biophobia, and Natural Landscapes," in Kellert and Wilson, *Biophilia Hypothesis.*

12. A. Katcher and G. Wilkins, "Dialogue with Animals: Its Nature and Culture," in Kellert and Wilson, *Biophilia Hypothesis;* J. Serpell, *In the Company of Animals* (Oxford: Basil Blackwell, 1986).

13. J. Steinbeck, *Log from the Sea of Cortez* (Mamaroneck, N.Y.: Appel, 1941), 93.

14. S. McVay, prologue in Kellert and Wilson, *Biophilia Hypothesis.*

15. A. Ohman, "Face the Beast and Fear the Face: Animal and Social Fears as Prototypes for Evolutionary Analyses of Emotion," *Psychophysiology* 23 (1986): 123–145; Ulrich, "Biophilia, Biophobia, and Natural Landscapes."

16. R. Nelson, "Searching for the Lost Arrow: Physical and Spiritual Ecology of the Hunter's World," in Kellert and Wilson, *Biophilia Hypothesis,* 224.

17. B. Bloom, ed., *Taxonomy of Educational Objectives,* handbook 1, *Cognitive Domain* (New York: McKay, 1956).

18. J. Diamond, "New Guineans and Their Natural World," in Kellert and Wilson, *Biophilia Hypothesis.*

19. E. Lawrence, "The Sacred Bee, the Filthy Pig, and the Bat out of Hell: Animal Symbolism as Cognitive Biophilia," in Kellert and Wilson, *Biophilia Hypothesis;* P. Shepard, *Thinking Animals: Animals and the Development of Human Intelligence* (New York: Viking Press, 1978); P. Shepard, *The Others: How Animals Made Us Human* (Washington, D.C.: Island Press, 1996).

20. M. Oelschlaeger, *The Idea of Wilderness* (New Haven, Conn.: Yale University Press, 1991), 377.

21. K. Thomas, *Man and the Natural World* (New York: Pantheon Books, 1983).

22. H. Beston, *The Outermost House* (New York: Ballantine Books, 1971), vi.

23. M. Chandrakanth and J. Romm, "Sacred Forests, Secular Forest Policies, and People's Actions," *Natural Resources Journal* 31 (1991): 742–761; quote, 750.

24. Leopold, *Sand County Almanac.*

25. H. Beston, *Northern Farm* (New York: Henry Holt, 1948), 245–246.

Chapter 5. Religion and Ecology

This chapter arose from a conference series, "Religions of the World and Ecology," which I organized with my husband, John Grim, at the Harvard University Center for the Study of World Religions in 1996–1998. The conferences brought together some eight hundred scholars of the world's religions along with environmental activists to rethink views of nature and the potential for environmental ethics in the world's religions. The papers from the conferences are being published in a ten-volume series distributed by Harvard University Press; details are available on-line at http://www.hds.harvard.edu/cswr/ecology.

We also initiated a Forum on Religion and Ecology, which has three major goals: to continue the research, to encourage educational initiatives, and to foster outreach to other disciplines such as science, education, economics, and public policy. To this end, we mounted an Internet site under the Harvard University Center for the Environment, accessible at http://environment.harvard.edu/religion.

Sections of this chapter were published in *The NAMTA Journal* 23, no. 1 (winter 1998).

1. T. Berry, *The Great Work: Our Way into the Future* (New York: Random House, 1999).
2. We might discuss this in terms of transcendent and immanent experiences of the divine, but I hope to find some language that goes beyond this kind of dualism, useful as it may be.
3. B. McKibben, *The End of Nature* (New York: Doubleday, 1989).
4. T. Berry, *The Dream of the Earth* (San Francisco: Sierra Club Books, 1988).
5. W. Capps, *Religious Studies: The Making of a Discipline* (Minneapolis: Fortress Press, 1995), 58.
6. It can be suggested that this latter dialogue may spark the most significant evolution of religious thinking in the past several hundred years. The Institute on Religion in an Age of Science (IRAS), with its journal, *Zygon,* has been one of the leading forces in fostering this dialogue since the mid-1950s. More recently, the John Templeton Foundation has supported conferences, workshops, courses, and publications in this field.
7. See, e.g., M. Eliade, *The Sacred and the Profane* (New York: Harcourt Brace, 1959) and M. Eliade, *Images and Symbols* (New York: Sheed and Ward, 1969).
8. L. Eiseley, *The Immense Journey* (New York: Vintage Books, 1946).
9. Ibid., 16, 20.
10. Ibid., 175.
11. Ibid., 26.
12. Ibid., 26–27.
13. This phrasing was suggested by Stephen Kellert in an e-mail communication.
14. See E. N. Anderson, *Ecologies of the Heart* (New York: Oxford University Press, 1996).
15. In my use of the term *worldview,* I am indebted to Clifford Geertz's articulation of

worldview and *ethos* as well as Ninian Smart's use of the idea of worldview to describe religious traditions. See C. Geertz, "Religion as a Cultural System," in *Reader in Comparative Religion: An Anthropological Approach,* ed. W. Lessa and E. Vogt (New York: Harper and Row, 1965), and N. Smart, *Worldviews: Crosscultural Explanations of Human Beliefs* (New York: Scribner, 1983).

16. M. Sahlins, foreword to G. Schrempp, *Magical Arrows* (Madison: University of Wisconsin Press, 1992), x.

17. Robin Lovin and Frank Reynolds edited a volume of provocative essays from cross-cultural perspectives on this topic. R. Lovin and F. Reynolds, eds., *Cosmogony and Ethical Order* (Chicago: University of Chicago Press, 1985).

18. Schrempp, *Magical Arrows,* 4.

19. See T. Berry, *The Great Work: Our Way into the Future* (New York: Random House, 1999).

20. B. W. Anderson, *Understanding the Old Testament,* 4th ed. (Englewood Cliffs, N.J.: Prentice-Hall, 1986), 541.

21. Ibid., 550–551.

22. Ibid., 551.

23. K. G. Zysk, ed., *A. L. Basham: The Origins and Development of Classical Hinduism* (Boston: Beacon Press, 1989), 10–11.

24. Ibid., 25.

25. Ibid., 23.

26. T. Berry, *Religions of India: Hinduism, Yoga, Buddhism* (Beverly Hills, Calif.: Bruce, 1971), 22.

27. J. Blofeld, trans. and ed., *I Ching: The Book of Changes* (New York: Dutton, 1965), 85.

28. H. Wilhelm, *Heaven, Earth, and Man in The Book of Changes* (Seattle: University of Washington Press, 1977), 18.

29. H. Wilhelm, *Change: Eight Lectures on the I Ching,* trans. C. F. Baynes (New York: Harper Torchbooks, 1960), 69.

30. There are many pioneers in the field of ecological design, including John and Nancy Todd, Amory and Hunter Lovins, David Orr, William McDonough, Janine Benyus, and Paul Hawken.

31. T. Berry, *The Dream of the Earth* (San Francisco: Sierra Club Books, 1988), 137.

Chapter 6. Gaia and the Ethical Abyss: A Natural Ethic is a G[o]od Thing

1. D. Sagan and L. Margulis, "Facing Nature," in *Biology, Ethics, and the Origins of Life,* ed. H. Rolston III (Boston: Jones and Bartlett, 1995), 196.

2. Ibid., 48.

3. E. D. Schneider and D. Sagan, *Into the Cool: Thermodynamics and the Purpose of Life* (Princeton, N.J.: Princeton University Press, in press).

4. A. K. Dewdney, *Hungry Hollow: The Story of a Natural Place* (New York: Springer-Verlag, Copernicus Books, 1998).

5. J. A. Moore, *Science as a Way of Knowing* (Cambridge, Mass.: Harvard University Press, 1993).

6. L. Margulis and D. Sagan, *What Is Life?* (Berkeley: University of California Press, 2000).

7. J. Lovelock, *Homage to Gaia* (Oxford, England: Oxford University Press, 2000).

8. L. Margulis and D. Sagan, *Gaia to Microcosm,* videotape and booklet (Dubuque, Iowa: Kendall/Hunt, 1994). Available from Sciencewriters, P.O. Box 671, Amherst, MA 01004-0671; http://www.sciencewriters.org.

9. Margulis and Sagan, *What Is Life?*

10. V. I. Vernadsky, *The Biosphere* (1926; translation, New York: Springer-Verlag, Copernicus Books, 1999).

11. R. Morrison, *The Spirit in the Gene: Humanity's Proud Illusion and the Laws of Nature* (Ithaca, N.Y.: Cornell University Press, 1999), xiii, xv.

Chapter 7. Religious Meanings for Nature and Humanity

1. For recent and useful discussions of the many issues involved here, see D. Christiansen, "Ecology, Justice, and Development," *Theological Studies* 51 (1990): 64–81; J. M. Gustafson, *A Sense of the Divine: The Natural Environment from a Theocentric Perspective* (Cleveland: Pilgrim Press, 1994); J. M. Gustafson, *Intersections: Science, Theology, and Ethics* (Cleveland: Pilgrim Press, 1996); K. W. Irwin and E. D. Pellegrino, eds., *Preserving the Creation: Environmental Theology and Ethics* (Washington, D.C.: Georgetown University Press, 1994); R. McKim, "Environmental Ethics: The Widening Vision," *Religious Studies Review* 23 (July 1997): 245–250; C. S. Robb and C. J. Casebolt, eds., *Covenant for a New Creation: Ethics, Religion, and Public Policy* (Maryknoll, N.Y.: Orbis Books, 1991).

2. L. White Jr., "The Historical Roots of Our Ecological Crisis," *Science* 155 (10 March 1967): 1203–1207.

3. Augustine, *The City of God,* trans. G. Walsh et al. (New York: Image Books, 1958), 11.16.

4. Ibid.

5. Augustine, *Confessions,* trans. R. Warner (New York: New American Library, 1963), 10.6.

6. See, e.g., T. Aquinas, *Summa Theologiae* I.44.1; *Summa Contra Gentiles* III.25; *De Veritate* 2.11 ad 4.

7. P. Teilhard de Chardin, *The Divine Milieu: An Essay on the Interior Life* (New York: Harper, 1960), 38.

8. See C. F. Mooney, *Theology and Scientific Knowledge: Changing Models of God's Pres-*

ence in the World (Notre Dame, Ind.: University of Notre Dame Press, 1996), 150–151.

9. See, e.g., L. Boff and V. Elizondo, eds., *Ecology and Poverty* (Maryknoll, N.Y.: Orbis Books, 1995).

10. See M. Buber, *I and Thou,* trans. R. G. Smith (New York: Charles Scribner's Sons, 1958), 100.

11. See C. S. Lewis, *Perelandra* (New York: Macmillan, 1944), 230–233.

Chapter 8. A Livable Future

This chapter is a revised version of an article that first appeared in *Johns Hopkins Magazine* (G. W. Fisher, "Finding Common Ground," *Johns Hopkins Magazine* 52 [2000]: 30–35), and I am grateful to Sue De Pasquale, the magazine's editor, for permission to reprint it here. Many of the ideas presented here appeared first in a book edited by Jill Schneiderman (G. W. Fisher, "Sustainable Living: Common Ground for Geology and Theology," in *The Earth around Us: Maintaining a Livable Planet,* ed. J. S. Schneiderman [New York: Freeman, 2000], 99–111), and I am grateful for her encouragement in preparing that essay.

1. P. R. Ehrlich, *The Population Bomb* (New York: Ballantine Books, 1971); D. H. Meadows et al., *The Limits to Growth: A Report for the Club of Rome's Project on the Predicament of Mankind* (New York: Universe Books, 1972).

2. National Research Council, *Our Common Journey: A Transition toward Sustainability* (Washington, D.C.: National Academy Press, 1999), 64–66.

3. P. M. Vitousek et al., "Human Domination of Earth's Ecosystems," *Science* 277 (25 July 1997): 494–499.

4. National Research Council, *Our Common Journey,* 67.

5. J. E. Cohen, "How Many People Can the Earth Support?" *New York Review of Books* (8 October 1998): 29–31.

6. J. M. Hayes, "The Earliest Memories of Life on Earth," *Nature* 384 (1996): 21–22.

7. J. Wu and O. L. Loucks, "From Balance of Nature to Hierarchical Patch Dynamics: A Paradigm Shift in Ecology," *Quarterly Review of Biology* 70 (1995): 439–466.

8. Vitousek et al., "Human Domination."

9. Cohen, "How Many People?"

10. P. Teilhard de Chardin, *The Divine Milieu: An Essay on the Interior Life* (New York: Harper, 1960).

11. J. B. Cobb Jr. and D. R. Griffin, *Process Theology: An Introductory Exposition* (Philadelphia: Westminster Press, 1976).

12. L. Gilkey, *Nature, Reality, and the Sacred: The Nexus of Science and Religion* (Minneapolis: Fortress Press, 1993); S. H. Nasr, *Religion and the Order of Nature* (New York: Oxford University Press, 1996); L. Zoloth, "The Promises of Exiles: A Jewish Theology of Responsibility," in *Visions of a New Earth: Religious Perspectives on Pop-*

ulation, Consumption, and Ecology, ed. H. Coward and D. C. Maguire (Albany: State University of New York Press, 2000), 95–109.

13. G. W. Fisher, "Sustainable Living: Common Ground for Geology and Theology," in *The Earth around Us: Maintaining a Livable Planet,* ed. J. S. Schneiderman (New York: Freeman, 2000), 99–111.

14. J. M. Gustafson, *Ethics from a Theocentric Perspective,* vol. 1, *Theology and Ethics* (Chicago: University of Chicago Press, 1981).

15. P. Tillich, *Dynamics of Faith* (New York, Harper, 1957).

16. Fisher, "Sustainable Living."

17. Tillich, *Dynamics of Faith.*

18. Fisher, "Sustainable Living."

19. Ibid.

20. H. R. Niebuhr, *The Meaning of Revelation* (New York: Macmillan, 1941), 68–69.

Chapter 9. *Alma De'atei,* "The World That Is Coming"

I'd like to thank the Heschel Center for Environmental Learning and Leadership, Tel Aviv, Israel, for making possible my participation at the conference "The Good in Nature and Humanity," and the director of the Heschel Center, my friend and colleague Eilon Schwartz, whose encouragement and ideas are present in every paragraph of this chapter. I'd also like to thank my great and good friend Dr. Noah Efron for a very helpful critical reading. All translations in this chapter are my own.

1. W. Berry, address at conference "The Good in Nature and Humanity," Yale University, May 12, 2000.

2. S. J. Gould, "The Power of This View of Life," *Natural History* (June 1994): 6–8.

3. We might add to these humbling (in the eyes of some, humiliating) slaps to the collective human ego the unseating of Western patriarchal "enlightenment" via the less heroic, but no less far-reaching, movements of postcolonialism and feminism. Yet these are already different stories, for they are not a global affront to human self-perception (or, more accurately, Western biblically influenced perception of the human project). Rather, they are a challenge to the primacy or, to use the term most in vogue, the hegemony of part of that humanity—the West over the rest, the male and masculine over the female and feminine. These movements are relevant here, though, because inherent in postcolonialism and feminism are deep critiques of two of the central pillars of that narrative of technological progress: the tenet of objectivity regarding the methods of science and the pursuit of technology, and the assumed universal applicability of the policies and tools of what is termed development by its proponents (and economic imperialism by its critics, indigenous and otherwise).

4. Interestingly, these three great scientific revolutions were met with trenchant, at times violent, opposition from religious (that is to say, Christian) authorities. Does religion only pay lip service to the ideal of human humility? Or is humility

desirable only in the face of divinity (or similarly sanctioned human authority)? Humility in the face of creation, arguably one of the central messages of the book of Job, seems much less important than the traditional "task" of asserting dominion. But without humility in the face of something greater than ourselves—whether divinity or nature—the biblical doctrine of potential human dominion, a message of hope for human dignity in a pretechnological age, becomes, in our own era of technological firepower coupled with unbridled hubris, a veritable nightmare of exploitation and destruction.

5. This is not to say that the insight was lost on all traditional religious thinkers. The great Jewish medieval Bible commentator Joseph ibn Kaspi (fourteenth-century Provence and Spain) wrote in his commentary *Adnei Kesef* to Deuteronomy 22: "Besides the eradication of cruelty the Torah wished to make us conscious of our own status . . . a sense of our modesty and lowliness, that we should be ever cognizant of the fact that we are of the same stuff as the ass and mule, the cabbage and pomegranate and even the lifeless stone."

6. Or is it *fewer* things? Part of the phenomenon of globalized consumerism is a sort of material homogenization (indicative of a parallel cultural homogenization, of course). So we're certainly dealing with more and more *things,* but perhaps of fewer types, with a lot more of certain narrowly defined, globally standardized merchandise.

7. Indeed, as I suggest, there may be a quasi-causal connection, with an existential vacuum being created that was gradually filled by the sort of techno-materialism I describe.

8. Obviously, there is no one traditional society, and this is an impossibly broad generalization. But I think the point holds in relation to a secular forward-looking progress or "knowledge" paradigm, as opposed to a more theistic "wisdom" perspective. I think that religious environmentalism at its best expresses a spiritually based critique of the former.

9. This is not to say that all traditional worldviews, or religions in general, are environmentally sound or wise. Parallel to the approach known as technological optimism—the belief that we need not worry or fundamentally change our lifestyles, for technology has the power to solve all our problems—is an interesting phenomenon that I term theological optimism. This is simply the similar belief that we need not worry or fundamentally change our lifestyles, for God has the power (and the will) to solve all our problems. This approach has Jewish as well as Christian variants. A very environmentally aware ultra-Orthodox Jewish friend of mine, a mother of eight (who wanted more), when confronted with the facts of the population explosion, responded: "God brings the children into the world; He will find the room for them." And James Watt, as secretary of the interior under President Ronald Reagan, was reported to have said in testimony against the protection of forests for future generations: "My responsibility is to follow the Scriptures. . . . I don't know how many generations we can count on before the Lord returns." J. B. Callicott, *Earth's Insights* (Berkeley: University of California Press, 1994), xix.

10. A. E. Imhof, *Lost Worlds: How Our European Ancestors Coped with Everyday Life and Why It Is So Hard Today* (Charlottesville: University Press of Virginia, 1996).

11. Ibid., 171–172.

12. See James Watt's comments quoted in note 9.

13. Of course, this can be and has been abused, with religious institutions perpetuating worldly oppression and deprivation in the name of heavenly promises. Certain proponents of progress—or, rather, proponents of a certain type of progress— claim that the church did indeed impede social and technological progress on these grounds or by these means.

14. G. P. Nabhan, address at conference "The Good in Nature and Humanity," Yale University, May 12, 2000.

15. F. Rosenzweig, *Der Stern der Erlosung* (Frankfort on the Main: Schocken, 1921; 2nd ed., 1930); F. Rosenzweig, *The Star of Redemption,* trans. W. W. Hallo (Boston: Beacon Press, 1970).

16. It is interesting to note that the Hebrew term *olam* has both spatial and temporal meanings: It means both "world" and "eternity." *L'olam,* then (with only a slight variation in vocalization of the initial consonant), can mean both "for the sake of the world" and "forever" or "for all time." It is practically a one-word encapsulation of the notion of sustainability.

17. Babylonian Talmud, Tractate Kiddushin, folio 39b.

18. The same Rabbi Ya'akov has given us two of the most trenchant maxims regarding the insignificance of this world in relation to the next, in *Pirkei Avot* (The Ethics of the Fathers): "This world is like a vestibule to the world to come; prepare yourself in the vestibule that you may enter into the banqueting-hall" and "Better is one hour of bliss of spirit in the world to come than all the life of this world." J. Goldin, *The Living Talmud* (New York: New American Library, 1957), 4:16, 4:17.

19. See Maimonides, *The Guide of the Perplexed,* trans. S. Pines (Chicago: University of Chicago Press, 1963), III:48.

20. Nachmanides was a Jewish commentator in thirteenth-century Spain. In this context, he also gives one of the clearest statements applying biblical law to the question of the preservation of biodiversity. He interprets this commandment of sending away the mother bird globally, as categorically forbidding actions leading to species extinction: "Scripture does not allow the total destruction of a species, although it allows us to slaughter some of its kind" (see his commentary to Deuteronomy, ad loc.).

21. W. Berry, *The Gift of Good Land* (San Francisco: North Point Press, 1981).

22. I. Abravanel, commentary to the Pentateuch, ad loc.

23. P. Gorman, address at conference "The Good in Nature and Humanity," Yale University, May 11, 2000.

24. Once again, Rabbi Ya'akov expressed this thought most pithily: "One, who while walking along the way, reviewing his studies, breaks off from his study and says, 'How beautiful is that tree! How beautiful is that plowed field!' Scripture regards him as if he has forfeited his soul" (Ethics of the Fathers, 3:7). For a detailed study of this pas-

sage, its commentaries, and related ideas in the context of Jewish environmentalism, see J. Benstein, "Nature versus Torah," *Judaism Quarterly* 44, no. 2 (spring 1995): 146–170. Republished in Arthur Waskow, ed., *Torah of the Earth: Exploring 4000 Years of Ecology in Jewish Thought,* vol. 1 (Woodstock, Vt.: Jewish Lights Press, 2000).

25. According to traditional Jewish values, this act of mastering one's urges and inclinations is the definition of true courage, or heroism: "Who is a hero? One who conquers his own impulses" (Ethics of the Fathers, 4:1).

26. Whether or not these are religious initiatives per se, they essentially have the force of religion, for they act to "bind together" (*re-ligio*). As both Ursula Goodenough and Calvin B. DeWitt point out in this volume, religion should act to religate, or reconnect, people with one another; the (heritage of the) past with (responsibilities to the) future; matter with spirit; science with ethics; and so on.

Introduction to Part II

1. A. Leopold, *A Sand County Almanac* (New York: Oxford University Press, 1968).
2. Ibid.
3. Ibid., 203–204.
4. T. Watkins, *Stone Time, Southern Utah: A Portrait and a Meditation* (Santa Fe, N.M.: Clear Light, 1994), 104.
5. Ibid.
6. Patriarch Bartholomew, speech delivered at the Symposium on Religion, Science, and the Environment, University of California, Santa Barbara, November 1997.

Chapter 10. Work, Worship, and the Natural World

1. M. Oliver, *Dream Work* (Boston: Atlantic Monthly Press, 1986).
2. W. Stegner, "The Gift of Wilderness," in *Learning to Listen to the Land,* ed. B. Willers (Washington, D.C.: Island Press, 1991), 114.
3. R. Nash, *Wilderness and the American Mind* (New Haven, Conn.: Yale University Press, 1967, 1973, 1982).
4. C. P. Estés, *Women Who Run with the Wolves* (New York: Ballantine Books, 1992), 3.
5. Quoted in O. Williams and E. Honig, eds., *The Mentor Book of Major American Poets* (New York: New American Library, 1962), 253.
6. Ibid., 254.
7. Ibid.
8. Ibid.
9. W. S. Merwin, epigraph in *The Forgotten Language: Contemporary Poets and Nature,* ed. C. Merrill (Salt Lake City: Gibbs Smith Publisher, Peregrine Smith Books, 1991).
10. S. Mitchell, *Tao Te Ching* (New York: Harper and Row, 1988), 1.
11. W. S. Merwin, "The Last One," in Merwin, *Forgotten Language,* 110.

12. D. Wagner, *The Heart Aroused: Poetry and the Preservation of the Soul in Corporate America*, ed. D. Whyte (New York: Doubleday, 1994), 259–261.

Chapter 11. Leopold's Darwin

1. S. Donnelley, ed., "Nature, Polis, Ethics (Chicago Regional Planning)," *Hastings Center Report* (November–December 1998), special supplement.
2. J. B. Callicott, ed., *Companion to a Sand County Almanac: Interpretive and Critical Essays* (Madison: University of Wisconsin Press, 1987); A. Leopold, *The River of the Mother of God,* ed. S. L. Frader and J. B. Callicott (Madison: University of Wisconsin Press, 1991); C. Meine, *Aldo Leopold: His Life and Work* (Madison: University of Wisconsin Press, 1987).
3. E. Mayr, *One Long Argument* (Cambridge, Mass.: Harvard University Press, 1991).
4. A. Leopold, "Thinking Like a Mountain," in *A Sand County Almanac, with Other Essays on Conservation from Round River* (New York: Oxford University Press, 1966), 129.
5. A. Leopold, "Escudella" and "The Green Lagoons," in *Sand County Almanac,* 133, 141.
6. See S. Donnelley, "Human Nature, Views of," in R. Chadwick, ed., *Encyclopedia of Applied Ethics,* vol. 2 (London: Academic Press, 1998).
7. See E. Hamilton and H. Cairns, eds., *The Collected Dialogues of Plato* (Princeton, N.J.: Princeton University Press, 1961).
8. See W. K. C. Guthrie, *A History of Greek Philosophy,* vol. 1, *The Earlier Presocratics and the Pythagoreans* (Cambridge, England: Cambridge University Press, 1987).
9. A. Leopold, "On a Monument to a Pigeon," in *Sand County Almanac,* 108.
10. A. Leopold, "Wisconsin: Marshland Elegy," in *Sand County Almanac,* 95.
11. A. Leopold, "The Land Ethic: The Community Concept," and "Substitutes for the Land Ethic," in *Sand County Almanac,* 203, 210.
12. A. Leopold, "Land Ethic: The Land Pyramid," in *Sand County Almanac,* 214.
13. A. Leopold, "November: A Mighty Fortress," in *Sand County Almanac,* 73.
14. A. Leopold, "Odyssey," in *Sand County Almanac,* 107.
15. Ibid.
16. A. Leopold, "Conservation Esthetics," in *Sand County Almanac,* 165.
17. A. Leopold, "Wildlife in American Culture," in *Sand County Almanac,* 177.
18. A. Leopold, "Part III: The Upshot," in *Sand County Almanac,* 165 ff.
19. A. Leopold, "Monument to a Pigeon," in *Sand County Almanac,* 108.
20. A. Leopold, "April: Skydance," in *Sand County Almanac,* 30.
21. See S. Donnelley, "Nature, Freedom, and Responsibility: Ernst Mayr and Isaiah Berlin," *Social Research* 67, no. 4 (winter 2000): 1117–1135.
22. A. Leopold, "Land Ethic: The Ecological Conscience," in *Sand County Almanac,* 207.
23. See A. N. Whitehead, *Science and the Modern World* (New York: Free Press, 1967), 51.

Chapter 12. A Rising Tide for Ethics

1. A. Leopold, *A Sand County Almanac, with Other Essays on Conservation from Round River* (New York: Oxford University Press, 1966), 218.
2. H. B. Bigelow and W. C. Schroeder, *Fishes of the Gulf of Maine* (Washington, D.C.: Government Printing Office, 1953), 386.
3. K. R. Miller, *Finding Darwin's God* (New York: HarperCollins, 1999). The seeming contradiction between the concepts of human free will and an all-knowing creator has been a major stumbling block to reconciling faith and reason. Miller, a cell biologist at Brown University, proposes an interesting resolution to the problem.
4. L. Margulis, *Symbiotic Planet* (New York: Basic Books, 1998). Margulis makes a forceful case for the tenacity of life on earth and the impermanence of *Homo sapiens*.
5. E. O. Wilson, *The Diversity of Life* (New York: Norton, 1993). For a further discussion of the human aesthetic sense, see S. R. Kellert, *Kinship to Mastery: Biophilia in Human Evolution and Development* (Washington, D.C.: Island Press, 1997).
6. Leopold, *Sand County Almanac,* 219.
7. Ibid., 269.

Chapter 13. Hunting for Spirituality

Adapted from *Heartsblood: Hunting, Spirituality, and Wildness in America,* by David Petersen (Washington, D.C.: Island Press, 2000). Used by permission.

1. S. R. Kellert, *Kinship to Mastery: Biophilia in Human Evolution and Development* (Washington, D.C.: Island Press, 1997).
2. M. Buss, "Meditations of a Hunter," *Outdoor Canada* (November–December 1977).
3. S. R. Kellert, "Attitudes and Characteristics of Hunters and Antihunters and Related Policy Suggestions," in *Transactions of the North American Wildlife and Natural Resources Conference,* 1978.
4. D. Crockett, "Hunting Hope," foreword to D. Petersen, *Elkheart: A Personal Tribute to Wapiti and Their World* (Boulder, Colo.: Johnson Books, 1998).
5. P. Davies, quoted in C. Raymo, *Skeptics and True Believers* (New York: Walker, 1998).
6. R. Metzner, "The Psychopathology of the Human–Nature Relationship," in *The Company of Others,* ed. M. Oelschlaeger (Skyland, N.C.: Kivaki Press, 1995).
7. R. Schultheis, *Bone Games: Extreme Games, Shamanism, Zen, and the Search for Transcendence* (New York: Breakaway Books, 1996).
8. S. Giedion, "Constancy, Change, and Architecture," First Gropius Lecture, Harvard University, 1961; quoted in P. Shepard, "The Tender Carnivore," *Landscape* (Autumn 1964).

9. J. Ortega y Gasset, *Meditations on Hunting* (Bozeman, Mont.: Wilderness Adventures Press, 1995).

10. M. Z. Stange, "In the Snow Queen's Palace," in M. Z. Stange, *Woman the Hunter* (Boston: Beacon Press, 1997).

11. C. L. Langer, "Man and Nature: A Basic Relationship," in *The Art of Thomas Aquinas Daly: The Painting Season* (Arcade, N.Y.: Thomas A. Daly Studio, 1998).

Chapter 14. The Idea of a Local Economy

1. Wes Jackson writes about the influence of the Committee for Economic Development in *New Roots for Agriculture* (Lincoln: University of Nebraska Press, 1985), chap. 9. And Mark Ritchie deals with that committee in his pamphlet *The Loss of Our Family Farms* (Whitehall, Mont.: League of Rural Voters, 1986, fourth printing).

2. A. K. Coomaraswamy, *What Is Civilization?* (Ipswich, England: Golgonooza Press, 1989), 1, 8.

3. A. Schweitzer, *Out of My Life and Thought: An Autobiography,* trans. A. B. Lemke (New York: Henry Holt, 1990), 192.

About the Contributors

JEREMY BENSTEIN holds a master's degree in rabbinic literature and is currently a doctoral candidate in environmental anthropology at the Hebrew University of Jerusalem, researching joint Jewish–Arab environmental initiatives in the Galilee. He is the environmental fellowship director of the Heschel Center for Environmental Learning and Leadership and is a lecturer on environmental ethics and spirituality at the Arava Institute for Environmental Studies. He has published numerous articles on Judaism and environmentalism, including regular contributions to the current events magazine the *Jerusalem Report.*

WENDELL BERRY is the author of thirty-two books of essays, poetry, and novels. He is a former professor of English at the University of Kentucky and a past fellow of both the John Simon Guggenheim Memorial Foundation and The Rockefeller Foundation. He has received numerous accolades for his work, including an award from the American Academy and Institute of Arts and Letters, the Friends of American Writers Award, and most recently, the T. S. Eliot Prize. His books include *The Unsettling of America: Culture and Agriculture; The Gift of Good Land;* and *Another Turn of the Crank.* He lives and works on his farm in Port Royal, Kentucky.

CALVIN B. DEWITT is professor of environmental studies at the University of Wisconsin–Madison and director of the Au Sable Institute of Environmental Studies, which examines the connections between religion and ecology. He is also co-founder of the International Evangelical Environmental Network, a founding member and chair of the American Society of the Green Cross, chair of the Advisory Council of the Evangelical Campaign to Combat Global Warming and Climate Change, and an advisor to the National Religious Partnership for the Environment. His works are widely published and include *Caring for Creation: Responsible Stewardship of God's Handiwork* (1998) and *Earth-Wise: A Biblical Response to Environmental Issues* (1994).

261

STRACHAN DONNELLEY is director of The Hastings Center's Humans and Nature Program. He previously served as the center's president (1996–1999) and, earlier, as director of education and associate for environmental ethics. He received his doctorate in philosophy in 1977 and has published numerous articles in applied ethics, including works on animal ethics, biotechnology, and regional planning. He currently directs several projects under the Humans and Nature Program, including Nature, Polis, Ethics: Chicago Regional Planning and similar projects on the Hudson River watershed and South Carolina's Low Country.

MARGARET A. FARLEY is Gilbert L. Stark Professor of Christian Ethics at the Yale University Divinity School and co-chair of Yale University's Interdisciplinary Bioethics Project. She has written and edited four books and published more than seventy articles addressing issues in medical ethics, sexual ethics, social ethics, historical theological ethics, and feminist ethics. She is past president of the Society of Christian Ethics and of the Catholic Theological Society of America.

TIMOTHY J. FARNHAM is a doctoral candidate at the Yale School of Forestry and Environmental Studies. His research focuses on perceptions of nature and the history of environmental values in the United States, and his dissertation specifically examines the evolution of concern for biological diversity in contemporary conservation thought. He received the Teresa Heinz Scholars for Environmental Research award in 2000 and the G. Evelyn Hutchinson Prize in 1999. Before undertaking his doctoral study, he held positions with the National Wildlife Federation and the Society of American Foresters.

GEORGE W. FISHER has taught geology at Johns Hopkins University since 1966. His early work focused on the geology of the Appalachian Piedmont and the kinetics of metamorphic processes. Since the 1990s, his interests have broadened to include questions of how the earth functions as an integrated system and how the growing human population can live within the limits imposed by that system. He is the author of numerous articles and several books; his most recent work is on the history of the Chesapeake Bay watershed ecosystem.

URSULA GOODENOUGH is professor of biology at Washington University; her research currently focuses on analysis of the genes that mediate sexual differentiation and mating in the unicellular alga *Chlamydomonas,* with particular interest in the evolution of these genes in related species. She has served as president of the American Society for Cell Biology and of the Institute on Religion in an Age of Science. Her publications include a text on genetics and a book titled *The Sacred Depths of Nature* (1998), which explores the religious potential of our scientific understanding of nature.

STEPHEN R. KELLERT is Tweedy/Ordway Professor of Social Ecology at the Yale School of Forestry and Environmental Studies. His awards include the National Conservation Achievement Award from the National Wildlife Federation (1997), the Distinguished Individual Achievement Award from the Society for Conservation Biology (1990), the Best Publication of the Year Award from the International Foundation for Environmental Conservation (1985), and a Fulbright Research Fellowship. He has authored more than 100 publications, including *Kinship to Mastery: Biophilia in Human Evolution and Development* (1997).

BARRY LOPEZ is the author of eight collections of short fiction and six works of nonfiction. He received the National Book Award in Nonfiction for *Arctic Dreams* (1986). Other awards include the John Burroughs Medal (1976), the Pacific Northwest Booksellers Association Book Award (1979), the Christopher Award (1987), and the Parents' Choice Award (1990). Lopez grew up in agricultural southern California and New York City. He has lived in Oregon since the 1970s.

LYNN MARGULIS is Distinguished University Professor at the University of Massachusetts, Amherst. She is an elected member of the National Academy of Sciences (1983), the World Academy of Art and Science (1995), the Russian Academy of Natural Sciences (1997), and the American Academy of Arts and Sciences (1998). She was awarded the distinguished William Procter Prize for Scientific Achievement from Sigma Xi, The Scientific Research Society (1999) and was presented by President Bill Clinton with the National Medal of Science. Her publications include twenty-three authored or co-authored books.

WILLIAM H. MEADOWS is president of The Wilderness Society. Before joining the society, he was director of the Sierra Club's Centennial Campaign. A native of Tennessee, he served for many years as a leader within the Sierra Club at the state and local levels. He was a founder and board member of the Environmental Action Fund and has served on the board of the Tennessee Environmental Council.

ROBERT PERSCHEL is director of the Network of Wild Lands Program at The Wilderness Society. A graduate of the Yale School of Forestry and Environmental Studies, he spent fifteen years working as a consulting forester, first for the forest industry and then in his own business. He currently serves as chair of the Northern Forest Alliance, a coalition of forty-two environmental groups working to protect the forests of northern New England and New York State. He is also a co-leader of The Wilderness Society's Land Ethic Task Force, which develops programs to foster the connection between people and place.

DAVID PETERSEN is a former U.S. Marine Corps helicopter pilot, magazine editor, and college teacher who has invested fifty years in learning about natural wildness and fifteen years in writing about what he has learned. The author or editor of a dozen books, Petersen lives in the San Juan Mountains of Colorado. His most recent book is *Heartsblood: Hunting, Spirituality, and Wildness in America* (2000).

DAVE PREBLE descends from a line of Maine coast seafarers. His father was a commercial fisherman, and his eldest son is a U.S. Navy officer. Dave has a master's degree in biology from the University of Rhode Island and holds a merchant marine license as Master of Coastal Vessels. He has four decades of experience in commercial, sport, and charter fishing and is the New England editor of *Salt Water Sportsman* magazine. He has authored dozens of articles as well as two books on fish and fishing. His third book, *Fishes of the Sea,* a collection of essays and stories, was published by Sheridan House in the autumn of 2001.

CARL SAFINA is currently vice president for marine conservation at the National Audubon Society. He is the author of more than 100 scientific and popular publications on ecology and marine conservation. His book, *Song for the Blue Ocean* (1998), was chosen as a *New York Times* Notable Book of the Year, a *Los Angeles Times* Best Nonfiction selection, and a *Library Journal* Best Science Book selection. He also received the American Fisheries Society's Carl R. Sullivan Fisher Conservation Award and The Pew Charitable Trusts' prestigious Scholar's Award in Conservation and the Environment.

DORION SAGAN is the co-author of twelve books, including *Microcosmos* (1986) and *What Is Life?* (2000). His essays and reviews have appeared in publications ranging from the *New York Times Book Review* to *Wired* and *Tricycle,* a Buddhist review. Currently, he is completing a book with Eric D. Schneider titled *Into the Cool: Thermodynamics and the Purpose of Life*. He lives in New York City.

MARY EVELYN TUCKER is professor of religion at Bucknell University. She has edited several books that examine the intersection of religion and ecology, including volumes specifically addressing Buddhism and Confucianism. She and her husband, John Grim, directed a conference series, "Religions of the World and Ecology," held at the Harvard University Center for the Study of World Religions in 1996–1998. They are series editors for the ten volumes arising from the conference, which are being published by Harvard University Press. She has been a committee member of the Environmental Sabbath Program of the United Nations Environment Programme since 1986 and is vice president of the American Teilhard Association.

TERRY TEMPEST WILLIAMS is the author of many critically acclaimed books, including *Refuge: An Unnatural History of Family and Place* (1992) and, most recently, *Leap* (2000). Her work has been widely anthologized, appearing in the *New Yorker*, the *Nation, Outside, Audubon, Orion*, the *Iowa Review*, and the *New England Review*, among other national and international publications. In addition to her writing, she has served on the Governing Council of The Wilderness Society and is currently on the advisory boards of the National Parks Conservation Association, The Nature Conservancy, and the Southern Utah Wilderness Alliance. She was recently inducted into the Rachel Carson Honor Roll and has received the National Wildlife Federation's National Conservation Award for Special Achievement.

RICHARD J. WOOD is dean emeritus of the Yale University Divinity School and adjunct professor of philosophy. His career includes top positions in academic institutions, as president of Earlham College prior to his work at Yale and as vice president for academic affairs and professor of philosophy at Whittier College. He has researched and taught in Japan and is recognized for his work in Asian studies.

Index

Island Press Board of Directors

Chair
HENRY REATH
President, Collector's Reprints, Inc.

Vice-Chair
VICTOR M. SHER
Environmental Lawyer

Secretary
DANE NICHOLS
Chairman, The Natural Step, U.S.

Treasurer
DRUMMOND PIKE
President, The Tides Foundation

ROBERT E. BAENSCH
Professor of Publishing, New York University

MABEL H. CABOT

DAVID C. COLE
Sunnyside Farms, LLC

CATHERINE M. CONOVER

GENE E. LIKENS
Director, The Institute of Ecosystem Studies

CAROLYN PEACHEY
Campbell Peachey & Associates

WILL ROGERS
Trust for Public Land

CHARLES C. SAVITT
President, Center for Resource Economics/Island Press

SUSAN E. SECHLER
Director of Global Programs, The Rockefeller Foundation

PETER R. STEIN
Managing Partner, The Lyme Timber Company

RICHARD TRUDELL
Executive Director, American Indian Resources Institute

WREN WIRTH
President, The Winslow Foundation